COMMUNITY LITERACY PROGRAMS

AND THE POLITICS OF CHANGE

COMMUNITY LITERACY PROGRAMS

AND THE POLITICS OF CHANGE

Jeffrey T. Grabill

State University of New York Press

Published by
State University of New York Press, Albany

Printed in the United States of America

For information, address State University of New York Press,
90 State Street, Suite 700, Albany, NY, 12207

Production by Christine L. Hamel
Marketing by Jennifer Giovani

Library of Congress Cataloging-in-Publication Data

Grabill, Jeffrey T., 1968.
    Community literacy programs and the politics of change /
    by Jeffrey T. Grabill.
        p. cm.
    Includes bibliographical references and index.
    ISBN 0-7914-5071-6 (alk. paper) —
    ISBN 0-7914-5072-4 (pbk.: alk. paper)
    1. Literacy programs—United States—Case studies. I. Title.

LC151.G69 2001
374'.0124'0973—dc21   00-067087
                                                          CIP

10   9   8   7   6   5   4   3   2   1

Contents

Figures and Tables

Tables

Preface

> "Women attended our literacy classes only as long as it took them to find work, anything to help them augment the family's meager monthly income. They bluntly told our teachers to go away, or stick to teaching children. Learning how to sign their names or write the alphabet would not help to fill empty bellies." (Anderson & Irvine, 1993, pp. 96–97)

I frankly don't blame these women for telling their teachers to go away. There is no inherent value to becoming "literate;" it does not guarantee better self-esteem, a job, or any other social or personal benefit. But for English teachers like myself, belief in the power of literacy is an article of faith, eagerly embraced by some, more skeptically and even cynically agreed to by others (akin to Pascal's wager about the existence of God— if literacy isn't particularly important, then there is no harm done in my pushing it; if it is important, then Amen). But as Elspeth Stuckey (1994) reminds us, there is violence both in the process of becoming literate and in the imposition upon others of the ideological values associated with a certain literacy. Sure, literacy doesn't put food in anyone's belly, and it certainly won't guarantee anyone a living wage, but it is important because of the good and the violence done in its name.

The teachers referenced in the epigraph above eventually moved away from "literacy itself," or a disembodied literacy, as the focus of their work. Given the situation in which they and their students found themselves, they helped identify problems in the lives of their students and worked to resolve them. They began with lived experiences of their students and worked to understand ways in which more traditional school-based literacies fit and didn't fit their students' situations. Anderson and Irvine worked, in other words, to narrow a perceived gap between literacy and life. Yet we enforce this separation between literacy and life by the ways in which we design literacy programs because we rarely ask students and workers what they need. We rarely ask them to make their lived experiences the center of our collective educational experience, to make those experiences the touchstone for educational planning and pedagogy. So we set out on our mission to make them literate, and in a variety of ways, they tell us to go away.

A personal example might help explain what I mean about literacy and life. This particular example is one reason for the study detailed in this book. As an undergraduate student I worked for a program in Fort Wayne, Indiana, funded by the Federal Jobs Training Partnership Act, legislation targeting at-risk teenagers for summer employment. In this program, teens were paid to attend intensive classroom modules focusing on a range of literacy issues: reading, writing, math, job skills, and life skills. The curriculum was designed and packaged by a private firm in Florida to be delivered according to strict Federal rules of accountability. As trainers, we were to follow the curriculum and exhaustively document our compliance. Complicating "compliance" were the social and personal issues found within the communities we worked with. A few students were in gangs, and many were gang "wannabes." Most weren't quite sure why they were there. Keeping kids out of gangs became an implicit role of the program; however, arguments against gangs and their allure were difficult for us to make—kids in gangs made money, had identities, and perhaps ironically, felt safe. Fort Wayne was particularly bloody that summer due to one of the first crack problems in the Midwest. A few of us had students who were killed; some just drifted away from the program; many stayed through the summer, "distracted" by more pressing concerns.

Did the program accomplish its goals to provide meaningful job and life skills training? According to the government and program designers, absolutely. According to documentation, our students learned a great deal. But did they? Many of our students felt disconnected from the material and the program. As a trainer in this program, I was faced with an uncomfortable contradiction. The program was both a success and a failure. I felt at the time that this tension was located in the design of the program, not in the strengths and weaknesses of individual teachers and students and not in the theories of language and learning that informed program practices. I became interested in institutional systems and in how such systems give meaning and value to certain practices and not others. This book, therefore, is an attempt to understand institutional systems with an eye toward changing them. My view is that those of us interested in changing the dominant meanings and values associated with literacy must focus on institutional systems. This book is an extended argument for how to make institutional systems visible, how to locate spaces for change, and how to enact an alternative institutional design. It is an argument for radical change that I hope encourages new ways of thinking about literacy and new tactics for changing the meaning and value of literacy.

Perspectives and Audiences

Discussions of literacy are inherently interdisciplinary, and so I think it is useful to understand who I am and where I come from because such information will go a long way toward explaining the contents of this book. I was trained in a department of English in a program that focused on rhetoric/composition and professional writing, and so I am concerned most specifically with "writing." Given that training, the following terms are important to this book:

> *Rhetoric*. For some, rhetoric is the historical study of rhetorical theory and practice. For others, it is a master term encompassing all discursive practice. I see rhetoric as a particular though flexible perspective on language, action, power. One of the most powerful notions of rhetoric sees it as comprising three elements: ideology, practice, and method (Sullivan & Porter, 1997). Ideology tells us something about what human relations should be or about how humans should relate to each other through writing. Practice tells us something about how people actually do relate to each other and/or how they actually write. Method tells us something about how people inquire—their tactics, heuristics, and procedures for invention. All involve the practices of power as well. These three elements of rhetoric can help us understand writing and institutions by providing a framework for examining and understanding what exists in a given situation and why. Rhetoric, then, constitutes the most general framework I employ for understanding community literacies and programs: a way to understand situated values, actions, relations of power, and the discourse that makes it all possible.

Composition. The discipline of "composition" is concerned primarily with the first-year writing classroom at the university level. Fueled mostly by the historical need to focus on writing instruction at the university, work in composition theory has created an active and dynamic field of inquiry into written literacies.

Professional Writing. My professional writing perspective is perhaps the oddest aspect of this book because my concern with community literacy and program design is not a concern of most in professional writing. Conversely, the focus on work and institutions that I bring from professional writing is not a concern of those who are interested in community literacy. Professional writing where I teach means a focus on teaching those whose primary career identities will be as writers—technical writers, Web-based writers, corporate communications specialists—and a secondary focus on training professionals who write—business and technology students. What I take from professional writing is a concern with understanding the purpose and function of writing within organizations and the importance of work and writing in contemporary society.

While I will draw on work from a range of disciplines, my frame of reference is rhetorical and my pragmatic concerns focus on writing. At the same time, I am trying to write for audiences that are quite diverse. My primary audience is certainly those like me: writing and composition researchers, students, and others, more generally, interested in what Ralph Cintron (1997) calls the "rhetorics of the everyday." Since scholars from across the spectrum of academic disciplines are interested in literacy, however, I hope this book is useful to researchers and students in education, linguistics, and others who see themselves as part of what Gee (2000) calls the New Literacy Studies. Writing for these audiences has been a considerable challenge. My hope is that knowing where I come from makes the book easier to navigate.

Methodological Frames

The goal of this book is to theorize literacy by constructing a localized framework for understanding it within a given institution in order to change that institution. The key questions that drive this project and book—what is literacy, who decides, in whose interests, and how can a program be designed collaboratively so that the answers to those questions are meaningful to those most affected—demand methodological flexibility. Yet "theory" and "local" are not comfortably linked. The concept of "theory" is the object of extensive examination and holds the privileged position in any number of binaries (e.g., theory/practice). Theory is extremely powerful and therefore important for fostering understanding and planning action. But theory is also limiting and harmful if accepted uncritically and used to construct unhelpful or inaccurate generalizations. The problem, therefore, is not with theory itself but with how theory gets done. It is a problem of methodology, which is why this issue needs to be foregrounded.

The problem of methodology is most clear at the level of concrete cases. Literacy theories—everything from notions of language use derived from some principle or paradigm to theories of cultural politics and liberation—seem to some degree to fall apart when run through the rubric of particular program experiences. At first, I saw this solely as a problem with theory—that it was useless or irrelevant. Later, enamored of theory as I tend to be, I saw the problems of particular cases as dismissible exceptions. Both positions miss the point that there *ought* to be a relationship between the general and the specific. Here that relationship is described by my goal to *theorize* community literacies, to engage in research and writing that is situated and contingent yet robust. My approach is an explicit attempt to move between the general and the specific, which necessitated the following methodological mix.

Institutional Case

In order to situate my study, I have embedded an empirical case of a community literacy program, called Western District Adult Basic Education, within a largely theoretical project. This case becomes a way to theorize community literacy that attempts to remain local and contingent. Because I construct Western District as an institution, I call this method an Institutional Case (see chapter 1 for a discussion of institutions).

My use of the term "case" does not come from traditional notions of case studies (e.g., Yin, 1984, rev. ed). One will not see, therefore, much of the apparatus typically constructed to conduct case study research, and I will make limited claims about what we can know about Western District based on my empirical work. Instead, I use cases as reasoning practices. A "reasoning practice" is another way of talking about building arguments with concrete, empirical examples, a tactic I have taken from casuistic moral theory. For Jonsen and Toulmin (1988), casuistry is a type of moral reasoning based on paradigms and analogies and not, in contrast, on universal maxims. Of importance in this definition are the paradigms and analogies upon which casuistic moral reasoning is based. These paradigms and analogies are cases: concrete, particular moral situations and decisions. Cases are important as reasoning tools because they encompass both the general (Theory) and the specific (concrete experiences). In their work on the National Commission for the Protection of Human Subjects of Biomedical and Behavioral Research, Jonsen and Toulmin (1988) saw that real cases made members of the Commission confront ambiguity. General principles were relatively easy to agree with; specific decisions, however, were difficult because they often lay at the margins of theoretical generalizations. In this study, a case like Western District Adult Basic Education is a concrete example of an institutional arrangement established in a community context for the purposes of dealing with literacy needs. Such a case can then be used as a heuristic that can help theorize what community literacy is and can be.

An institutional case, then, is both a site and a method; it focuses on a specific site but looks at that site in a particular fashion. While scholars in rhetoric and composition often look at students, teachers, and classrooms, an institutional case looks at the larger material and discursive structures that provide classroom space and make the work of teachers and students possible. An institutional case sees institutions as rhetorical systems and seeks to collect data that might enable one to understand how these structures work to make certain practices possible and others impossible. So an institutional case, at least in this project, is concerned with understanding the degree to which the institution—like a community literacy program—warrants certain notions of literacy and literate practices. An institutional case is much like cases in professional writing that focus on the ways in which institutional power relations constitute a site's literate practices and individual identities (e.g., Richardson & Liggett, 1993).

Therefore, the primary methodology for this project is an institutional case that describes a community literacy program. Not only does this case help make an institution "visible," but it provides resources that assist in constructing how an institution defines literacy, who makes those decisions, and in whose interests those decisions are made. An institutional case, then:

- focuses on institutional power relations;
- is both a site and a method (a specific location and a particular way of looking at/constructing that location);

• sees institutions as rhetorical systems and seeks to collect data that might enable one to understand how these systems work to make certain practices/identities possible and others impossible.

In an effort to construct Western District as an institution, I collected the following data:

Descriptions of funding sources (or who makes the program possible and for what reasons). This information gets at who makes the program possible, both financially and legislatively, and why they "authorize" the work of the program. Data for this information comes from legislation, grant proposals, reports, policy documents, and interviews.

Institutional definitions of literacy (e.g., mission statements). Some of this material is also provided by funding agencies and mechanisms and in teacher training material. Data for this information comes from legislation, promotional materials, policy documents, and interviews.

Descriptions of institutional arrangements with employers (e.g., definitions of literacy specific to this arrangement and the writing practices developed as a response). This information describes what employer-clients see as their needs and how the program positions itself to address them. Some of this information is visible in grant proposals, and some of it will be visible in other documents created with regard to workplaces. Relationships with workplaces is an important part of the work of the ABE program in my study; my sense is that this is increasingly common nationwide.

Interviews with tutors, "students," and workers as well as program administrators.

Examples of writing practices taught and used to fulfill institutional expectations (including sample texts and actual pedagogical practices of instructors). Data for this material comes from classroom observations and interviews.

Postmodern Mapping
I use mapping to conceptualize, organize, and present what I think current

literacy theory says about the phenomenon of "literacy." I also use this mapping strategy when dealing with theories of ethics and politics. Sullivan and Porter draw from postmodern geography (e.g., Soja, 1989) in their development of this methodology within rhetoric and composition, and it has a range of uses in rhetorical and methodological discussions as well as in geography itself. Postmodern mapping is a visual practice that emphasizes movement, change, and partiality. Sullivan and Porter write that mapping is "one tactic for constructing positionings of research that are reflexive" and for making visible frames of reference in research (p. 78). Tactics for reflexivity and visibility are ways to get at the problem of how to *do* theory. Mapping is simply and not so simply how I represent the work of others. Of course, this is not an innocent practice. Acts of representation are also acts of interpretation. Mapping is a practice of representation that doesn't allow one to forget this.

Perhaps a quick example of the type of mapping practice outlined here would help. At Georgia State University, we recently moved from quarters to semesters, refigured the English curriculum, and began to develop a professional writing program. This was all complicated by the fact that Georgia State is an urban university with a significant number of non-traditional students. In order to think about what courses we needed to offer and when, we had to understand our students and their needs. We talked to them, of course, but we also developed profiles of them, and this proved to be a difficult process because the taxonomies we developed seemed too flat, too uncomplicated, and therefore conceptually inadequate. So we tried to map them and therefore create a conceptual tool that is more useful (see Figure P-1).

Figure P-1 is a rather simple map showing the students who take the two core classes in professional writing. In addition, this figure shows that we need to offer certain classes in certain proportions at times of day that are best suited to certain types of students (e.g., evenings for non-traditional students). Finally, this map shows that unlike business writing, which has fairly stable patterns, the makeup of our technical writing classes moves, which makes it a more difficult course to plan. The point is that mapping allows more multivariate positioning and relationships than other taxonomy and placement procedures do. In addition, mapping allows the opportunity to show movement and change.

The openness and self-reflexivity of mapping is meant to ensure that these maps are seen *as maps*, not as "reality." Pragmatically, mapping in this project is a type of visual taxonomy, a method of representation

Figure P-1
Mapping Georgia State English Students

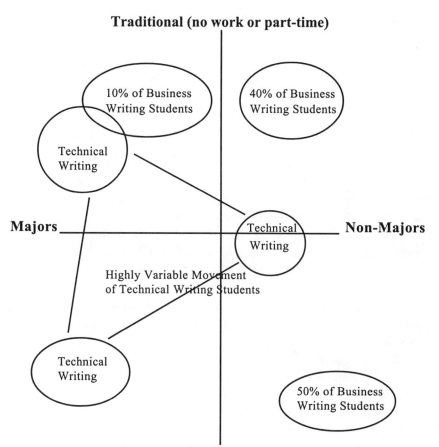

attentive to changes in time and space. It is a heuristic strategy that allows one to:

- construct complicated theoretical positions for others
- represent differences within positions that share similarities
- reveal the frames by which I am positioning others
- position myself within that process
- locate places where work is useful and work is needed

As a theoretical practice, then, the maps allow me to construct—and then change—theoretical realities regarding literacy and Western District, always looking for the ambiguities where institutions can be changed.

Chapter Overviews

The book's seven chapters work through previous theoretical work on literacy, toward an understanding of literacy as institutionally situated, and toward a critical rhetoric for understanding and changing institutions.

Chapter 1 frames the study of community literacy in terms of the disciplinary interests commonly grouped under the "rhetoric and composition" umbrella, introduces the concept of "institution" and the importance of institutional power, and similarly introduces Western District Adult Basic Education as an institutional system.

Chapter 2 poses the question "what is literacy" and works through various theories of literacy for answers. In contrast to theoretical answers, the chapter returns to the case of Western District to show how institutional systems locate the meaning and value of literacy. The contrast between theoretical methods and answers and institutional procedures is important and relocates the power to give literacies meaning and value within institutional systems.

Chapter 3 takes up questions of ethics and politics in the determination of which literacies count and which literacies are meaningless. It is a chapter about power. Although it is a critique of the relative lack of discussions of power in literacy theory, the chapter also begins to develop the language necessary for a theory of institutional design.

Chapter 4 focuses on computer technologies in community contexts and argues for community literacy programs as key access sites to sophisticated networked computer technologies. Western District serves as such a site, and this chapter uses Western District as an example of both the problems and promises of a community literacy program as a place to access computer literacies.

Chapter 5 is an examination of the concept of "community." The chapter seeks to develop a useful notion of community for community literacy practice, seeks to articulate a relationship between communities and institutions (a relationship filled with tension in much of the community development literature), and seeks to develop a method for seeing and understanding community literacies.

Chapter 6 is an argument for participatory institutional design and works most clearly with material developed in chapters 3 and 5 to make this argument. The chapter develops a theory of institutional change based on a two-fold process of critique and redesign. Given the argument of this book that specific institutional systems give literacies meaning and value, this chapter is an argument for how participatory communities can intervene to change institutional systems and therefore alter the meaning and value of literacy.

Chapter 7 is a pragmatic extension of the sixth chapter, focusing on specific tactics researchers, teachers, and students can use to participate in the development and redesign of community literacy programs.

Acknowledgments

In many ways it took me nearly six years to write this book, and in those six years, it has taken many forms: course papers, research proposals, articles, a dissertation, scribbled notes on bar napkins. Despite the singular author, it was collaboratively written, and so I would like to thank my co-authors.

Pat Sullivan and Jim Porter have been wonderful teachers, mentors, and friends. More than anyone else, Pat has taught me how to think carefully and creatively about research and to believe that researchers and teachers can make a difference. She has made a difference. Jim has been generous and supportive, and his council has been and will continue to be indispensable to me.

Stuart Blythe and Libby Miles have been constant colleagues and friends whom I treasure. Mary Hocks, Lyneé Gaillet, Elizabeth Lopez, and George Pullman, my colleagues at Georgia State, have been remarkably supportive; I couldn't ask for a better group of people to work with.

Finally, my deepest thanks go to my parents for their unwavering support, and to Chandra and Megan, my sources of energy and joy.

Permissions have been granted for the use or reproduction of the following material:

Figure 5–1 is reprinted from John P. Kretzmann and John L. McKnight, *Building Communities from the Inside Out*, Evanston, IL: Institute for Policy Research, Northwestern University (1993). Distributed Exclusively by ACTA Publications, Chicago.

Chapter 4 is a revised version of an article reprinted from *Computers*

and Composition, 15, Jeffrey T. Grabill, 297–315, 1998, with permission
from Elsevier Science.

The epigraph to chapter 1 is reprinted from pages 4–5 of Barton, D.
(1994). *Literacy: An introduction to the ecology of written language.*
Oxford: Blackwell.

The epigraph to chapter 2 is reprinted from page 106 of Street, B. V.
(1995). *Social literacies: Critical approaches to literacy in development,
ethnography and education.* London: Longman.

The epigraph to chapter 4 is reprinted from pages 33 and 34 of Cerf,
V., Huber, P., Duggan, E., Gilder, G., Nader, R., Irving, L., Breeden, L.,
Perelman, L., Robinson, K., Schrader, W., & Weingarten, R. (1995).
Universal access: Should we get in line? *Educom Review,* 30(2), 33–37.

The epigraph to chapter 6 is reprinted from the inside front cover of
Lindsay, V. (1968). *Earth man & star thrower: Adventures, rhymes and
designs.* New York: The Eakins Press.

The epigraph to chapter 7 is reprinted from pages 215–216 of Street,
B. V. (1984). *Literacy in theory and practice.* Cambridge: Cambridge
University Press.

Chapter 1

Disciplinary Gaps, Institutional Power, and Western District Adult Basic Education

> "The main area for research on reading and writing up till now has been education. The main focus has been on individual learning. The main research paradigm has been psychological. However, it is not just educators who are interested in literacy." (David Barton, 1994, pp. 4–5)

When I first started to conceive this project, I knew that I was interested in written literacies and community contexts, but I wasn't sure what "community literacy" was. People in composition studies had written about it (e.g., Peck et al., 1995), and while such discussions were important, I knew they only described certain types of community literacy programs. Based on my reading of work outside rhetoric and composition (e.g., Barton, 1994), I appreciated the importance of vernacular literacies and the range of locations where people learned new literacies. The diversity of literacies and locations made my attempts to start this project more difficult.

My solution was to map local community-based literacy programs. This activity was revealing because it destroyed the rather romantic notion I had that there were many neighborhood-situated programs. There was actually less program diversity than I anticipated. While there is no doubt that numerous neighborhood programs exist, they are rare relative to what I found: community-based programs with strong ties to larger institutional systems: state and federally funded workplace training,

1

public library systems, and school districts. I wanted to focus on "community," yet I found that I couldn't completely distance myself from institutions (more in chapter 5 on the relationship between the two). While I agree with David Barton's (1994) assertion that "school," "work," and "community" constitute three domains of literate activity because of the

Figure 1-1
Mechanic's Work Order/Work Description

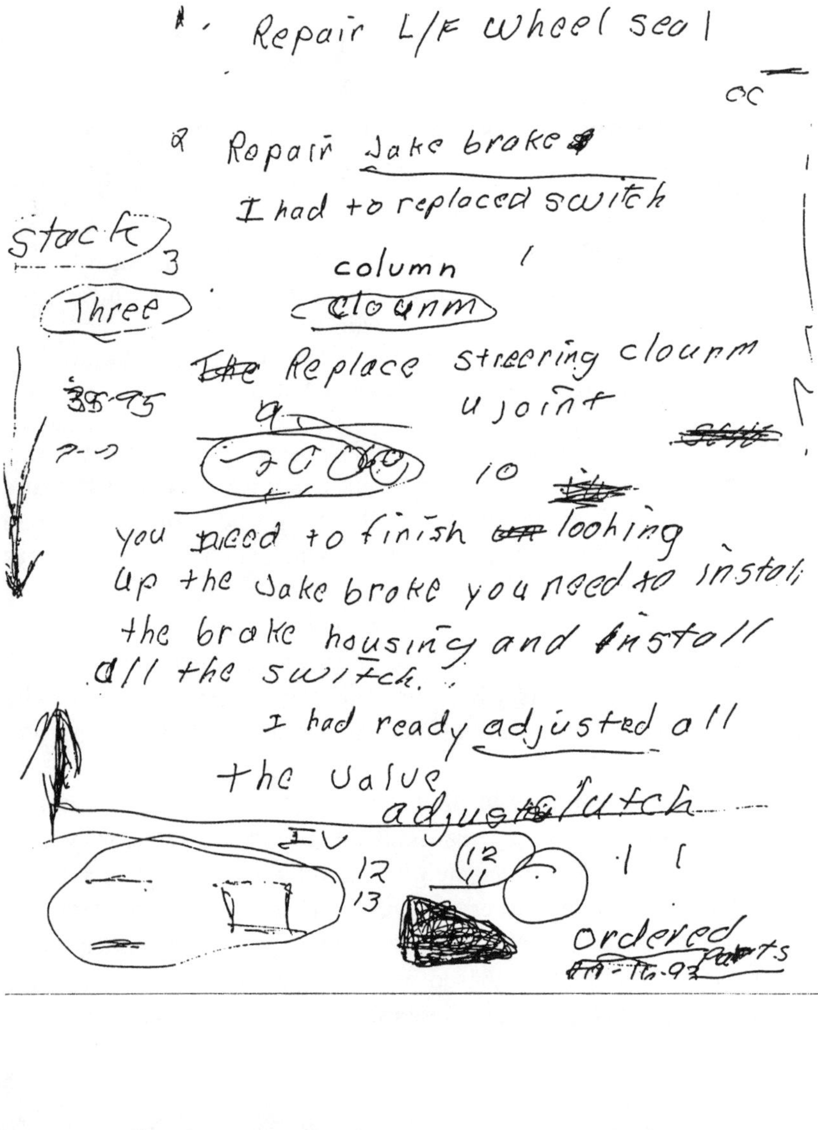
1. Repair L/F wheel seal
2 Repair Jake brake
I had to replaced switch
stock 3
column
Three cloanm
Replace streering clounm
u joint
10
you need to finish looking
up the Jake brake you need to install
the brake housing and install
all the switch.
I had ready adjusted all
the value
adjust clutch
IV
12
13
ordered parts

social institutions that shape the literacies of each domain, the three domains overlap. As I tried to understand "community literacy" outside schools and workplaces, they kept pulling me back in, and nothing made this point more clear to me than the document I found while I was mapping local programs (see Figure 1–1). It was this document that crystallized how I needed to approach "community literacy" because I began to understand that community literacy programs linked to powerful social institutions are important because they are generally well-known, stable, and have the resources to help people. I began to understand that "community literacies" cannot be separated from the literacies necessary to be successful in more structured social institutions like workplaces and schools. I began to understand why it is important to listen to others when we design community-based programs.

The document represented in Figure 1–1 was given to me by a professor at a small university in the city where I was mapping community-based literacy programs. What was actually given to me was a short story written by a man taking classes at a library-based program where the professor volunteered her time. It was only when I turned over the page that I saw a very different type of text. While many literacy programs focus only on reading, this program also worked on writing. The writing done in the program was largely personal narrative with the goal to increase confidence, fluency, and voice. The program eventually published a book of participants' narratives. I was given this particular story because the professor thought it was both representative and good. But the most interesting part of the document is not the story but what was photocopied on the back of it. When I asked the professor about the writing on the back of the paper, she nodded gravely, sighed, and told me the story.

Like many others in the class, the author of the story/document was struggling with the literacy demands of work. If you aren't sure what Figure 1–1 represents, it seems to be a work order or a report of work completed for an auto repair shop. The document, while seemingly chaotic, actually has a logic to it. The author attempts to list work done on a car (toward the top of the document), and there is a short narrative toward the bottom of work yet to be completed. In addition, there seem to be attempts to draw diagrams or at least represent visually concepts that may not have been easy for the author to write alphabetically or that are simply better represented visually. The author of the document brought it to literacy class to illustrate the difficulties he was having at work. The professor confessed to me that nobody had any ideas about how to help him with writing such as this.

Did the author lose his job? I don't know, but it seems possible. Should the literacy program have helped him with his work-related writing? Perhaps, but then again, the program was not *designed* to do so, and unfortunately, most of us in English don't know how to work with a document and writer such as this. Even more unfortunate is the fact that those who do know how to work with writing such as this, such as technical and professional writing students and teachers, are focused on white collar workplaces and professions. This document helped crystallize the importance of institutions, work, and program design to my examination of community literacy, and it also pointed out that current academic divisions and disciplines don't fit very well the needs of those in community-based programs. This is the problem of "gaps" that I turn to in the next section, a justification of sorts for my own interests and an argument aimed at those from similar disciplinary backgrounds to expand their vision a bit.

The goal of this chapter is to introduce problems that I wrestle with throughout the book, problems related to the argument that the meaning and value of literacy is situated within specific institutions and that in order to change the meaning and value of literacy, features of a given institution must change. Therefore, this chapter also has the primary function of introducing the community literacy institution that is the focus of my inquiry: Western District Adult Basic Education. Throughout this book, I ask a set of related questions that attempt to establish how the meaning and value of literacy is established at Western District. These questions, what is literacy, who decides, and in whose interests are these decisions made, are questions that focus on the discursive and material power that has the ability to create and shape reality.

Why Study Community Literacy? The Problem of Gaps

As David Barton (1991; 1994) and Shirley Brice Heath (1990) correctly point out, the world of literate practices extends far beyond schools and workplaces, yet most literacy discussions occur within these two domains. As I illustrate in Figure 1–2, scholarly discussions often focus on a rather narrow though powerful range of people and literacies. The case site I focus on in this book, Western District, actually intersects in important ways with both schools and workplaces, yet significantly, it is neither. The lack of significant overlap of the "school" and "workplace" circles in Figure 1–2 expresses the fact that there is little interest—for good reasons—on the part of scholars in these domains for the concerns of those in other domains. While professional writing does move between workplaces and schools, the disciplinary focuses of rhetoric and composition and professional writing make it difficult to pursue work with community-based literacy programs. This situation results in a gap, a situation in which people in schools, workplaces, and community contexts may all be studying writing (or literacy more generally), yet they don't talk with each other. Crossing this gap seems important because it might result in a more integrated understanding of written literacies.

Figure 1–2
Literacy Domains and an Institution

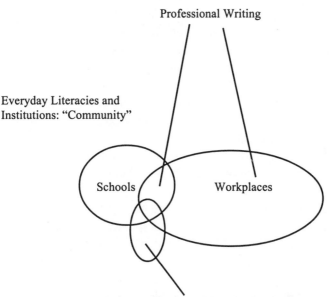

Barton (1994) argues that people in universities have paid little attention to writing in peoples' everyday lives, which means that literacy theory is constructed from a rather limited set of writing practices found in schools (see more recently, Barton & Hamilton, 1998). Barton (1994) writes that the locus of work on reading and writing has been education, the focus on individual learning, and the paradigm psychology. Yet, he notes, it isn't just educators who are interested in literacy (p. 5). Ivanič and Moss (1991) continue this line of reasoning by suggesting that since the nineteenth century, school-based definitions of literacy have dominated discussions, often abstractly, so that literacy appears "neutral, standard-ized, and measurable" (p. 197). Such a move to define literacy in terms of schools has not been an innocent practice (see Street, 1984; Graff, 1979; Cook-Gumperz, 1986), and has served to push into the background "more pluralistic literacies of early nineteenth-century Britain and the United States" (Ivanič & Moss, 1991, p. 197). Such pushing often continues today such that people find it "hard to articulate their theories of literacy except in relation to schooling" (Barton et al., 1992, p. 7). Closely related to the politics of defining literacy is the periodic announcement of literacy crises. For example, in *Why Johnny Can't Read*, Rudolf Flesh (1955) attempted to signal a reading crisis connected to poor schooling (later we learned that Johnny can't write either). Jonathan Kozol (1985; 1991), for his part, connects socioeconomics to school failure but also expands the literacy crisis to include an examination of illiteracy in the general population and the existence of communities and generations of illiterates (see also Purcell-Gates, 1995). While some argue about whether there is a "literacy crisis"—Ohmann (1987), for example, links moments of crisis with war; Kaestle et al. (1991) argue that people are about as literate or illiterate as they always have been—it seems clear that certain communi-ties and groups of people lack the literacies necessary to function successfully within various social institutions like schools, government agencies, and workplaces. Literacy clearly is embedded in such institu-tional successes or failures.

And so, by ignoring or dismissing a wide range of literate practices that take place outside schools, rhetoric and composition theorists risk the same blindness of which Barton (1994) and others accuse scholars in education: ignoring a wide range of significant literate practices that must be accounted for in theories of writing. The same is true for professional writing. By failing to look outside schools and a limited range of workplaces, scholars in professional writing run the risk of ignoring perhaps the bulk of literate practices in workplaces, and for my purposes here, the community-based institutions where workers go to learn them.[1] My point is that the gaps between schools, workplaces, and community sites are unnecessary at this point in the development of rhetoric and composition and professional writing. Our notions of writing and writers will change by working outside traditional boundaries, and this can only be helpful.

We should study community literacy, then, for two general reasons. First, if we are to take seriously the study of writing, then we can no longer ignore the nonacademic writing that takes place with greater regularity and variety outside the comfortable domains of certain schools and workplaces. Second, for those interested in change and agency, community-based literacy institutions are fundamental spaces for access to literacies. These literacies, in turn, are one way in which individuals who lack such access can attempt to enter powerful institutions in their communities. Access to institutions through the use of certain literacies is important, then, and a significant social and public policy issue.

Institutions

Perhaps the key concept in this book is "institution." I will argue that institutions give literacies existence, meaning, and value, but I don't really mean to give inanimate systems life and agency. Institutions are people; they are the systems by which people act collectively, whether you call that system a school, a particular corporation, or a community literacy program. Yet when we talk about literacy, we tend to talk about "illiterates" or literacy "itself"—linguistic, psychological, and/or textual practices. But as Peter Freebody (1992) argues, "reading" and "writing" are terms that gloss a wide range of practices that cannot be described adequately in some theoretical sense (p. 67). Instead, they are "given shape and significance differently in different institutional settings and at different moments within any one setting" (p. 67). Therefore, Freebody continues, both local and distant authority relations are "*inside* all literacy activities . . . built into literacy practices at their definitional core from setting to setting" (p. 67). Further highlighting the ideological function of institutions, David Barton (1991) writes that "behind home, school, and work can be seen particular institutions [and that] particular definitions of literacy and associated literacy practices are nurtured by these institutions" (p. 5). Institutions, then, are definition-sustaining, selecting "categories of activities that count, for teacher and student alike (as well as for parents and administrators), as reading and writing" (Freebody, 1992, p. 65). Therefore, nearly all literate activity takes place *within* or *with reference to* specific social institutions, and any attempt to understand literate practices without understanding the institutions that make certain practices possible and valuable fails to account for how and why literate practices look the way they do. Without understanding the power relations of local and distant institutions, we struggle to understand why certain classrooms look the way they do, why individuals speak and write in certain ways, or why some citizens have difficulty gaining access to the resources and knowledge necessary to better their lives.

The concept of the institution is extremely important, yet it is largely undeveloped in the literacy work from which I have taken it. We are accustomed to thinking of institutions in the abstract: The Law, Family, Business, Government, the Liberal Arts. But institutions are also local- ized manifestations of such larger systems: local public schools and community literacy programs, for example. I am particularly interested in how such local institutions function as ideological systems that give literacy meaning. I am particularly interested, in other words, in the situated institutional systems within which people read and write every day. David Harvey (1996) writes that institutions are "produced spaces," or relatively stable "domains of organization and administration" (p. 112). He also writes that institutions are composed of "semiotic systems" (e.g., writing) that organize practices that affect people subject to or active through a particular institution. Institutions are the systems that we are subject to every day. They are also the systems through which we act every day. Institutions are the universities where we teach, the schools our children attend, and the locations of a great number of public interactions (the department of motor vehicles; social service agencies; parent-teacher groups; neighborhood committees). Institutions are local, concrete spaces (discursive and architectural) that are written. They are given life discur- sively through the writing that makes them possible (e.g., legislation, regulation, business plans), and they act through other forms of writing (e.g., policy, procedures). Institutions, then, are local systems of decision- making within which people act rhetorically in ways that powerfully affect the lives of others, including decisions about the meaning and practice of literacy. Institutions, in other words, are written, and if they are written, they can be rewritten.

A short example might help. Ellen Cushman's (1998) work illustrates the power of institutions to give literate practices meaning and value. Cushman's ethnographic study explores how African-American citizens used language to participate in and struggle with institutional systems. As most of these citizens were poor, the institutions with which they had significant contact were the Department of Social Services, Housing and Urban Development, the Housing Authority, and local ministries. In her project, Cushman chronicles the elaborate and complex literate practices and events her participants engage in: collaborative discussions, form-filling behaviors, letter writing, audience and institutional analyses. She illustrates the sophistication of these practices with reference to the institutional systems that demanded them and contrasts this perspective with common ways of seeing literacy that focus on the surface simplicity of texts or the apparently "limited" abilities of her participants. Engaging complex institutional audiences and procedures demanded considerable thought and effort to accomplish what some might incorrectly see as "simple" literate practices. What an institutional framework asks us to see about Cushman's example is that the events and practices in which these people participated were warranted—demanded and determined—by the institutions themselves and given meaning and value by the ideologies of those institutions and their importance in the community. The power of these institutions demands, in turn, the sophisticated literacies of Cushman's participants. Outside an explicit connection to particular institutions and their related practices, we are tempted to see mere form-filling or letter writing and the problems her participants had *only* in terms of cognition, expression, or technical considerations. We would miss, in other words, the power of the institutions for which the documents were produced. And so we would miss, as I argue in this book, nearly everything.

A focus on institutions in the process of understanding literate activity, then, entails a focus on power. The power to make an order, and the power to order new acts of making. The power, in other words, to make a certain literacy. Institutional orders need a rhetoric that can help us understand their existence and operation and therefore what is possible within their domain. I spend much of this book attempting to make institutions visible in order to understand the contexts that give literate practices meaning. Without such an understanding, we are limited to changing people who are subject to institutions or tinkering with texts. Therefore, the use of Western District as an institutional case is crucial to the success of the argument I make in this book. I am arguing, like others, that it is impossible to understand literacy in the abstract. Unlike most others, I argue that literacy only has meaning because it is given meaning by institutional systems like Western District Adult Basic Education. To change the meaning and value of literacy, one must change institutions.

Western District

I chose Western District as a case site because it was established and well-connected to area schools and workplaces. As an Adult Basic Education

(ABE) site, Western District is a node in a much larger federal and state network of literacy funding and initiatives. As an ABE program, Western District is similar to other programs nationwide. In the state and community in which Western District is located, it is also closely tied to the local school district (through funding lines), area businesses and industry (through grant programs), and local government (through welfare reform). Because of these connections and the significant presence of school-related literacies implied by these relationships, some might not consider Western District a *community* literacy program. This strikes me as reasonable; however, I think my description of Western District in this chapter and my argument about the pervasiveness, power, and interrelatedness of institutional systems will show why Western District is indeed a community literacy program. In fact, my argument in this book is that it is probably impossible to find or design a community literacy program outside institutions.

Western District is a visible presence in its part of the city—an area of working and middle class neighborhoods, heavy and light industrial parks, and a large airport. In fact, Western District is located in a light industrial area sandwiched between two major interstate highways and busy state and local roads that feed the airport. There are just a few houses in the immediate area and public transportation is poor. So like most in this Midwestern state and city, those who attend classes must drive their own cars or find other reliable transportation. Western District is located in an area, in other words, with no neighborhood feel or spatial community. Western District is an institution that serves a community in need, but the precise nature of this community and the relationship between the institution and the community is difficult to determine.

Because of its relationships with area schools and workplaces, Western District is relatively well-funded and has multiple "streams" through which participants come to the program. During the time I was at Western District, the participants were mostly working-class white women. Western District is often the last and best place for these participants to return to their education at a location that is well-connected to area schools and workplaces, and therefore, serves as an interface between these participants and admissions and human resources personnel. Western District, therefore, is an important part of the web of social services available in that part of the city.

I developed and maintained contact with the Western District Adult Basic Education (ABE) program over the course of two years. During five months of the second year, I had my most intensive contact with specific classes run through that program as part of my data collection. The classrooms I focused on at Western District were those that seemed most appropriate for my study: one of the general ABE classes, a workplace-situated class, and the computers class.[2] I chose these classes because they formed a representative picture of the types of classes offered at Western District. In addition, each of these classes dealt in some way with writing. It is worth emphasizing at this point that my classroom observations are not the core of my study and not my primary interest. Classroom practices and experiences are only part of a larger institutional picture.

I spent most of my time in the computers class (five months of observation and interviews from 4/10/96 to 9/12/96), which I came to call the "professional writing" classroom, and I spent less time in the general ABE class (only about 16 hours). My time at the Rosewater Publishing class, because access was so difficult, was confined to four weeks during the summer. While in class, I took field notes, participated in classroom activities (mostly in the computers class), and interviewed twelve students about their experiences in the program (two in the general ABE class, five in the computers class, and five at Rosewater Publishing). In addition, I interviewed all five teachers and the director of the program, most of them more than once. The bulk of data collection concerned constructing Western District as an institution, and this entailed research from the most general (e.g., legislation, rules, and interviews with state government officials) to the most local (classrooms).

An Outline of Western District as an Institution
Western District is both a literate institution—a space that requires certain literacies to function effectively—and a literacy institution—a space that provides literacy instruction. But I think it is a mistake to speak of Western District exclusively in the singular. In actuality, understanding the literacies warranted by Western District means understanding Western District as an articulation of institutions: governments, school corporations, work-places and their rules, regulations, and assessment practices. The literacies given definition and meaning within Western District are directly con-nected to how these institutions exercise power in making such decisions. Brian Street (1984) argues that his ideological model of literacy "stresses the significance of the socialisation process in the construction of mean-ing of literacy for participants and is therefore concerned with the general social institutions through which this process takes place and not just the explicit 'educational' ones" (p. 2). In short, Street's ideological model seeks to understand literate practices within the institutional systems that

define and give meaning to certain practices (and not others). In the case
of Western District, the general social institutions that exercise power on
the meaning and value of literacy are most clearly federal and state
governments through both legislation and assessments and the workplaces with which Western District collaborated. The particulars of how
those within institutional systems make such decisions and how they
affect other's lives are the subject of subsequent chapters. By way of
introduction, I want to construct a more general picture of Western
District as an institution in order to better understand its position and role
within larger social systems. My method here will be to trace the flow of
power—a hierarchical flow in this case—in order to outline the sources
for decisions about literacy. The evidence that I use to trace the power
relations at Western District comes from federal and state legislation and
Western District policy documents. In later chapters, I will draw on
assessment and placement practices and classroom observations to continue this process. What one sees, in general, is how legislation helps
determine policy and assessment, and that these practices, in turn, affect
classroom literacies. My argument is that the exercise of power is
traceable and determines, in various ways, what literacy is and in whose
interests those decisions are made at Western District.

The purpose of the Western District program is tied directly to the
federal legislation that created Adult Basic Education (ABE). The
program's statement of purpose is a gloss of the purposes of adult
education as first articulated in the original (1966) Federal legislation (see
Adult Education Act [P.L. 100–297] as amended by the National Literacy
Act of 1991 [P.L. 102–73]). Western District's purpose is to:

1. Enable all adults to acquire basic literacy skills necessary to
   function in society;
2. Enable adults who so desire to continue their education to at
   least the level of completion of secondary school;
3. Make available to adults the means to secure training and
   education that will enable them to become more employable,
   productive, and responsible citizens. (Western District Adult
   Basic Education, "Adult Basic Education Center," p. 4)[3]

The mission of Adult Education, according to Indiana, is to provide
literacy, ESL, GED preparation, secondary credit (in Secondary Education Programs not offered at Western District), life skills, and basic and
secondary academic skills, and to provide these services to adults
whose skill levels "range from minimal or no literacy skills to GED

level" (Division of Adult Education, "Indiana's Adult Education Teacher Handbook," p. 2-2). The state program is intended to serve those people who:

a) need that education to gain the mastery of skills that lead to the completion of grade 8 or to a high school equivalency diploma;
b) need that education to receive high school credit to obtain a high school diploma; or
c) have graduated from high school (or received a high school equivalency certificate/diploma) but who demonstrate basic skill deficiencies in mathematics or English/language arts. (Division of Adult Education, "Indiana's Adult Education Teacher Handbook," pp. 2-5, 2-6)

Furthermore, the purpose of Indiana's ABE programs is to design flexible services customized in response to individual, workplace, and community needs; collaborate with other community organizations to maximize services; employ professional adult educators; and prepare adult learners for productive participation in the community (p. 1). The centerpiece of the program's philosophy is that "every adult has a right to an education with the ultimate rewards and responsibilities" (Western District Adult Basic Education, "Adult Basic Education Center," p. 5). The program further articulates a concept of adult students as "persons who are unique, learn throughout their lives, have the potential for growth and self-fulfillment, have a right to be involved in the process of making decisions that affect them, and have a right to learn how to effectively and positively manage their own lives" (Western District Adult Basic Education, "Adult Basic Education Center," p. 5).

Western District is a "Comprehensive Program" funded under a Federal Comprehensive Program Grant. A comprehensive program is designed to serve those adults within the district at low proficiency levels and "special populations that are particularly impacted by functional illiteracy" (Division of Adult Education, "Indiana's Adult Education Teacher Handbook," p. 2-12). Programs like Western District typically also offer multiple services at a number of sites, and they also are expected to work with other community agencies, governmental and non-governmental agencies, and business and industry. The Western District program offers classes at its center, libraries in neighboring towns, area centers that serve the needy and handicapped, and numerous businesses and industry sites.

Indiana sees Adult Education as a second chance, a chance the state has been involved with since the 1940s (Division of Adult Education, "Adult Education Handbook," p. 1). The 1966 Adult Education Act (P.L. 100–297) was the federal government's bid to assist the states in this endeavor. But with their entry into Adult Education, the federal government also changed state efforts by further systematizing them through additional rules and regulations. Legislation and appropriations acts provide the mechanism for federal funds to move to the state level. States receive funds "according to a statutorily defined formula based on the proportion of individuals, at least 16 years of age, who have not graduated from high school or its equivalent" (Division of Adult Education, "Indiana's Adult Education Teacher Handbook," p. 2-5). Indiana then disburses the funds to local levels where instruction is provided (see Figure 1–3).

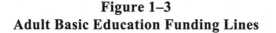

Figure 1–3
Adult Basic Education Funding Lines

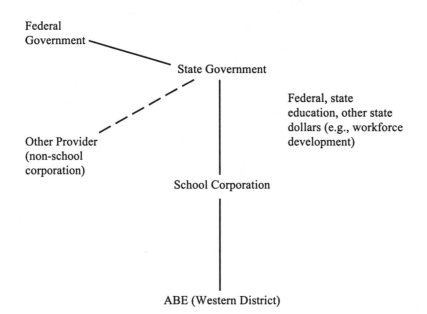

Federal
Government

State Government

Federal, state
education, other state
dollars (e.g., workforce
development)

Other Provider
(non-school
corporation)

School Corporation

ABE (Western District)

Federal money is viewed by Indiana as a supplement, not the primary means of program support. Priority for funding is assigned to those programs that can "consolidate efforts with others in the community," thereby further spreading the responsibility for program support. The federal money comes with the requirement that states develop assessment procedures to ensure that programs are meeting the needs of adult students.[4] It is important to note, however, that while federal dollars can go to any recognized education provider who successfully submits a grant, in Indiana, under House Enrolled Act 1599 (specifically IC 4-22-2), only school corporations can receive adult education dollars (Division of Adult Education, "Indiana's Adult Education Teacher Handbook," p. 2-5).[5] Thus, as Figure 1–3 illustrates, while federal legislation allows various educational providers, such as universities, technical programs, non-profits, or job training programs to compete for federal money and provide programming (represented by the dotted line), Indiana funds school corporations (Division of Adult Education, "Indiana's Adult Education Teacher Handbook," p. 2-12). This makes school corporations a powerful centerpiece in the required collaboration between agencies and organizations for the design of program services.

In Indiana, then, Adult Education is a partnership of federal, state, and local agencies; this flexibility avoids complete dependence on one funding source and, in the words of the Indiana handbook, "allow[s] programs to meet the unique needs of learners" (p. 1). In terms of state policy, meeting the unique needs of learners is a mission connected to flexible funding, but it is also at the center of Adult Education's *ethos*. Indeed, Indiana's philosophy seems very much concerned with "learner-centered education," emphasizing that the state *"assures* individual learner goal achievement" (Division of Adult Education, "Policy on ABE/GED Standardized Testing," p. 1, emphasis in original). In part, this assurance is delivered through demonstrated gains via standardized testing, part of Indiana's "commitment to results" (p. 1). The reliance on standardized testing is, of course, mandated by the funding legislation that makes the programs possible. In chapter 2, I discuss how assessment practices, in turn, help give specific literacies meaning and value. State policy on assessment is therefore largely determined by the need to show systematic learning gains:

> The Division of Adult Education embraces the philosophy that pre- and post-testing with standardized instruments is but one piece of the picture. The documentation of learning/competency gains, as individuals meet goals and/or exit the program, will tell the real story. The development of specific indicators for learning gains for adult basic education programs and learners is "work in

progress." However, consistent with our state's philosophy, learning gains will be defined to reflect the achievement of steps
important to the learner's life. (Division of Adult Education,
"Policy on . . . Testing," p. 1)

Some in the state Department of Education have expressed concern to me
about how standardized assessments are given and interpreted, and they
are increasingly looking into "alternative assessments" like portfolios and
dialogic/collaborative methods (interview with Ed Cotton, 8/12/96).
These efforts manifest themselves in teacher training workshops, but in
my observations, not significantly in practice. In short, the mechanisms
of funding connect Adult Education's purpose to assessment, and this is
the power that government has to make assessment central to the ABE
process. This power flows through the system beginning with legislation
and assessment controls, and as I will discuss later, drives practice to a
significant degree.

Power, then, is an obviously important concept and one that occupies
a central place in this book. Yet in my home disciplines, power and the
procedural mechanisms by which power operates are often invisible. In
rhetoric and composition, for example, research typically focuses on
individual students, teachers, or classrooms, either as the object of interest
or as a way to examine a theory of learning, composition, and/or a
pedagogical practice. Yet with Western District such a focus will not work
because it leaves invisible the processes people use to shape the contexts
within which students and teachers work. As I have tried to show in this
chapter, relations of power at Western District begin with legislation,
become more concrete in rules and regulations that determine who gets
what money, why, and how that money is determined to be well-spent.
The result of these relations of power is "literacy."

The rest of this book continues to use the case of Western District as
a touchstone, focusing first and in greater detail on how and why a
particular literacy is given meaning and value within an institutional order
and then moving toward understanding how institutions can be changed.
The result is a framework for understanding the decision-making processes through which people create "reality" about literacy. This framework amounts to a rhetoric of institutions and a critical rhetoric for
institutional change.

Chapter 2

Locating the Meaning and Value of Literacy

> "The question that concerned us was: if, as we argue, there are multiple literacies, how is it that one particular variety has come to be taken as the only literacy?" (Brian Street, 1995, p.106)

While literacy theory can serve a number of purposes, it typically does three things. It can present an understanding of how people acquire the ability to read and write. It can present a picture of how people actually do read and write. It can and often does present an argument for how one should think about reading and writing. Regardless of the specifics, theory locates the meaning and value of literacy and at the same time creates a universe of possibilities—conceptual, ideological, practical— associated with a literacy's meaning and value.

This chapter poses the question "what is literacy?" and serves as the beginning of my argument for how to locate literacy and create a vision of the possible with respect to literacies in community-based institutions. The purpose of the chapter is to locate literacy in two senses. The methodological sense focuses on how various theoretical formulations of literacy provide certain understandings of its meaning and value. The pragmatic sense focuses on how, in contrast to theoretical work, institutional systems construct a reality with respect to literacy. My strategy in this chapter is to move between the general and the specific, between various theoretical conceptualizations of literacy and the case of Western District. I begin by mapping relevant literacy theory in order to understand various positions on the question of literacy and to pinpoint those that I find most useful. Then I turn to the case of Western District to explore an alternative way in which literacy is given meaning and value. I hope to work back to Street's question: how is a particular literacy taken to be the only one? And so the important question really isn't *what* literacy is but rather *how* it came to be.

Mapping Literacy Theory

A general survey of literacy theory would be unwieldy and tedious, so I focus on the literacy theories produced and cited by scholars in rhetoric and composition that constitute a focused concern with the social practices of writing outside the first-year composition classroom.[1] This literature is still substantial and interdisciplinary, drawing particularly from educational psychology and various approaches in anthropology, sociology, and linguistics. One can see scholars in rhetoric and composition articulate this literature in a set of texts that began appearing regularly in the late 1980s. Among the first of these is the collection *Perspectives on Literacy* (Kintgen, Kroll, & Rose, 1988). This book contains few essays not previously published, but its organizational principle names four approaches to understanding literacy—theoretical, historical, educational, and community—that is noteworthy for its gaze outside the classroom. Likewise, the book that followed the 1988 MLA "Right to Literacy" conference is another important text for rhetoric and composition because it contains a range of articles covering differing disciplinary and institutional backgrounds and focuses on a variety of writing practices and contexts (Lunsford, Moglen, & Slevin, 1990).

As the number of books and articles dealing with literacy outside the first year writing classroom has proliferated, so have the taxonomies of literacy theory. These publications have made available important interdisciplinary work: studies from psychology like Scribner and Cole (1981), critical approaches from education, and perhaps most importantly, scholarship from anthropology (e.g., Street, 1984; 1995) and ethnographic approaches to language and learning (e.g., Barton, 1994; Barton & Hamilton, 1998; Heath, 1983). The result of these interdisciplinary discussions is a rich but confusing picture. Table 2–1 is an attempt to compare relatively recent literacy taxonomies.

The top of the table lists the various categories scholars have used to taxonomize literacy work. The left side of the table lists the authors and

Table 2-1
Terms Used to Categorize Literacy Work in Rhetoric and Composition

	Cultural Literacy	Social & Cultural Critique	Critical Literacy	Community Literacy	Strong Text	Functionalist	Literacy as Contextual Practice	Literacy as Involvement	Literacy as Personal Growth	Literacy as Social Practice	Ideology	Ecology
Knoblauch 1990	No Source		Critical Literacy; Freire		Ong Olson et al.	Basic Skills Technical Writing; Workplace Literacy			Expressive rhetoric			
Walters 1990					Great Leap Theory: Ong et al.							
Brandt 1992					Ong, Olson et al.			Socio-Cognitive Work				
Barton 1994			Freire		Ong, Olson et al.					Scribner &Cole	Street	Heath; Barton
Peck et al. 1995	Hirsch; Bloom	"Straw-Person"		Themselves								
Minter et al. 1995					Ong; Olson et al.		Heath; Street; White; Robinson					

19

20 *Community Literacy Programs*

dates of publication. To read how a particular theorist places others in their taxonomy, one should read horizontally across the table. Deborah Brandt's (1990) taxonomy, for example, is relatively small, contrasting a set of theorists she calls "strong text" with her own "literacy as involvement." Knoblauch's (1990) entry is more properly a taxonomy, encompassing a number of scholars and researchers in five categories. As a whole, this table shows a number of things, such as a few overlapping and confusing categories (e.g., "critical" and "social and cultural critique" or the various placements of Heath and Street) and a few strong consistencies (like the Strong Text category).

This table also shows that literacy theorists are concerned with a wide range of issues—politics, psychology, expression, texts. But I use this table to make another point: it is confusing. There isn't much holding together the work represented in the table. The table is map with too few (or too many?) road signs. Certainly the scholars cited here can't all be talking about the same thing. But they are. Thus it is what this table masks that is important for me. Masked yet running through this table are four general themes: mind, (social) culture, autonomy, and context. These themes provide one way to make sense of the literacy literature, and remapping this literature in terms of these themes is a way to make this work more useful for understanding how scholars locate literacy's meaning and value.

What is Literacy?
Mapping Table 2–1 in terms of the four themes of mind, (social) culture, autonomy, and context is a more powerful representation than previous taxonomies because it allows for change and for various notions of literacy to reflect more than one theme (see Figure 2–1). I hope it is immediately possible to see that these theories of literacy are rich, that in my reading each embodies a variation on these themes in order to locate meaning and value. The map itself is composed of two interrelated continua. The horizontal continuum moves from theories that focus on the *Mind* (internal) to theories that focus on *Socio-Culture* (external):

> *Mind.* This label marks those theories that locate the meaning and value of literacy internal to human beings: expressive theories that focus on self-expression or the development of voice, approaches to literacy that focus on the cognitive and intellectual effects of literacy, or various cognitive approaches to literacy that likewise focus on the cognitive processes associated with the development and use of written literacy.

Socio-Cultural. This label marks those theories that locate the meaning and value of literacy external to human beings, often as a function of social processes and actions and/or culture. Theorists who locate literacy

Figure 2–1
Theories of Literacy

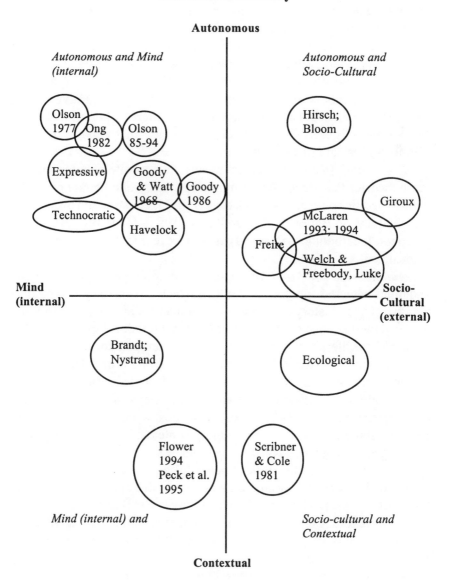

in the social see it as having meaning primarily within the social practices of institutions and communities. Theorists who focus on culture (the terms "social" and "culture" are used almost synonymously) similarly locate literacy in social life but sometimes tend to focus on literacy as cultural knowledge or struggles over cultural meaning. Examples of approaches that most clearly illustrate a cultural focus are Hirsch's (1987) "cultural literacy," which sees literacy as a body of cultural knowledge, and approaches from critical theories of education, like Giroux (1993), which see literacy as a cultural politics.

The vertical continuum expresses another tension that I see running through most literacy theory, the tension between *Autonomy* and *Context*.

Autonomous. Brandt (1990) and Street (1984) use the term "autonomous" to describe work that claims "revolutionary" cognitive consequences from the acquisition and use of written literacy. For my purposes, "autonomous" describes any theory of literacy that decontextualizes people, places, and literate practices.

Contextual. In a sense, context means the opposite of autonomy, or those theories that locate the meanings of literacy and literate practices within specific contexts, like Peck et al.'s (1995) construction of community literacy or Barton and Hamilton's (1998) focus on "everyday" practices. If autonomous theory is generalized, contextual literacy theory is localized.

Autonomous and Mind (internal). The combination of autonomous and mind-centered approaches should not be too surprising; this combination reflects a history of talking about human cognition and consciousness and their connection to historical and cultural development. For the most part, the literacy theories in this section attempt to focus on "literacy itself" by characterizing the qualities of a literate mind. This work is Theory in the way I characterized it in the preface—abstract and general in its scope and application. Because of the ways in which this work decontextualizes people and places, I find most work here inappropriate for understanding writing in community contexts. In fact, public policy and program design based on this work can be harmful to the very people who need help. Yet this work is powerful and therefore necessary to understand. I begin my discussion with expressive approaches, move to the set of approaches Brandt (1990) and Street (1984) call "autonomous" or "strong text" and end with a gloss of what some call functional literacy, and what others (e.g., Flower, 1994) label "technocratic" notions of literacy.

Expressive approaches to teaching writing are commonplace in composition theory. However, expressive practices are less common as attempts to understand writing issues outside of schools. Still, expressive theory and practice are deeply ingrained as a kind of lore about how people learn to read and write and are pervasive in both school and community contexts (see, for example, Writers of the Greater Indianapolis Literacy League, 1994). Proponents eschew models of communication that are more pragmatic or based on paradigms, like cognitive science, that fail to capture the complexity of literacy (see, for example, Smith, 1985). So the individual in acquiring a literacy is really acquiring a new way of experiencing the self and the world (an insight I agree with), but too often that world exists only in the mind, experience, and texts of the individual. The purpose of literacy here is to "create worlds," to facilitate individual expression regardless of context. Western District, like most educational institutions, makes ample room for expressive literacies.

In contrast to the expressive focus on individuals and self-expression, the vast range of other autonomous approaches are concerned with general, macro-level statements about literacy. Many of these autonomous theories of literacy primarily come from two disciplinary concerns—cultural anthropology and educational applications of cognitive psychology. In both cases, scholars typically focus on differences between oral and literate societies and cultures. In anthropology, the concern is often with large-scale changes over time. In psychology, represented here by David Olson, the concern began with one conceptualization of school failure: students who struggle in school come primarily from "oral" situations and have trouble adapting to the "literate" world of school (see Cook-Gumperz, 1986, for a critique and alternative). Both focus on understanding and arguing for the consequences of acquiring written literacy.

Autonomous approaches often begin with the Greek alphabet, and because of that, with Havelock (1982), for whom the Greek alphabet is "a piece of explosive technology, revolutionary in its effects on human culture . . ." (p. 6). For Havelock, written language means distance and abstraction, while oral language marks the local and particular (1986, p. 124). The alphabet "converted the Greek spoken tongue into an artifact, thereby separating it from the speaker and making it into a 'language,' that is, an object available for inspection, reflection, analysis" (Havelock, 1982, p. 8). Such inspection, reflection, and analysis—made possible by written records—gives us historical sensibility (Goody & Watt, 1968, p. 34) and the consciousness that is "absolutely necessary for the development not only of science but also of history, philosophy, explicative understanding of literature and of any art, and indeed for the explanation of language (including oral speech) itself" (Ong, 1982, pp. 14–15). Thus, if written language or literacy equals increasing abstraction of mind and the subsequent dissemination of tradition, custom, law, and culture (Havelock, 1982, p. 126), then the objective of literacy is "the mastery of that kind of language which deals in concepts, the ability to express oneself abstractly, and so to think logically and clearly" (Havelock, 1986, p. 124).

The discourse on language, history, and culture that I have just summarized is ubiquitous to the extent that many will see it as common knowledge or common sense. My reaction to this work is that it might be overstated but probably isn't wrong. Regardless, my point is not to argue with these positions on their own terms but rather with their effects on how we think about literacy. This can be seen clearly in the work of David Olson. Early, Olson (1977) makes an explicit link between textuality and literacy, between the qualities of text and the qualities of the literate mind, arguing that written language is "able to stand as an unambiguous or autonomous representation of meaning" (1977, p. 258). In later publications, Olson (1985; 1986; 1994) still demonstrates these formalist tendencies while acknowledging that "literacy" marks a set of culturally situated cognitive skills. Unlike others I will discuss, however, Olson makes little effort to actually situate his discussion either in a culture or a specific context. What remains clear in Olson, I think, is the consistent connection between the autonomous qualities of written literacy and literacy's cognitive consequences. This is one unfortunate legacy of the work of Havelock, Ong, and others. Their philosophical histories of literacy were so successful and persuasive that they became fundamental to a common way of thinking about literacy that encouraged simplistic links between thought and language, between literacy and culture, and between writing and historical progress.

These simplistic links are nowhere more clear than in literacy work that some call "technocratic" and others "functional" or "basic skills" literacy. This work has been influential in shaping school curricula and community-based literacy programs. Technocratic approaches seem to embody "common sense" principles of language and learning and appear more practical and straightforward. And technocratic literacies figure prominently in how literacy is defined and practiced at Western District.

DeCastell and Luke (1988), for example, attribute the rise of technocratic approaches to literacy with the post Second World War drive to make education more scientific. Drawing on developmental and cognitive psychology as they operated in education, "literacy was ... scientifically dissected into individually teachable and testable subskill units" (p. 170). Reading programs like SRA proliferated as did other basal readers and worksheet approaches to language arts instruction. The teacher, in turn, was "encouraged to see the educational process in medical and managerial metaphors. In technocratic pedagogies, students are diagnosed, prescribed for, treated and checked before proceeding to the next level of instruction" (DeCastell & Luke, 1988, p. 172). Instruction became "individualized" and "neutral" skills were taught based on scientific assessment, but significantly, the same skills were taught to students across North America in packaged curricula. Typically, technocratic literacy is a generalized literacy in that while it is a functional, skill-based process of education, the process is conceptualized as the same for all students. This is done by focusing on cognitive skills, normalized behavioral objectives, and as Flower (1994) argues, correctness, thereby abstracting both student and teacher from context, culture, difference. In "occupational" or workplace literacy, technocratic curricula focus on functional literacies with a limited scope—literally focused on specific job tasks such as reading labels. Yet often, these "specific" job skills are the same for all workers, regardless of job or situation; the result is a generalized list of necessary skills (Rush, Moe, & Storlie 1986; Diehl, 1980). These approaches to literacy, while different from others in this portion of the map because of their pragmatism, are still quite similar because of the abstraction of students and literate practices.[2]

Harvey Graff (1988), referring to what I have been calling autonomous and mind-centered literacy theory, suggests that:

> Writings about the imputed "consequences," "implications," or "concomitants" of literacy have assigned to literacy's acquisition a truly daunting number of cognitive, affective, behavioral, and attitudinal effects. These characteristics usually include attitudes ranging from empathy, innovativeness, achievement-orientation, "cosmopoliteness," information- and media awareness, national identification, technological acceptance, rationality, and commitment to democracy, to opportunism, linearity of thought and behavior, or urban residence. (p. 83)

Graff is working from a position of critique. He argues that the consequences of literacy are more dependent on issues of power (structures of

authority), ideology, and economy. Still, his gloss is an effective sum-
mary of autonomous positions. What are the characteristics of literacy
according to this work? What kind of language are we given to describe
the meaning and value of literacy? There is a clear focus on expression,
rationality, and consciousness; there is a related focus on texts and
artifacts; and there is a powerful concern with functionality, skills, and
work. One important result is a concrete and clear "good" associated with
literacy. Yet this work is not situated in any recognizable context and is
not concerned with any specific group of people. And it has no theory of
institutional procedures and power; it has no rhetoric. One will see in
Western District, however, many of these same tendencies toward abstraction, particularly the decontextualized way in which workplace
literacy is conceived and programs designed.

Socio-Cultural and Autonomous. We remain in the abstract portions
of my map, yet, perhaps ironically, move into the social and cultural.
Because of this and because of the odd grouping of work here, this
quadrant is a strange place. My goal here, in fact, is to make strange a set
of well-known and powerful ways to understand literacy in order to
highlight similarities despite obvious differences. The key similarity is
the way this work continues to abstract people and places. Most often,
theories in this quadrant focus on literacy as cultural knowledge or
struggles over cultural meaning. Yet this focus makes for some strange
political bed-fellows.

In rhetoric and composition's approaches to literacy theory, the work
of Hirsch (1987) and Bloom (1987) has come under consistent critique.
Their work is the most articulate and persuasive presentation of an
approach to literacy and education more generally that is often associated
with political and ideological conservatism and which conceives of
literacy as a problem of knowledge, standards, and values. To be literate
is to be culturally literate, "to possess the basic information needed to
thrive in the modern world. . . . Cultural literacy constitutes the only sure
avenue of opportunity for disadvantaged children" (Hirsch, 1987, p. xiii).
Indeed, for Hirsch cultural literacy is the knowledge necessary for greater
economic prosperity, social justice, and democracy (p. 2). It would be a
mistake, however, simply to equate Hirsch's cultural literacy with a list
of cultural facts or a static body of knowledge. Cultural literacy as the path
to opportunity and democracy is predicated on a theory of community
held together by knowledge and communication: in order to have a better,
freer, and more prosperous democracy, society needs to retain a sense of
common community and culture. In effect, we must be able to communi-

cate "our national community" as well as within that community. The shared culture or community is the "oxygen of social discourse, " excluding nobody (Hirsch, 1987, p. 21), or what Bloom (1987) calls the "shared goals or vision of the public good" necessary for maintaining the social contract (p. 27). A shared community is necessary for democracy and freedom.

While there is a clear political rift in this quadrant, the work of others here, particularly Henry Giroux (1987; 1988; 1989a; 1989b; 1993) is similarly generalized. Giroux's position on literacy is fundamentally political; that is, he foregrounds politics and conceptualizes literacy as a form of cultural politics (1988, p. 63). Literacy is also a struggle over the construction and meaning of subjectivity within a broad range of cultural practices. When Giroux sets out to define literacy and name possible emancipatory subject positions, the generalized tendencies of his approach to literacy become clear. Giroux (1987) writes, "in the broadest political sense, literacy is best understood as a myriad of discursive forms and cultural competencies that construct and make available the various relations and experiences that exist between learners and the world" (p. 10). In later efforts, Giroux writes that literacy is:

- a notion "synonymous with an attempt to rescue history, experience, and vision . . . from dominant social relations" (1987, p. 10)
- a "means of developing the theoretical and practical conditions through which human beings can locate themselves in their own histories . . ." and become agents of their own liberation (1987, pp. 10-11)
- a precondition for struggles of power (1987, p. 11); being literate is not being free, it is "to be present and active in the struggle for reclaiming one's voice, history, and future" (1988, p. 65)
- "a form of cultural citizenship and politics that provides the conditions for subordinate groups to learn the knowledge and skills necessary for self and social empowerment . . . an emerging act of consciousness and resistance" (1993, p. 367)

I present these quotations because I think they illustrate two things about Giroux's conception of literacy: (1) literacy is a necessary early condition for cultural and political struggle; and (2) it is nearly impossible to locate or situate the site of this struggle. In one important sense, the locus of literate struggle is the subject. Giroux writes that a radical theory of literacy is concerned with intervening in the "dialectical relationship between human subjects and the objective world," or with helping subjects to locate their own histories (1987, p. 12). And there is no doubt that all social institutions must be the subject of critique and revision. Giroux's focus on how discourses about literacy often mask concrete asymmetries of power and resources by focusing on the "skills" "illiterates" lack is another part of his focus on subjectivity. But still, I cannot locate his work with more specificity than a concern with postmodern society and culture and a concern with discourse, subjectivity, and democratic citizenship. Is Giroux talking about schools? About workplaces? About community literacy programs? Perhaps all of them. What types of literate practices is he interested in? What types of practices are important for people to be able to utilize so that they can "locate themselves in their own histories"? Who decides? I'm not sure. In other words, I'm not sure where, exactly, Giroux locates the meaning and value of literacy because his theorizing practices are never situated.

Giroux's tendency toward the abstract is a problem shared by most critical literacy theories. Paulo Freire (1992; 1995) influences in many ways a wide range of literacy discourses by placing issues of subjectivity, politics, and power at the forefront of literacy discussions. The irony in reading Freire, however, is that while his work has tried to counter the harmful abstractions of much contemporary educational practice—abstractions that isolate individuals from their communities and the value of their lived experiences—his own work lacks the rhetorical sense and methodology that would allow us to locate meaningful institutional contexts.[3] The devil, as I will insist throughout, is in these details.

Yet not all critical literacy work has such strong tendencies toward the universal. The work of McLaren (1993; 1994) and Lankshear and McLaren (1993) argues that literacy is "entirely a matter of how reading and writing are conceived and practiced within particular social contexts . . . where access to economic, cultural, political, and institutional power is structured unequally" (Lankshear & McLaren, 1993, pp. xvii–xviii). Literacies are "indices of power" (p. xviii), but they are also situated within the particular institutions that warrant them (Luke, 1993; Welch & Freebody, 1993). The promise of Freire and others is found in their descriptions of local practice and arguments that we look at local institutions in order to understand their power to shape literacies; the problems are found in the tendency to theorize without recourse to those local practices.

While I am attracted to the power of theory, I also think it is dangerous, and despite the political edge of some theorists, fundamentally disengaged. Stories with epic scope are often narratives with simple histories and characters. The work I have glossed here does provide some useful language and perspectives on literacy. We learn that literacy is tied to culture in some way, and because of this, we are told differently by both Right and Left that literacy is inseparable from politics. Most importantly, the critical theorists here provide a language of liberation, a focus on power, and a theory of action (praxis), all of which form part of a critical rhetoric of design. And so despite the problems, I will rely on critical literacy throughout this book.

Mind (internal) and Contextual. For the field of rhetoric and composition, socio-cognitive approaches to understanding composing processes have been important, and these same theoretical approaches drive literacy theory as well, both within rhetoric (as in the case of Brandt and Flower), and within other disciplines (like the psychologists and linguists Scribner and Cole). I use the label "socio-cognitive" to describe a situated and therefore useful way of understanding written literacies, particularly Brandt's (1990) and Nystrand's (1989) formulation of literacy as intersubjectivity, Scribner and Cole's (1981) important study of the literate practices of the Vai, and Flower's (1994) and Peck et al's (1995) interrelated formulations of socio-cognitive approaches to literacy.

Brandt's (1990) *Literacy as Involvement* is one of the few texts in rhetoric and composition to counter autonomous notions of literacy (she calls them "strong text"). For Brandt, there are no fundamental differences between the oral and the literate; they pose "the same basic interpretive puzzles," the same social interactions, and the same deeply contextual references for meaning (p. 7). Brandt offers a literacy of involvement, by which she means a mode of inquiry that seeks to understand how writers and readers "do" writing and reading together. Literacy as involvement conceives of literacy as "knowing what to do now" in the process of making meaning through reading and writing (pp. 7, 38).

Brandt's theory of literacy depends on Nystrand's (1989) social-interactive model of writing. According to this model, readers and writers are essentially solitary individuals "struggling mainly with their thoughts" (p. 70). The skilled writer "senses, in typically tacit manner, when her purpose is likely either to mesh with or to run against the grain of her reader's expectations and purposes" (p. 78). Similarly, Brandt's intersubjective agreement comes down to the writer possessing the writing strategies necessary in order to keep the process of writing going until the reader will understand the meaning of a writer's text—a drama that plays out in the mind of the writer. Brandt's approach to literacy is an important argument from within rhetoric and composition against autonomous approaches to literacy and is an important argument for contextualizing literacy. Generally speaking, I think this is what rhetoric and composition as a discipline has to offer larger discussions of literacy: rich understandings of written literacies that are deeply situated within specific contexts.

Perhaps the strongest socio-cognitive work in the area of literacy— certainly for community literacy—has been the work of Linda Flower and others working at Carnegie-Mellon and with the Community Literacy Center in Pittsburgh. According to Flower's (1994) socio-cognitive perspective, literacy entails:

- a shift from a focus on texts to a focus on practices
- a notion of practices as socially situated problem-solving processes
- a sense of practices as purposeful literate actions performed in social/cultural situations
- a knowledge of discourse conventions and communities in order to function effectively within social/cultural situations (pp. 2–30)

For Flower literacy is not conceptualized in the singular or as something that can be possessed. Literacies, rather, are situated actions geared toward solving problems. In terms of community literacies, literate acts are geared toward collaborative problem-solving, critical awareness, strategic thinking, and reflective learning, all with the goal of building community and enacting social change (Peck et al., 1995, pp. 203–205, 215). Still, like Brandt and Nystrand, Flower ultimately is interested in the inner, cognitive processes of individuals.

The socio-cognitive work of Scribner and Cole (1981) does not focus exclusively on the individual or see contexts as fundamentally static. Their project sought to separate literacy from schooling; that is, to test whether or not the acquisition of written literacy has cognitive consequences separate from the effects of schooling. To do this, they used both experimental and ethnographic methods to study the Vai people of Liberia because Vai society was one in which there were not only multiple written and oral literacies (English, Vai, and Arabic), but there were also certain written practices that fell outside school domains (Vai literacy). Their findings were interesting and important. First, they found that the Vai people developed highly diversified uses for writing sustained by a host of ideological, intellectual, and pragmatic concerns and partitioned across scripts (English, Vai, and Arabic). Second, with the exception of some school situations, literacy rarely led to the acquisition of knowledge, as most autonomous theories assert. Third, the roles of written literacy were confined to cultural functions, and each script fit within a specific cultural framework. For example, Arabic literacies, which were mostly oral, were used for Koranic learning, Vai writing for correspondence.

What Scribner and Cole call their descent from the general to the specific—from autonomous assumptions to culturally specific conclusions—led them to develop a notion of literate practices. By a practice account of literacy, Scribner and Cole mean a "recurrent, goal-directed sequence of activities using a particular technology and particular systems of knowledge . . . A practice, then, consists of three components: technology, knowledge, and [cognitive] skills" (p. 236). Thus, they approach literacy as a set of "socially organized practices which make use of a symbol system and a technology for producing and disseminating it" (p. 236).

The connection between Scribner and Cole and socio-cognitive work in rhetoric and composition should be clear, and all of the work described here is useful for understanding written literacies. Like certain autonomous perspectives, it is interested mostly in the individual, but it is much more situated. Meaning, for example, is contextual, not Textual, and the meanings and values associated with particular literacies must be situated culturally and ideologically to be understood. Perhaps most importantly, this work insists on conceptualizing literacies as actions, as practices. So despite the lack of institutional awareness, work such as this has had a significant impact on how we understand written literacies.

Socio-Cultural and Contextual. Work here goes even farther in attempting to locate literate practices within specific, concrete, and local contexts, situations, and institutions. I am grouping the particular approaches in this quadrant under an umbrella term, "ecological," that I take from David Barton (1994), although an alternative way to describe this work would be in terms of the New Literacy Studies (see Gee, 2000). This umbrella includes work by Barton and his colleagues at Lancaster University in England, including the closely associated work of Brian Street (1984; 1993; 1995), and the similar work of Heath (1983; 1986; 1990). Barton (1994) takes the term "ecology" from biology and uses it as a way to name an approach to literacy that sees it as part of a complex and interrelated social environment. For Barton, it is important to understand not only that literacies are "tied up with particular details of the situation, and that literacy events are particular to a specific community at a specific point in history" (p. 3), but also to understand that these local contexts are what give literacy its social meaning from which technical and functional aspects follow. In other words, to generalize a discussion of literacy is to lose any sense of the meaning of literacy.

But Barton's work also raises a new set of terms taken from linguistics that mark conceptual categories and allow one to understand the social sphere within which particular, local literacies are practiced (see Barton & Hamilton, 1998; Barton, Hamilton, & Padmore, 1992; Ivanič & Moss, 1991; Bloome, 1993; & Davies, 1994). It is important, then, to understand what Barton means by these terms:

> • *Domain.* Domain is a macro-level term. It marks larger, sociological spheres of activity: school, work, and the everyday (or "community" in Barton & Ivanič, 1991). The concept serves to partition social life into three fluid and overlapping categories that allow literacy scholars to make distinctions not made by school-based theorists; that is, workplaces and community sites may constitute "distinct social situations" that cannot be accounted for by theory produced within schools.

> • *Event.* According to Heath (1983), a literacy event is "any occasion in which a piece of writing is integral to the nature of participants' interactions and their interpretive processes" (p. 350). Rooted in the linguistic notion of a speech event, a literate event is a purposeful interaction supported by literate practices.

> • *Practice.* Literate practices are described by Barton and Hamilton (2000) as "general cultural ways of utilizing written language which people draw on in their lives" (p. 7). They note that practices are what people do with literacy, but they also write that practices are not "observable units of behaviour" (p. 7). There is some confusion, it seems to me, as to what a practice is. It is an action, but it is not observable. For my purposes—and drawing on a wider notion of practice—literate practices are indeed observable actions that are also part of the larger fabric of cultural practices associated with literacy.

> • *Institution.* Barton (1991) writes that "behind home, school, and work can be seen particular institutions that support ... distinct domains. Particular definitions of literacy and associated literacy practices are nurtured by these institutions. They are definition-

sustaining institutions ... [defining] and influenc[ing] different aspects of literacy or different literacies" (p. 5). By focusing on institutions, Barton, and Street (1984; 1995) as well, want to say more than literacies exist in social contexts or that there are social dimensions to literacy; they are arguing that the very definition and meaning—the existence and power—of certain literate practices is embedded in institutions.

The concept of the institution is extremely important, yet this is the only literacy work that I know of that highlights the role of institutions.

The literacy theory I have represented in the first part of this chapter is clearly influential. There is much work here that I find an exercise in myth-making when it comes to understanding how certain literacies are given meaning and value. There is other work, in contrast, that is extremely useful: the focus on power, oppression, and resistance on the part of critical literacy theorists; the attention to specific acts of meaning making on the part of socio-cognitive theorists; and the framework for conceptualizing literacy that is provided by an ecological perspective. The influences of work from each category will be clear throughout the rest of the book. However, while the importance of social institutions is generally acknowledged, there are few examinations of how specific institutions shape the meaning and value of literacy. And so one purpose of this mapping exercise is to create a space for a look at institutional systems and how they give meaning and value to certain literate practices and therefore shape what is possible.

Literacy at Western District

The question "what is literacy" at Western District is answered *by* institutions. The most consistent and powerful set of answers comes from the laws that fund Adult Basic Education, the state documents that regulate it, and the assessment tools that measure it. The Indiana "Adult Education Handbook," for instance, provides its definition of literacy within the acts governing adult education (from The National Literacy Act of 1991 [P.L. 102–73]). This definition expresses what I would term an "autonomous" or abstracted sense of literacy, perhaps necessary given its origin (in law) and use (in a state regulatory document). Still, this definition, as I hope to show, is powerful and operates at specific, local levels in the Western District program itself. The definition reads as follows:

> An individual's ability to read, write and speak in English and compute and solve problems at levels of proficiency necessary to function on the job and in society, to achieve one's goals, and to develop one's knowledge and potential. (Division of Adult Education, "Adult Education Handbook," p. 5)[4]

This definition does not localize literacy in any meaningful way, nor, more importantly, does it acknowledge the need to do so. It does not recognize that literacies "on the job" and "in society" vary significantly. Furthermore, the definition is connected to the belief, expressed elsewhere in this and other documents (e.g., Division of Adult Education, "Indiana's Adult Teacher Handbook"), that the skills that correlate with the abilities in the definition are "basic skills" that lay the foundation necessary to function in society (functional reading, writing, and numeracy skills). Sometimes the required basic skills seem synonymous with credentials, like a diploma or a GED (e.g., Division of Adult Education, "Indiana's Adult Education Teacher Handbook," p. 2-4). Here the vocational motif in Adult Basic Education surfaces. A credential means not only proof of a certain level of education, but more importantly, it increases the probability of employment, at least in theory, which is a goal of the state and the students who attend ABE programs. Most students check "GED" as their reason for attending Western District, and as my interviews with students showed time and time again, both students and the state share the belief that with a GED comes enhanced employment opportunities. Perhaps this is true. Still, as soon as literacy becomes synonymous with credentials, it seems to lose meaning as a set of actions/practices that people can use to act effectively within a range of situations. Literacy becomes an object, a possession.

The meaning and value of literacy is established first through the relationship between legislation and assessment. The two are intertwined: legislation mandates the assessment practices, the assessments reinforce legislated rules and goals. The assessment process begins with the intake assessment of students, which is mandated by the federal government and regulated by the state. The state designates which tests are to be given at intake, which in turn determines student placement. The initial assessment is the baseline from which learner gains are measured and documented, a key to Indiana ABE philosophy (Division of Adult Education,

"Policy on Testing," p. 1), and a key to Western District goals of student recruitment, student retention, and learner gains (Western District Adult Basic Education, "Grant Application," 1994, p. 6). Once students are in classes, the effect of assessments on the meaning and value of literacy varies. For example, not all students are working toward their GED; they may have been placed in classes at a level for which the GED is not an immediate reality. Still, these students are assessed at prescribed times, both "informally" by curricular exams when they finish a unit and "formally" by the Test of Adult Basic Education exam, one of the standardized assessments. For students working toward their GED, their curriculum reflects the skills and knowledge necessary to be successful on that exam. In both cases, the literacies of the exams become the literacies of the classroom, and by extension, the program. The exams drive the curriculum, and the pervasiveness and power of the exams is significant. Therefore, the most concrete way to see how an institutional system like Western District gives certain literacies meaning and value is to look at its assessment practices.

Eligibility, Assessment, and Placement of Students
For Western District and likely for any program that must demonstrate effectiveness, assessment begins with the intake of students and follows them throughout their time in the program in order to track learning. Assessments literally construct student identities and trigger the flow of money through the system. In ABE programs, this begins with eligibility. Eligibility is linked to reimbursement of federal and state money and is therefore important. In effect, eligibility and reimbursement define the population of ABE programs, and in a sense, define the "community" directly served by a program like Western District. The following constitutes the parameters for who can be served by Western District:

- at least 16 years old
- officially withdrawn from a K–12 program
- does not have a diploma or equivalent
- if a graduate, needs basic skill development in math or language arts (i.e., tests below a 12.9 grade level). (Division of Adult Education, "Indiana's Adult Education Teacher Handbook," 2-7).

It is possible for adult students (16+) who do not fit the above criteria to participate in the program, but the program cannot be reimbursed for their attendance.

Reimbursement, however, is more complex than the recruitment of eligible students. Both federal and state guidelines specify a *registration* and *enrollment* status as part of an elaborate intake process. Registered students are "those participants who have attended, but have not yet accumulated the hours needed to be enrolled" (Division of Adult Education, "Indiana's Adult Education Handbook," p. 2-8). Enrollment, then, is the status students obtain when they have attended 12 hours of instruction. Thus, the registration process constitutes those hours prior to twelve during which the student goes through the intake process (which includes assessment). After the twelve hour enrollment period, the student then "counts" in terms of reimbursement, and is considered, at least from a strict funding standpoint, served by the adult education program.

The process represented in Figure 2–2 moves through initial orientation, various form-filling moments, a battery of pre-test assessments, and the development of the most important form for instruction, the Adult Learning Plan (ALP). Everything represented in this figure takes place *before* instruction. This process of intake and assessment is fundamental to the ways in which literacy is defined and ultimately practiced at Western District. The process begins at the top with an evening of orientation, registration, and testing at Western District. Key to that orientation are decisions about "testing appropriateness" and the collection of background information from participants about their educational and work histories, current skills, and vocational plans (Division of Adult Education, "Indiana's Adult Education Teacher's Handbook," p. 5-1). Each piece of information contributes to the decision to test or not:

> All learners who attend ABE programs must be assigned to an instructional level. A learner's instructional level is determined by standardized test scores in a two-step process: first, the goals and expressed needs of the learner are usually used to select an area in which further assessment will be made; second, the student's competencies are determined through standardized testing in the area selected. (Division of Adult Education, "Adult Education Handbook," p. 25)[5]

Almost every student is tested and moves through the process as represented in the left-hand column of Figure 2–2. The process begins with their initial exams (either CASAS or TABE) and continues with the IN

Figure 2–2
Intake, Registration, Enrollment

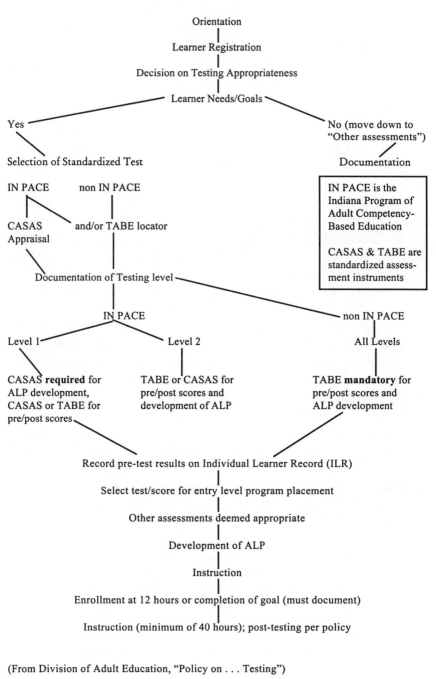

Orientation

Learner Registration

Decision on Testing Appropriateness

Learner Needs/Goals

Yes

No (move down to "Other assessments")

Selection of Standardized Test

Documentation

IN PACE   non IN PACE

IN PACE is the Indiana Program of Adult Competency-Based Education

CASAS   and/or TABE locator
Appraisal

CASAS & TABE are standardized assessment instruments

Documentation of Testing level

IN PACE   non IN PACE

Level 1   Level 2   All Levels

CASAS **required** for ALP development, CASAS or TABE for pre/post scores.

TABE or CASAS for pre/post scores and development of ALP

TABE **mandatory** for pre/post scores and ALP development

Record pre-test results on Individual Learner Record (ILR)

Select test/score for entry level program placement

Other assessments deemed appropriate

Development of ALP

Instruction

Enrollment at 12 hours or completion of goal (must document)

Instruction (minimum of 40 hours); post-testing per policy

(From Division of Adult Education, "Policy on . . . Testing")

PACE curriculum and the development of the Adult Learning Plan (which I will discuss in some detail below). As a program, IN PACE covers assessment and instruction and is designed to be a "comprehensive, learner-centered, performance-based program to meet the needs of adults who wish to improve fluency in English, develop skills necessary to get a GED, enhance employment opportunities or function more effectively in society" (Division of Adult Education, "Indiana's Adult Education Teacher Handbook," p. 2-9).[6]

After the initial assessments are scored, the student is placed in one of three levels—Beginning ABE, Intermediate ABE, or Adult Secondary Education/GED. Each level corresponds to a grade assessment from the testing instrument: 0–5.9; 6–8.9; 9–12.9. (Division of Adult Education, "Adult Education Handbook," p. 26). Following those results, the student and program, represented by the intake person or teacher, set "realistic" short- and long-term goals (Division of Adult Education, "Indiana's Adult Education Teacher Handbook," p. 6-5). In effect, IN PACE instruction attempts to make an explicit connection between "basic" and "life" skills, and so the goals set are framed in terms of grade level improvement and basic skills acquisition. Basic skills, like reading, writing, computing, speaking, and listening are "enabling skills" which allow students to learn life skills related to employment. The teaching imperative, then, is to help students see the connections between the two, and as often as possible, use real-life materials to learn basic skills. These goals form the basis for the Adult Learning Plan (ALP), perhaps the single most important document/practice at Western District.[7] The ALP is a tool required for federally funded programs (Division of Adult Education, "Indiana's Adult Education Teacher Handbook," p. 2-18). The ALP is designed to document learner gains as well as the needs and plans of the student. It is seen by Indiana as a document that moves beyond standardized testing, is consistent with learner-centered approaches, yet also meets increased federal standards of accountability. The ALP was designed to do the following:

1. To enhance the learner's sense of ownership of his/her learning plan and increase the learner's enthusiasm and commitment to the learning process, allowing the learner to realize success more quickly;

2. To provide a "roadmap" of learner and program staff decisions about a course of study based on the reasons the learner chose to attend the program;

3. To serve as a tool for better communication among staff members, volunteers, and referral agencies in implementing a learner's plan;

4. To provide a method by which learner progress is reviewed on a regular basis; and,

5. To provide documentation of learner achievement for the learner, local programs, funding sources, and referral agencies. (Division of Adult Education, "Purpose of Adult Learning Plan," p. 1)

From my observations, however, it is important to note some mismatches between policy and practice. The description of the intake process in these policy documents paints a picture much more collaborative than my observation of intake procedures at Western District suggest (the issue of collaboration is an important "who decides" issue for questions of literacy and one I will discuss in later chapters). Intake is a process that takes approximately two hours per evening for three evenings (all material from fieldnotes taken 9/16/96). The first night consists of a general introduction to Western District and the policies of the program. After the general/ policy introduction, which on the night I was there took about a half hour, students fill out their registration forms and materials. Among these forms are the "Referral Form," the "Registration Form," and the Adult Learning Plan (ALP). In filling out the referral form, students are taken through a step-by-step process by the intake leader, who demonstrates how the form should be filled out using the chalkboard and overhead. On this form, students choose the classes they wish to attend in terms of day and time, and they confirm when they will continue their intake testing. The registration form asks for biographical and socio-economic data, and it also has a checklist that allows students to articulate their goals (e.g., get a job, get off public assistance, get GED). Finally, students fill out their ALPs, what one of the intake leaders called "a charming sheet the state dreamed up." The ALP is the center of Indiana's implementation of "learner-centered education," and is meant as a collaborative and goal-directed assessment tool that allows students and teachers to set short-term goals (interview, Ed Cotton, 8/12/96).[8] During the first evening of intake, the students merely filled out the portions of the ALP that asked for their name and their reasons for participation in the program; the rest of the form is left for the students to work through with their teachers.

The remainder of the evening was spent with students taking the TABE (Test of Adult Basic Education) locator exams in vocabulary and math. Based on the results of these exams, on day two of intake, students take the TABE math pre-test, followed by a math lesson. On day three of intake, students take the TABE pre-test in language. After these intake hours, students can join their classes of choice (in terms of time of day) and level (determined by the exams). After twelve hours of instruction, they are officially enrolled and not assessed again using the TABE or other standardized instruments until they leave the program, finish the term, or complete 40 hours of instruction.

The process of eligibility, intake, and assessment is complicated and bureaucratic, and it is extremely important because it is a key procedure for establishing the meaning and value of literacy. Because the focus in rhetoric and composition is often on individuals or single classrooms, the procedures I have just outlined here are often invisible, yet they are absolutely relevant for individuals and classrooms. At Western District, a significant number of crucial decisions about literacy are made prior to a student or worker ever setting foot inside a classroom. Legislated definitions of literacy are operationalized—given concrete meaning and value—through the processes of intake and assessment. The parameters for what literacy can be are established, and this standardized, basic skills literacy is what students must work with in the classroom.

Monday/Wednesday Afternoon Class

The class title may seem odd, but the title, which the teacher, Joanne Tipton, put on all her handouts, reflects two principles about Western District: students chose classes based largely on time of day, and they did so because one class could accommodate many students at different skill levels. Therefore, while the class was geared toward the GED, not every student in the class was attempting to pass the GED in the near future. In other words, because the program was designed to be highly individual-ized, there was space in the class for individual pacing and widely varying skill development (material in this section is taken from field notes and collected class handouts).

Joanne told me that the class, as a general ABE class, was focused on math, reading, and language. I only attended the class on language days. At the time I was attending the class, there were about 15 students, and Joanne had a para-professional to help her when needed (personal interview, 5/20/96). Joanne characterized her students as mostly wanting to improve skills, although some wanted to work toward their GED. And in response to those needs, Joanne attempted to design classes accordingly. For example, while Joanne's personal definition of literacy—and the definition she felt her students and the program held as well—was a generalized notion that literacy is the ability to read, write, and do math "to function in society," she was more specific in class, including concrete ways she adapted classes to meet specific student needs (personal interview, 5/20/96). Writing for Joanne was purpose driven, and depending on the needs of her students, Joanne would teach a significant amount of job related writing like memos, job applications, and resumes (personal interview, 6/12/96). In the classes I observed, Joanne taught the writing techniques necessary for success on the GED.

Figure 2–3
Reproduction of Class Outline Handout

Class Time: 12:30–4:00 P.M.

12:30–1:15   Text: Word Definitions—the word today is "accurate"
                Task: dictionary skills, parts of speech,
                sentence structure

1:15–2:00   **Language Lesson**
                Text: Contemporary's GED Writing Skills pages 151
                and 152 and Writing Skills Exercise Book page 44
                Task: combining sentences

2:00–2:15   Break

2:15–4:00   **Writing Lesson**
                Topic: given by teacher
                Task: write an essay

After completing your essay, work in language according to your ALP.

In general, the classes followed a set pattern Joanne said changed little from class to class (see Figure 2–3). Class functioned much like the outline suggests, right down to the timing. Students would begin the word definition task with time to work alone on a worksheet which asked them to (1) write the definition of the word (from a dictionary), (2) give an example of the definition, and (3) use the word in three sentences (the word-of-the-day was usually suggested in advance by a student). The word definition tasks would begin for the entire class with a phonetic breakdown of the word. The class would then go over what part of speech the word was, then a few students would read their definitions and sample sentences, and after the sentences were on the board, the class would name the parts of speech for every word in the sentences.

The language lesson was similar to the exercise on word definitions. The language lesson would deal with an issue like sentence combining (using portions of sentences from workbooks), or a worksheet on comma rules. Students would listen while Joanne went over the lesson for the day, and then they would work through their worksheets individually, asking for and receiving help from Joanne throughout the process.[9] In general, I observed that this seemed a frustrating process for students (sighs, looks of frustration), yet the literacies students were asked to learn and the method of instruction were related to the GED. There was a clear connection between the exercises and the exam. It was also clear from comments Joanne would make to me and to the class that this was how language arts instruction was supposed to proceed—from the word to the sentence to the paragraph—including the methods of instruction used, which were heavy on worksheets and issues of correctness. These principles and methods were unquestioned by Joanne and driven by a combination of program expectations and Joanne's own philosophy.

The writing portion of the class was scripted as well. Students would be asked either to turn to an essay prompt in the GED writing books, or Joanne would provide a prompt. She would then provide some strategic advice that was GED driven (e.g., use examples and watch the word limit), and then give students time to write in class. During one of my observations, Joanne reviewed the exam's essay structure (the five paragraph theme), but her review was actually geared toward development advice as well, emphasizing how to generate content for each portion of the essay. As students finished their essays, Joanne would walk around, read essays, suggest content and correctness revisions, and allow students more time to revise. The most elaborate comments from Joanne in terms of writing instruction came during her interaction with a struggling student. With this student, Joanne stressed that the student should not worry about issues of correctness, but instead should become "comfortable with writing" and generating ideas. In a class that overwhelmingly stressed issues of correctness, Joanne's shift was significant, and indicative, I think, of her commitment and attention to the needs of individual students and of a more complex approach to language arts instruction than I was able to observe.

Despite my persistent concerns that my observations were too partial, the literacies I saw were rather limited. The literacies in this class were the same basic skills given meaning and value by the assessment practices of the program. The literacies within this classroom were connected to larger, institutionally defined literacies—GED preparation and basic skills training. And this fact is the most important and consistent connection between policy definitions of literacy and classroom practices. Still, the students seemed to love the class; the two with whom I spoke at length certainly did. Attendance was good, and one of them told me that:

> Here the teacher takes time to study you. It ain't like in a classroom in regular school. I can remember when I was in school. Like I say, when it came time for reading, Selden had his hand up, I gotta go to the bathroom. They didn't pay no attention to me. You know, day after day after day. Here, she takes and she looks at these here essays that I'm writing, this is my fourth one I've ever written. 57 years old in August, and this is my fourth one. And she says it's good; that's a pat on my back! (Selden Johnson, personal interview, 6/12/96).

Selden and his wife Gertrude were extremely happy with the class, and more importantly, with Joanne. She provided them with the attention and encouragement they needed, and they were learning the skills they wanted. Selden, for instance, wanted to learn certain words to put in papers he was writing so he could sound better; spelling was also important to him. Gertrude was learning to read again after a stroke, so again, vocabulary work was important to her. I take their satisfaction seriously, and I also take seriously Joanne's expertise and experience. What for me is a classroom that demonstrates a functional view of literacy overdetermined by assessment practices with little clear connection to literate practices beyond exams is for Selden and Gertrude just what they wanted and needed. I see a limited and limiting set of literacies. The students, in contrast, see a type of liberation, or at least some satisfaction.

There is a very real tension, then, between my perception of the program as limiting, the program's perception of student needs, and the students' satisfaction. This tension will exist throughout the rest of the book. What is equally clear from my observations of this class is that the meaning and value of literacy is established and situated institutionally in

rather mundane ways. The mundane, the institutionally routine, is important because it is powerful and often invisible. Thus it is not surprising that
most literacy theory does not locate the meaning and value of literacy
within institutional systems. Yet literacy theory absent a sense of how
specific social institutions warrant certain literacies misses something
significant. If theorizing about literacy does not account for institutional
systems in locating literacy, the possibilities for changing the meaning
and value of literacy are constrained. And this is the real problem.

Chapter 3

Exercising Power: Who Decides
Which Literacies Count?

> "[R]adical educational theorists have virtually ignored
> any attempt to develop a theory of ethics in order to
> provide a referent for justifying either their own language
> or for legitimating the social practices necessary for
> defending a particular version of what schools might
> become. Caught within the paradox of exhibiting moral
> indignation without the benefit of a well-defined theory
> of ethics and morality, radical educators have been un-
> able to move from a posture of criticism to one of
> substantive vision" (Henry Giroux, 1989, p. 131).

This chapter begins the process of moving toward what Giroux calls a
"substantive vision." I take up two additional questions that are necessary
for conceptualizing literacy and thinking about program design in community contexts: who decides which literacies count and in whose
interests are those decisions made? These questions move us toward
conceptualizing and enacting a vision of what community literacy practices should be, or more properly, how people, working together, might
decide these issues. To do this, as Giroux suggests, we must have an ethic,
a vision of the good and how the good ought to be decided. The purpose
of this chapter is to continue to focus on Western District as an institution,
this time examining power relations (or ethics and politics). I do so not
only to present different facets of Western District as an institution, but

to begin the process of developing a design language, a process that will culminate in chapter 6.

Politics and ethics are central to the ways we understand literacy. They should also be considered jointly, as distinct yet closely related ways of thinking, and they should be seen as exercised institutionally. Both politics and ethics describe acts of constituting relations or processes of making commitments and acting with respect to one's commitments (see Sullivan & Porter, p. 103, and of course Foucault [1979; 1984; 1991]). Therefore, I see my questions about who makes decisions with respect to literacy and in whose interests those decisions are made as questions of politics and particularly as questions of ethics. But what kind of ethics? My ethics is a particular kind of postmodern ethics, one that "differs from traditional ethics primarily in its contingent nature; it sees ethics as grounded in fluctuating criteria, in difference, or in community or local practices. It does not rely on, nor would it attempt to seek, a universal ground for ethical action" (Porter, 1998, p. 50). This ethic, following Foucault, understands that all acts of power require commitment; following Lyotard and Thebaud (1985), this ethic understands that there is no escaping commitment. Finally, following Young (1990) and certain theologies of liberation, this ethic understands the importance of difference and the possibilities of solidarity through difference. This becomes my rough framework for talking about ethics and politics: power, commitments, and difference and solidarity. And so my work here is concerned with developing processes for making commitments to local communities and others within those communities which are in various ways "liberating" for them. The nature of these processes will be taken up in subsequent chapters. For now, this framework is important to understand because it informs, along with political and ethical positions I see in other literacy theories, the maps which follow. These maps are an attempt to understand the politics and ethics of current literacy theories; they are a way of beginning, a framework for understanding decision-making at Western District, and a horizon of current possibilities.

Mapping Politics and Ethics

These maps of politics (Figure 3–1) and ethics (Figure 3–2) are presented together yet kept separate in order to illustrate my point about the relationships—both in the overlaps and the differences—between politics and ethics. Furthermore, these maps should be read together with the map in chapter 2. All three maps constitute my reading of literacy theory, a reading that I hope illustrates the complexity, movement, and diversity that I see in this body of work. The silence of much literacy theory on issues of politics and ethics, however, is one of the problems this project seeks to address, and it is a silence that may surprise some. Because of the success critical theorists have had in foregrounding the politics of literacy and the large number of conservative responses (glossed in Berlin, 1996, chapter 1), politicized discussions of literacy may seem the norm. They aren't. The silence on issues of ethics shouldn't surprise anyone, however, although it ought to bother all of us.

Table 3-1
Mapping Terms

Politics

Individual/Institution: This continuum expresses both a focus on identity and the related interest in "who decides" what literacy is. Some approaches are almost impossible to map in these terms because they have abstracted literacy from specific contexts and situations. Still others construct the individual (e.g., "the writer") at the center of their theory and the principal arbiter of questions of power (Flower, 1994). Those at the "institution" end of the continuum see identity as a function of institutional structures of various kinds, like programs, schools, or theories themselves, and see decisions about literacy as a function of those institutional relations.

Neutral/Critical: This continuum has a dual purpose. First, neutral/critical designates the degree to which politics is foregrounded in a given theory, with those approaches that are silent on issues of politics to the left (neutral), those that foreground politics to the right (critical). Second, neutral/critical also functions as a political spectrum, moving from the most conservative (neutral) to the most radical (left/critical).

Ethics

Generalized/Concrete: This continuum is focused on understanding how fully the "subjects" of literacy theories are constructed in ways that are capable of agency. The terms themselves are taken from Benhabib's (1992) critique of "universalistic moral theories" that tend to define individuals and groups (like women) in terms of paradigmatic, "human" cases, which are necessarily generalized and most often "male" (1992, pp. 152-153). In contrast, Benhabib argues for a position that seeks to account for concrete situations, differences, and identities in the articulation of moral theory.

Individual/Communal: This continuum is meant to express the primary focus of ethical commitments. Simply put, the continuum moves from a focus on the good of the individual to a concern with the good of the community.

The vertical axes on both the maps of politics and ethics are continua of identity, or rather, continua which express how the subject is conceived within a range of political and ethical positions. On the map of politics, this continuum is expressed in terms of "individual" and "institution." (see Table 3–1: Mapping Terms). On the map of ethics, this continuum is expressed in terms of language I have taken from Benhabib (1992). The horizontal continua on both maps are based on my reading of literacy theory itself. In terms of politics, I see a concern with the question of politics itself, which expresses itself in a number of ways, everything from ignoring the question to foregrounding it. Likewise, when one finds an explicit concern with ethics, literacy theorists tend to assume terms

Figure 3-1
Political Positions of Current Literacy

Politics

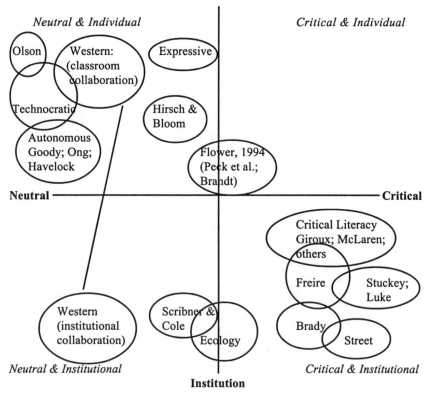

common to ethical debates elsewhere. In North American contexts, the tension is between the individual and the community. The usefulness of these maps is the relationships they create, the movement (and lack) they show, and the possibilities they highlight. Note as well that these maps position the practices of Western District as an institution, positions that I will discuss later in this chapter. What I will not discuss, at least in detail, is each positioning decision I have made. Instead, I want to focus on those positions—those areas of the maps—that are most problematic and most exciting, both in terms of understanding Western District and developing a substantive vision of community literacy practice.

Figure 3-2
Ethics in Current Literacy Theory

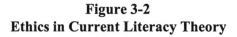

Ethics

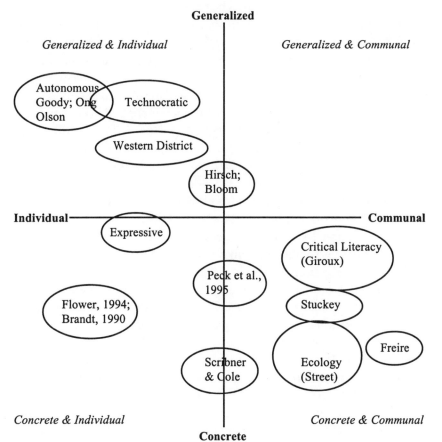

What Literacy Theory Tells us about Politics and Ethics

The work that is most powerful and useful is clustered around two distinct positions. One body of work deflects or ignores questions of power or focuses myopically on the generalized individual. Another body of work foregrounds issues of power yet lacks a developed ethic. The contrast, I hope, will be revealing. So I begin with work that is in some way generalized, neutral, and individualized. As I discussed in chapter 2, autonomous theorists remove literate practices from local contexts, from the institutions in which issues of power would become visible. Literacy is therefore a neutral and decontextualized variable, a viewpoint also voiced by technocratic views of literacy, which often strive, as DeCastell and Luke (1988) argue, to specify educational objectives in "value-neutral" terminology and highly individualized curricula (p. 171). Thus questions of politics and ethics are avoided altogether.

While most expressive approaches aren't nearly as abstract and are often politically more variable, their sharp focus on the individual is most salient for my purposes here; there is almost never a focus on the institution or the individual's relationship to social institutions.[1] To cite one example, for O'Donnell (1996), policy and political questions become philosophical ones, "the solution to which (if there is one) cannot help involving the consultation of one's experiences and how they have been named, categorized, and explained (to the self and others) *by language*" (p. 428, my emphasis). Questions of politics become questions about the meanings of words (p. 430), and perhaps more accurately, the meaning of words for individual readers and writers.

Both Hirsch (1987) and Bloom (1987) pick up this focus on the individual; their work is based on the classical liberal notion of the social contract, or a model which sees society as constituted by individuals freely constructing social forms like institutions based on principles of "rights" over obligations (Elshtain, 1995, pp. 103–104). The contract is threatened when the "light of natural rights, which give men common interests and make them truly brothers" is subordinated to multiculturalism and/or leftist critiques of natural rights and the social contract (Bloom, 1987, p. 27). Their politics, then, and even Hirsch's sense of community are based on a classically liberal politics in which individuals are the ultimate arbiters of political decisions. They are committed to the individual's right to the literacy necessary to participate in civil society.

What we see in my brief discussion here is the result of common ways of thinking about literacy: as a phenomenon or state of mind or set of knowledge-based activities completely separate from most political or ethical concerns. This allows intellectuals and literacy programs to consider literacy without simultaneously considering issues of power. This is easier and more elegant, but it is harmful. Absent a focus on power and institutions, literacy is seen as something that language teachers can deal with as they work with their students in their classrooms. It is an issue of language, of knowledge, of individual consciousness. Teachers and students have agency here. By placing literacy in its own box, theorists successfully have isolated literacy as a variable, thereby "neutralizing" it with respect to its various functions in specific contexts. When we get an explicit acknowledgment that literacy is not removed from the larger political processes of everyday life, our gaze is still fixated on the individual who is largely free from relations of institutional power. Therefore, the politics of literacy theories that fail to account for institutional power miss instances of coercion and violence and possibilities for agency. Critical theory calls attention to these issues.

In contrast to work that is abstract and individualized, we come to work that is in some way critical, concrete, and institutional. This is the location of a viable alternative to more commonplace views of literacy. The one thing all approaches here share is a concern with how institutions shape identities and exercise power. Some, like Scribner and Cole (1981), provide only the traces of such a concern, while others, like the "ecological" work of Barton (1994), have a strong sense of institutions but a much weaker notion of power. And still others, like Giroux (1993), are primarily concerned with power, identity, and oppositional politics.

Thus critical literacy theorists foreground literacy as a cultural politics and so are concerned with identity and difference (Giroux 1987, 1988, 1989, 1993; McLaren 1994; Welch & Freebody 1993; and many others). As Giroux (1987) writes and Lankshear and McLaren (1993) echo, a radical theory of literacy wishes to intervene in the "dialectical relationship between human subjects and the objective world," or with the formation of subject positions (Giroux, 1987, p. 12). While the focus on issues of identity and power is important, there is often a failure to link this focus to specific institutional practices. Identity is a function of "Discourses" more generally. When critical literacy work looks to specific institutions, like schools, to focus on how particular institutional practices impact identity and agency, their work is more meaningful (see, for example, McLaren, 1993; Stuckey & Alston, 1990). Luke (1993), for example, argues that

> pedagogic discourse and power are realized differently in local
> institutional sites—the same pedagogy, the same curricula, even
> the same textbooks or materials, can generate varying, if not
> outright contradictory effects. What might appear an emancipatory
> agenda for a specific clientele can have very different effects and
> consequences in other educational systems and contexts. (p. 3)

Luke's conceptual move here begins to locate typical critical
literacy concerns within specific locations, thereby complicating
both what literacy is and what emancipatory practices can and
should be.

A more significant move, perhaps, is the attempt to articulate an ethics
of literacy, and critical literacy work is nearly unique in this regard.
Though tentative, the concern with ethics follows closely a focus on
power and identity. Giroux (1989) provides perhaps the most significant
critical literacy commentary on ethics.[2] Giroux argues that "literacy is a
form of ethical address that structures how we construct relationships
between ourselves and others" (p. 368). The relationship between "ourselves" and "others" marks a border, a relation of power, which can be
constructed oppressively or not. Yet as Giroux argues in the epigraph to
this chapter, radical theorists have failed to adequately present ethical
positions as part of a viable alternative to the status quo. While Giroux
does not offer the needed theory of ethics, Freire's (1992) ethic of
solidarity, an ethic taken from the communitarianism of theologies of
liberation, is a step in that direction. Freire writes that when one is
confronted with the reality of oppression, guilt or rationalization are not
appropriate final responses. Rather, one should take a position of solidarity, which "requires that one enter into the situation of those with whom
one is in solidarity; it is a radical posture . . . [and] means fighting at their
side [the oppressed] to transform the objective reality which has [op-
pressed them]" (1992, p. 34). Solidarity is an important and complicated
principle in liberation theologies, and as such, it is a concept I will discuss
in later chapters. For now it is important to note that in liberation
theologies and for Freire, solidarity is an ethical position and commitment
which enables the articulation of a "we," the construction of a community.
A position of solidarity requires that one stop seeing the oppressed in
abstract and generalized terms and see them as human beings inhabiting
concrete realities and possessed of real needs. Solidarity requires, Freire
(1992) writes, that one stop making "pious, sentimental, and individualistic gestures and risk an act of love" (p. 35). The love of which Freire

speaks is not the love of *eros*, but the love of *agape*, the "love for the other *as other*, for the sake of that other," and not for individualistic reasons (Dussel, 1988, p. 10). Love and solidarity are impossible within a literacy discourse which sees individuals as non-persons or as objects of knowledge (and power). Love and solidarity are possible when individuals are seen as subjects of their own lives and learning. This is the contribution of Freire's ethics. He initiates a discourse which begins to articulate a "we" in the interests of which the good of *community* literacy practices can be articulated.

We can learn a great deal, I think, from critical approaches to the politics of literacy. Only work like this allows us to ask and answer questions about who participates in decision-making and who constructs identities and enacts change. This work links the meaning and value of literacy to institutional systems and from there to larger ideological systems of value and belief. Critical work carries with it a fundamental concern with others, particularly with those left behind by social, political, and educational systems. This work acknowledges that literacy can hurt as well as help. And this work sees literacy as part of an unequal system of power and privilege. Most importantly, critical literacy work focuses on the need to understand how power operates in specific institutional locations and the related commitment that agency in such locations is collective, not individual (to draw rough distinctions).

My own position is that we ought to make clear our ethics, our commitments to *how* and *why* we establish "the good" of literacy in a given situation. And part and parcel of this commitment is *with whom* we participate in the establishment of a good. However, much like literacy theory that ignores questions of power or that frames it in terms of individual interactions, issues of politics and ethics at Western District are largely invisible and individualized. They are invisible, that is, unless one focuses on decision-making processes, which are an important way to understand power at Western District.

Decision-Making at Western District

As an institution, Western District is governed, though not consciously, by thinking I have characterized as generalized, neutral, and individualized. And so what the case of Western District will show in terms of politics and ethics is decision-making power exercised asymmetrically by institutional systems, the related and relative disempowerment of class-rooms and those who have agency there, and perhaps most importantly, the incredible complexity of power relations at Western District. At Western District, the answer to the question of who exercises the power to make decisions about literacy moves in two distinct directions. Both federal and state government make many decisions through law and policy. Yet policy emphasizes that many decisions are to be made collaboratively, between the program and the students. On the surface at least, power seems to flow in both directions (top-down; bottom-up). Collaboration is clearly important, although the types of institutional practices considered "collaborative" makes the situation complicated.

I discussed in chapter 2 the significant degree to which institutionally defined notions of literacy were prominent at Western District. The mechanisms by which definitions of literacy were established are not limited to actual definitions; in fact, definitions *per se* may be the *least* significant factor. Rather, regulations, policies, and observations of compliance through reports and funding applications are the mechanisms which help decide what literacy can be. Indiana, after all, legislatively has given itself the ability to "prescribe" a program of Adult Basic Education, and this appears to be the case. What I think my discussion in chapter 2 and my statements here suggest is that to a significant degree, the most powerful agents in decision-making about literacy are a set of institutions acting jointly and separately at different points in time. The means of this agency are discursive: legislation, rules, policy grants, approved cur-ricula, and so forth. In the most general sense, this agency *is* collaborative.

Institutional collaboration happens when Western District looks to other institutions to help design a program. Western District's promo-tional documents describe this type of collaboration in terms of "educa-tional consultants," "community representatives," and students and in-structors joining government officials in the design of "flexible goals and outcomes of appropriate curriculum" (Western District Adult Basic Education, "Adult Basic Education Center," p. 8). I saw little of this sort of collaboration, but by looking at old program files, I do know that consultation with various stakeholders has taken place. More current program files at Western District contained short surveys (1–2 pages) of organizations Western District had worked with, often through workplace arrangements, which were designed to gauge how programming was meeting their needs. Indeed, the most significant collaboration in terms of needs assessment appears to happen with Western District's workplace partners, who are not subject to federal regulation and therefore can work more flexibly with Western District.[3] All of this "institutional collabora-tion" takes place within the context of a program policy to develop learner-centered education, which would seem to imply significant learner participation in decision-making. This doesn't seem to be the case, as I saw no opportunity for significant interaction with learners. Collabora-tive decision-making here means consultation with other stakeholder institutions in addition to the powerful role played by government. The most powerful collaborative relationships then are institutional—be-tween professional governmental and non-governmental bodies of deci-sion-makers.

Where collaboration does involve students is in the determination of needs at the level of teacher-student interaction. This, finally, is what the state means by learner-centered education, and both the state and Western District have instituted good-faith mechanisms to achieve collaborative needs assessment. Here as well, however, the notion of "collaboration" which appears in the documents does not have a stable meaning, and in practice, becomes even more complex. The Adult Learning Plan (ALP) is at the heart of collaborative decision-making. The ALP is initiated at intake, and developed and reviewed at various times during the student's time in the program (Division of Adult Education, "Indiana's Adult Education Teacher Handbook," pp. 2-18, 5-2). This arrangement sees the teacher and learner as "partners in the learning process," developing primarily short-term goals to increase the likelihood of achievement (Division of Adult Education, "Policy on Testing," unpaginated). This would seem to be the prime place where students could make decisions about what literacy is for them, and perhaps it is. I have some concerns about the extent to which students are allowed space and power to make such decisions. The ALP itself was developed by a committee that included teachers, intake coordinators, program directors, state staff, but no students. Thus, the Plan was designed and mandated without the input of students. I point this out because of my interest in design, and I feel strongly that if we want participatory program design, then the tools that we use to collect data about a program or that are used to facilitate collaboration must themselves be designed collaboratively. As I will discuss in later chapters, such practices can make a difference.

The fact that students can't participate in the design of the tools that govern their lives already constrains their space for agency. And again, by the time we examine the classroom, many significant decisions about literacy have already been made, decisions that can severely restrict even the best classroom tools. Still, in the classroom, the ALP seemed to work very well because it allows the student and teacher to chart an individualized student-centered curriculum. This is important to students. At the same time, however, the curriculum at Western District is so closely tied to assessment—a basic skills or GED curricula—that one has to wonder the extent to which this collaborative process of developing learner-centered curricula has much effect. In other words, given the powerful ways in which the context of ABE is established at Western District by funding, regulation, emphasis on credentials (GED), and documented learner gains, there seems relatively little room and power for students or teachers. There is choice, but only within tight constraints. Individualized instruction does not necessarily mean students have control over their learning. There is little space at Western District, in other words, for a literacy not consistent with the policies, procedures, and practices that result from institutional collaboration and decision-making.

Establishing the Good at Western District

The commitment to the idea that Adult Basic Education benefits those "most in need," those who need a "second chance," or more generally "students" pervades the data I collected from Western District. Sometimes this *ethos* is expressed in terms of "target group[s]" or geographic areas (Division of Adult Education, "Adult Education Handbook," p. 29); sometimes this is expressed in terms consistent with the state philosophy of learner-centered education—meeting needs important for a learner's life (Division of Adult Education, "Policy on Testing," p. 1). In policy documents, those who benefit tend to become generalized, but this is the nature of such documents. In practice, Western District knows who many of their "target" populations are, where they are, and how to reach them. In the case of welfare recipients, for instance, those most in need are often referred to Western District as part of new welfare-to-work programs. The commitments I am interested in, however, are related to whose interests the good of a literacy program is established.

According to statements of philosophy and program purposes, federal and state agencies as well as the Western District program are committed to the notion that they are providing services that are designed in the best interests of students. Furthermore, my observations of teachers show that they energetically work to benefit students. And my interviews with students overwhelmingly confirm their satisfaction and recognition that they are at the center of activity at Western District, although the students I had access to were those attending classes and participating, a generally satisfied population. Selden and Gertrude, for instance, spoke glowingly of class, could think of nothing else they wanted, and took my question asking for such information as an invitation to criticize the teacher, which they never would have done (see chapter 2). Again, at the classroom level, the professionalism and commitments of the teachers are clear; they are working on behalf of their students.

However, when commitments are mandated as part of policy, one sees a different story, particularly when those who are said to benefit are not part of the decision-making process. For example, to the intake person at Western District, the Adult Learning Plan (ALP) was another mandated document, not a tool to be developed, negotiated, and used locally. In other words, the most concrete tool for student involvement was seen by some teachers and staff as a tool from above. Even state documents reflect some ambiguity as to who benefits from a document and process like the ALP:

> The entire policy for learner assessment and documentation of gains remains a concerted effort to: maintain Indiana's learner-centered approach and commitment to results; meet increased federal accountability requirements; and expand opportunities for local programs to measure and report learner achievement data beyond standardized test measures. (Division of Adult Education, "Policy on Testing," p. 1)

I think state documents, while foregrounding the fact that programs are designed to benefit students, also show that such programs, especially in the ways they are conducted, are meant to benefit everyone involved. The ALP was designed as a way to set short-term, attainable goals separate from standardized testing because professionals at the state level were suspicious of the exclusive use of standardized results (Ed Cotton, personal interview, 8/12/96). But as the quotation above shows, the ALP benefits Western District and Indiana by meeting federal accountability standards, and the federal government, in turn, benefits in numerous ways from having their standards met. In fact, the notion that students might benefit from the ALP is nearly absent in this quotation. Finally, the definition of "adult education" found in The Adult Education Act (1966; amended in The National Literacy Act of 1991) contains information about those to be served by adult education (those "most in need") and states that such populations are in need of services to "raise the level of such individuals with a view to making them less likely to become dependent on others" (Division of Adult Education, "Adult Education

Handbook," p. 6). So even in the policy documents that assert those in need are the focus of educational programs, there is the acknowledgment that social programs like ABE are also designed to benefit others as well ("society").

In writing this, I don't intend to be either cynical or näive. I'm not dismayed that policy makers and planners and others more powerful expect to benefit from programs focused on others less powerful. I understand that if this were not true, such programs might not exist. Social and political altruism is rare. My point here has been to show how difficult it is to establish why programs exist—there are any number of answers that depend on their source. Sure, Western District exists to fill a set of needs, but in whose interests, really, is this or any program constructed? Furthermore, when those who are said to be the focus of a program don't participate in its design, how confident can we be that the program serves their interests?

I suggest, then, that the question "in whose interests" literacy is decided and programs designed is more complex than any set of institutional documents would suggest. The question I cannot answer on the basis of my experiences with Western District is whether various interests which can and do benefit from adult education result in a conflict that hurts students and workers. Institutions, like individuals, rarely act in ways that are not perceived to be in their interests. The issue for institutional critique and design is not finding ways to act in the interests of individuals against the oppressive power of institutions (because I believe this largely impossible). The issue is finding ways within institutions to design programs which benefit everyone, with a clear eye on those most in need of a given institution's services. Perhaps Western District and the other institutions involved have found that way—to a certain extent I believe this to be true—but "the way" of Adult Basic Education in this case strikes me as paternalistic and not in line with notions of collaborative design and empowerment which I will soon argue are more appropriate for commitments to those "most in need." Significant decision-making power at Western District is located at levels considerably "higher" than the classroom, where teachers, students, and the differences they represent are most visible and powerful, and such a situation calls into question the possibility of "learner centered" education within such an institutional design. Much more complicated, however, is the issue of who benefits or who is hurt by this design process. Gauging benefit and loss is complicated both by the difficulty of the question and by the limits of my study (i.e., what I saw, with whom I spoke, the limits of time). Still, design—

and the particular exercises of power associated with it—is important and does impact people's lives. I think the example of a class at Rosewater Publishing illustrates this well.

Rosewater Publishing. The workplace literacy program at Rosewater Publishing was initiated by a grant through the Indiana Department of Workforce Development (all information in this paragraph comes from Western District Adult Basic Education, "Workplace Literacy Grant Proposal," pp. 1-5). According to the grant proposal, Western District initiated contact with area employers who fit the grant profile (e.g., under 500 employees). Western District did a mass mailing, made phone calls and visits to alert and recruit possible employers, and through a referral, came into contact with Rosewater Publishing. Soon after, Laura Bush, the CEO of Rosewater Publishing, and Judy Rooney, the director of Western District, began collaborating on the grant proposal. An advisory group consisting of Laura, Judy, direct line supervisors, the ABE teacher intended for the program, and employees was formed to help with program specifics. The Indiana Department of Workforce Development was brought in to do a literacy task analysis for Rosewater Publishing. Rosewater Publishing was concerned with their high employee turnover rate and was also troubled by the low reading and critical thinking skills among prospective and current employees. Some 50 percent of new employees had no diploma or GED; about 30 percent of current employees lacked such credentials. Rosewater Publishing was one of the few companies in the area that hired people without such credentials. In response, a "multi-strand" program was developed covering the following areas:

- Basic Skills/Reading improvement
- Basic Skills/Preparation for the GED
- Basic Skills/ESL
- Thinking Skills
- Personal Qualities

According to Judy Rooney, the class on "Personal Qualities" was designed to improve self-esteem and employee skills (e.g., punctuality), issues cited by Laura Bush as important for her company (personal interview, Judy Rooney, 4/10/96).

The purpose of the program, once developed, was to "identify the gaps between job tasks and performance and basic skills, and to deliver an instructional program that reduces or eliminates that gap" (Western District Adult Basic Education, "Workplace Literacy Grant Proposal," p. 6). The curriculum was to include input from the planning group, tasks from the plant floor, results of the literacy task analysis, and feedback from employee needs assessments (Western District Adult Basic Education, "Workplace Literacy Grant Proposal," p. 6). When I began attending classes at Rosewater Publishing, the multi-strand program was reduced to the basic skills/GED preparation classes. At this point (about ten weeks into the program), the communication class that was developed to improve thinking skills and personal qualities had run its first four week session but did not generate enough interest to run a second four weeks. The job skills class, which focused more specifically on good employee behaviors, suffered a similar fate. Employees were generally not motivated to attend classes because they were not getting paid to do so and could not expect any benefit like higher evaluations or advancement. Class attendance and performance was entirely self-motivated, and the lack of external motivation was a program design flaw according to both Judy Rooney and Mary Robinson (one of the teachers). The attendance numbers were not good, and this worried Western District, who wanted to write a report about a successful program to the grant funders (Mary Robinson, personal interview, 6/19/96).

Because the program at Rosewater Publishing was reduced to two classes by the time I began my observations there, I attended classes that were much like those at Western District itself—GED preparation. The class at Rosewater Publishing where I spent most of my time was the math class, due largely to the fact that my presence made the teacher of the language classes uncomfortable, so I only attended one of her classes (I'm not sure why I made her feel uncomfortable; I never had the chance to ask her). Still, the same six to seven women attended both the math and language classes, so I got to know them well. The math class at Rosewater Publishing was driven by GED preparation and by the Adult Learning Plan; the literacies here were defined and connected to assessments. There were few whole-class lessons taught, and much of the time was spent with Mary working with individual students one-to-one. For most of the two hour classes, students worked non-stop on their individual lessons, at times working with neighbors on problems they shared. Once students moved through a skill or lesson in their books (typically GED math preparation materials), they were tested, scores were recorded, and students quickly moved on to their next area. In the language class, there was a structure more like Joanne's GED classes at Western District.

During the class I attended, students had structured lessons on capitalization and comma rules, worksheet exercises, and then a test on capitalization (because they had reached the end of that unit). My understanding, from talking to both the teacher of the language class and the students, was that this was a typical pattern for classes (field notes, 6/20/96). The entire language class structure was informed by a notion of language learning and use which emphasized correctness and GED testing situations, and moved from the word, to the sentence, and to the paragraph. This again was overdetermined by the need to show learner gains through assessments, but it was also a philosophy shared by the instructor (personal interview, Angie Langen, 5/23/96).

In short, the classes at Rosewater Publishing were much like the classes at Western District itself. And despite the grant's intention to focus on workplace literacy issues, there was little connection. Mary only alluded to workplace issues twice, and each time she asked if students used on the job the particular math they were learning, the answer was no. When I asked the seven students/workers in interviews and casual conversations about workplace and "real life" applications of the skills they were learning in class, they could see no connection, and in fact, were adamant that they did not use what they were learning in class anywhere else in their lives (group interviews, 7/03/96, 7/17/96; field notes, 6/19/96, 6/20/96, 7/03/96, 7/17/96). Furthermore, the management of Rosewater Publishing, as I remarked earlier, had given the students no incentive to attend classes. In fact, just the opposite was the case (see below). So the question "why are you here?" became important.

The answer was deeply personal. Each woman attended the GED preparation classes in order to get their credentials. They expected no compensation from the company, and in fact were cynical about any recognition they might receive. They had no intention of looking for new employment, but not because they were happy at Rosewater Publishing. They were used to working at Rosewater Publishing and enjoyed the company of the small group of co-workers/friends who were taking classes together. They were hesitant to change jobs and cut long-standing ties to co-workers. The women attended classes because the time was right for them to pursue their GED; most had grown children (many were in their forties and fifties), and most had few of the constraints younger employees had or felt they had. They came to the ABE classes for their own benefit, what each of them called "self-esteem," "to feel better about myself," or to avoid feeling like people were talking over their heads. Each woman spoke with passion about how personally important getting her GED was. I was surprised at the complete lack of economic motivation—at least expressed to me—for their attendance.

The fact that Rosewater Publishing made the GED classes available in-house was central to why the workers took the opportunity to pursue their GED. Had these classes not been offered at the plant, then few workers would have taken advantage of the opportunity. Because they had to take the classes either before or after their full shift, the women were often exhausted and would not have driven off-site to class. Their ability to work on math for two hours after a long shift with few breaks was remarkable to me. Furthermore, the women would not have taken the classes if they were not in-house because the women, to a person, were only willing to risk learning (or "looking stupid," they would say), in the presence of friends (group interview, 7/03/96). So the in-house opportunity was an important design decision for the Western District/Rosewater Publishing program. But according to the workers taking the class, it was one of the few good decisions. Management philosophy and practices, at least observed from the perspective of the student/workers in class, had a deep and negative effect on the success of the program.

One example can best illustrate this tension. Classes were held in the office of the CEO, Laura Bush. During one class, Mary, the teacher, remarked out-loud (as Laura left her office in the middle of class) how rare it must be for a CEO to give up her office (field notes, 6/19/96). Laura turned back as she left her office and said that the class was important. This simple, rather nice story lay at the surface of some deep tensions at the company that became visible during student/worker interviews. I learned later that Western District insisted that Rosewater Publishing supply an air-conditioned space for the classes (field notes, conversation, Mary Robinson, 7/03/96). Because the plant workers had no air-conditioned space, and because there was no space in the office that was large and private enough for a class, Laura gave up her office. But to the student/workers, Laura never gave up her office, and her interruptions of the class—to come into her office to work, make phone calls, and even meet with other management employees—was a sign of the general lack of dignity and respect that the women felt from the company (group interviews, 7/03/96; 7/17/96). According to the women in the class, the company had "no respect" for the classes or for them. I was surprised by how forcefully the women reacted to the interruptions, but they took their class time seriously and viewed the interruptions as a breach of agreement between the company and them.

But the problem of interruptions was connected to a history of poor relations compounded by the fact that the classes had no effect on worker evaluation or compensation (group interview, 7/17/96). This issue was salient to the women because fiscal year earnings had recently been announced, and the company had made a multi-million dollar profit. The employees told me they were congratulated on the day profits were announced, but later in the week when the women in the class asked for a raise, they were told that there was no money for such raises. One of the women remarked that she had never had a cost of living increase (group interview, 7/17/96). And the very week that our interview/conversation occurred (the 7/17/96 discussion was off-tape), the two women in the class who were preparing to take the GED exam were told that the company would not pay the cost of taking the exam and that the women would be docked pay and points (part of an evaluation system) for missing work on exam day. The women wanted to miss work to take the exam so they did not have to take the two-part, eight hour exam after working an eight hour shift. In the eyes of these workers, the company was punishing them for doing something they thought was encouraged.

Ultimately, the design of the Western District/Rosewater Publishing program seems faulty. Despite the talk of collaborative needs assessment and curriculum design in the grant proposal, none of this appeared to have taken place. Instead, Western District provided Rosewater Publishing with everything the CEO wanted (as expressed by Rosewater in the grant proposal). So the question "in whose interests" literacy and program decisions are made is key to understanding my experience of the Western District program at Rosewater Publishing. The program was designed according to management's vision, including classes geared toward problems management saw in employees, not classes employees felt they needed (meeting, Judy Rooney, 4/10/96). And so the program seemed unresponsive to worker needs—as indicated, I think, by the failure of the thinking skills and personal qualities classes. The only workers who took advantage of the classes were those who found themselves at a place in their lives when they had the time and desire to pursue the GED. Clearly, decisions were made by certain interests (and not others), and such decisions were made *for* certain interests (and not others). The few student/workers who were able to create success for themselves within this program were able to do so because they could resist the classes and literacies that did not interest them and take the classes that taught literacies which were important to them. So again, while the GED literacies that formed the core of this program seem limited and unconnected to the workplace, they met the needs of a few student/workers at Rosewater Publishing. At the same time, the program as a whole was headed toward failure because too few students/workers took advantage of the program. In the design process, power was exercised in ways student/workers found "oppressive" (my word), and this relation of power can account, at least in part, for the dynamics of this workplace program (for more on this, see chapter 6).

Toward a Critical Rhetoric for Program Design

At this point, I think it is useful to state clearly where I am heading: a theoretical framework for developing procedures for local decision-making. Later in the book, I call this procedure a critical rhetoric for the design of community-based literacy programs. This rhetoric is a situated procedure committed to participatory decision making within communities and institutions that gives preference to the least powerful.

As I noted at the beginning of this chapter, the relationships between politics, ethics, and rhetoric are significant. Both politics and ethics are concerned with how identities are established through relations of power, and rhetoric is the action component, the means by which certain identities are established or changed. Thus the critical rhetoric toward which I am moving must have a vision of the good, a critical procedure for thinking about how certain possibilities are established, and finally, a procedure for asserting an alternative vision of the good when appropriate. Most helpful in developing this rhetoric has been the work of critical literacy theorists, and my work here should be seen as an extension of that way of thinking about literacy. Most important, however, has been the way in which this framework for thinking about power and literacy has allowed me to read Western District as an institution.

Western District is an institution that creates a reality with respect to literacy that is powerful and deeply situated at the core of the program. It is reflected in its mission statement, its policies and procedures, and in the ways in which the institution enacts those policies. With respect to politics and ethics, decision-making processes at Western District—and I would argue at any institution—thus become the key rhetorical moments for determining what literacy is, and an examination of these processes reveals who makes these decisions and in whose interests they are made. A critical rhetoric for program design seeks to intervene in these decision-making processes, but to do so requires an alternative vision of what literacy ought to be, and ultimately, an alternative theory of institutional design. So in later chapters I will take up issues of participation, think carefully about notions of community and the relationships between institutions and communities, and finally, offer a theory of institutional design. In doing so, I will revisit key moments in this chapter—the class at Rosewater Publishing and the importance of the Adult Learning plan in particular—because this chapter provides a framework for how to think about power with respect to literacy institutions. It is one step toward a substantive vision.

Chapter 4

Utopic Visions, The Technopoor, and Public Access to Networked Writing Technologies: Community Literacy Programs as On-Ramps

> "Anyone seriously interested in universal access has to make a basic tactical choice between growth and re-distribution. . . The choice between the two ultimately depends on which we want more, abundance or equality. . . . But in many areas, the question will be whether policy makers have the strength, the vision—indeed the courage—to stand by and do nothing" (Peter Huber in Cerf, Huber, Duggan et al., 1995, pp. 33, 34)

> "It's available, and if it is available and you can't access it, then you're missing something." Diane, a student in one of the Western District Adult Basic Education programs

At the time that he wrote these words, Peter Huber was a senior fellow with the Manhattan Institute for Policy Research, a professional, well-educated, hyper-literate man voicing the ideology of market capitalism. Discussions of universal access to computers and online connectivity frighten him because they raise the horrific specter of "big government," "regulation," and "anti-competitive measures." His bogeymen. His solution is to leave the market to itself. As he argues, while there will be short-term inequalities, in the long run all will be taken care of. In the meantime, some of us will enjoy abundance. Some, of course, poverty.

Diane's comments come from an interview I conducted with a group of women who were attending literacy classes at Rosewater Publishing. Diane is working class, without her high school diploma or GED, literate, a woman. Unlike Peter Huber, she has never heard a discussion of "universal access," but she knows what it means. The "it" to which Diane is referring is the Internet. Diane's directness belies the complexity of access to computer resources, a complexity that Huber completely misses. Jim Porter (1998) sees access to computer resources as perhaps "the number one ethical issue for internetworked writing" (p. 102).[1] He writes that most discussions of computer ethics focus on the "haves" and deal with issues like electronic rights, censorship, and appropriate language use. These are important issues, yet they ignore the "have-nots." A focus on the have-nots would foreground issues of justice and deal with questions like "How are computer resources shared and distributed in the public realm? Who decides who gets what type of computer resources? Who has access to computers?" (p. 132). In a society where "full participation in the political life of the community may soon *require* computers" (p. 133), the concern for fundamental access to computer technologies is indeed an issue of justice.[2] As the epigraphs illustrate, however, it is difficult to talk about issues like access, justice, and literacy unless we consider the perspective of the speaker and the community or interests for whom he or she is speaking.

This chapter is about access to literacy technologies. Technology is often overlooked in discussions of literacy even though scholars like Ong (1982) and more recently Haas (1996) have made clear connections between literacy and technology. For them, literacy *is* a technology. Technology can be overlooked in discussions of literacy when literacy is seen as an abstract, decontextualized variable or when, as in many composition and workplace literacy discussions, "writing" is studied independently of its contexts of production and reception (see Sullivan and Dautermann, 1996, for this critique). Any consideration of written literacies must examine the role and function of writing technologies. Any discussion of community-based writing and writing programs must, as I will argue here, focus on how community-based programs can provide people with access to internetworked writing technologies.

My disciplinary frame for this chapter is the computers and composition community located mostly within English departments and concerned largely with writing with computers in composition classrooms in colleges and universities. I will rely on work from this community (of which I consider myself a member), and I will also suggest that the vision of scholars in this community ought to be expanded, that they (we) have something important to offer larger conversations about writing with computers in community contexts. Community-based contexts are key locations for creating access to computer technologies for those currently without. Yet because access to writing technologies in community-based programs is uneven, the literacy learning of students and workers suffers.

Access and Computers and Composition

In many ways, scholars in computers and composition have considered, explicitly or implicitly, one or more issues related to access. In one of the more explicit treatments of access, for example, Selfe and Selfe (1994) frame their article on interface design in terms of the subtle and often invisible "borders" English professionals establish and maintain, "contributing to a larger cultural system of differential power . . ." (p. 481). Porter's access framework, however, expands previous considerations and consists of three types of access: infrastructural or resource access, literacy (skills and expertise), and community or social acceptance (p. 103). In what follows, I will provide an overview of this framework to show how work within computers and composition already addresses access issues. In this way, I hope to show why computers and writing scholars have useful contributions to make to larger conversations about access.

Infrastructural access is the level at which most people tend to think of access—acquiring the means and then the machines. Piller (1992) provides perhaps the most vivid examples of the importance of infrastructural access in his *MacWorld* article on technology in public schools, and print and television newsmagazines have produced a number of similar pieces since 1992. Piller contrasts the access of students in public schools that can afford desktop publishing systems and wide area network access with students who may never see a computer that actually works (see Kozol's *Savage Inequalities* for similar contrasts). Many online discussions of issues like "affordable computing," for example, often wrestle with this issue (e.g., Negroponte, 1995; Kline, 1996), although at their worst such treatments champion bare-bones hardware solutions and gloss over issues like figuring out how to use the technology (e.g., Sandfort & Frissell, 1995). For years computers and writing teachers have been making a variety of arguments for computer class-rooms to university administrators. And administrative and scholarly work has similarly been marked with a concern for designing classrooms once the technology has been acquired (Selfe, 1989; Boiarsky, 1990; Myers, 1993; Lopez, 1995). Infrastructural barriers are obviously the primary economic and structural impediments to access, but in the work of Porter and others, this primary access issue acquires additional facets. Infrastructural access deals with issues of systems design and decision-making—how is hard and software configured and who participates in those decisions? Likewise, Selfe and Selfe's (1994) critique of interface design argues for English teachers to influence the "cultural project of technology design" (p. 484). And Selfe (1996) also takes up issues related to decision-making about technology use. Administrators and systems designers often dominate discussions of technology design and use and leave out students and many teachers. Thus infrastructural access deals with fundamental issues related to the distribution of computer resources within a given community, with questions like "which students and citizens in our community will have access to computer resources, what will they have, and where will they access them?" In addition, infrastructural access also is concerned with equally fundamental procedural issues related to design and decision-making, with questions like "who is making these decisions about technology?" and "how will these access spaces (both physical and virtual) be designed?" (see Lopez, 1995, for a discussion of physical and virtual classroom design).

The second part of Porter's access framework deals with literacy, the greatest strength of computers and composition specialists. Quite simply, literacy as an access principle deals with knowing how to use computer technologies as well as how to write effectively with such technologies. The mistake of many decision-makers is that they provide the hardware resources without the means to train teachers and students to use the technology. This is clearly an area of expertise for computers and writing teachers as numerous pedagogical and theoretical articles will attest (as perhaps best illustrated in the computers and composition history, Hawisher, LeBlanc, Moran, & Selfe, 1996). But significantly, Porter connects design to literacy access as well. Countering the tendency to design systems "rationally" or in a way most "efficient" for systems administrators, an approach to technology design that values what is best for student writing is an example of allowing student or user literacies to drive decision-making. Clearly not divorced from infrastructural issues, literacy in this sense means both the necessity of learning new literacies and letting user needs and literate practices drive design decisions (see Jones, 1996, for an excellent look at the intersection of literacies and design).

The third notion of access concerns acceptance. Here again, scholars in computers and composition have done important work. As Selfe and Selfe (1994) suggest, English teachers in computer environments have been acutely sensitive to constructing computer environments that are potentially more democratic and egalitarian (e.g., Cooper & Selfe, 1990; Faigley, 1992), that are accepting spaces for women (e.g., Selfe, 1990; Takayoshi, 1994; Hawisher & Sullivan, 1998), and that are accepting spaces for differences based on class (Salinas, 1997), race and ethnicity (Romano, 1993; Sims, 1997), and sexual orientation (Regan, 1993). Community acceptance (however that community is defined) is crucial for maintaining access. It is important to emphasize that acceptance is also an issue of design. In this case, participants must decide how to construct and implement accepting electronic spaces.

This framework for considering access is powerful because it foregrounds both distributive (economic) and procedural (rhetorical/ethical/political) issues and practices, and it emphasizes issues of design as locations for action. In addition, I think it is clear that computers and composition has consistently addressed some access issues in ways that are useful and successful. However, when considering writing and technology outside university classrooms, the terrain changes and the prospects for access and justice become more bleak. In what follows, I attempt to map the terrain as I see it, drawing on access statistics and my own experiences at Western District. From there I want to show how to conceptualize access problems in that community context and why the experience and expertise of computers and writing scholars is necessary.

Utopic Visions, The Technopoor, and Public Access

"Discussions of electronic mail," writes Selfe (1996), "have inspired some hope among educators that e-mail environments might offer enhanced possibilities for literacy education and literacy activity" (p. 257). Such hope includes, as many have noted and critiqued, claims that e-mail environments support more "democratic" and "egalitarian" spaces for communication, open discussion, greater collaboration, and access to more and better information (see Selfe, 1996, pp. 257-258). But as Selfe also notes, such hopes for e-mail have been voiced as part of larger public policy discussions that have called for, among other aspects of tele-communications policy, universal access to e-mail. Universal e-mail access, as a Rand research report (1995) argues, is not only possible but desirable.[3] The authors write that the use of e-mail is valuable "for the practice and spread of democracy, and for the general development of a viable National Information Infrastructure" (p. xiv). Citing other studies, they write that adults with access to computer networks have more information "about matters of political, professional, and organizational concern" than those without (p. 15). And they also write, citing work in organizational communications, that networks allow lines of social stratification to be crossed more easily.

Reading such praise for networked and internetworked writing—and I have cited only a few of many sources—it is a wonder that more universal access is not on the horizon. In fact, while feasible, universal access is not soon likely, and we are quickly creating, as Charles Piller (1992) has phrased it, a technological underclass. According to some estimates, computer access, usually defined as household ownership plus access afforded by school or work, is somewhere between 25–40 percent, a rather large range.[4] While it is difficult to count the number of people who are actually online, the National Telecommunications and Information Administration Office of Telecommunications and Information Applications (NTIA), in a 1995 report called "Connecting the Nation," estimated that there were 27 million people online at that time. At first glance, the fact that about 30 percent of households have access to personal computers and some 27 million people are online may (or may not) be good—it sounds like a significant number of people. But exactly who are these people? How are these resources distributed in society? And how are these decisions being made? If the raw numbers of people owning computers and gaining online access are increasing, why be concerned about the "technopoor"?

Like access to a number of other resources and institutions, access to computers and networks is uneven, and in some respects, getting worse. Both the NTIA (1995) and the Rand report (1995) write that access is highly correlated to household income and educational attainment. The Rand data is also revealing for the ways it has attempted to trace changes over time.[5] Consider the following data figures for household income (Figure 4–1) and educational attainment (Figure 4–2) based on numbers taken from the Rand report (pp. 24–28).

Anderson et al., the authors of the Rand report, find these numbers most revealing in terms of who does and does not have access to networks.

Figure 4–1
Differences in Computer Access and Network Use
by Household Income, 1989/1993

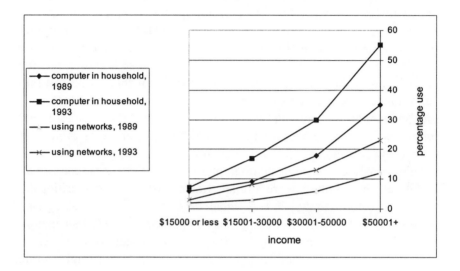

Figure 4–2
Differences in Computer Access and Network Use
by Educational Attainment, 1989/1993

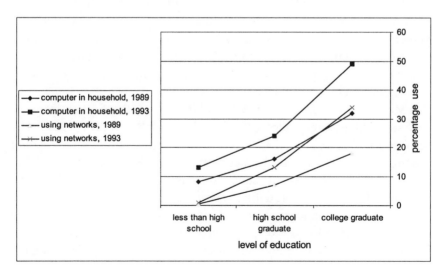

73

In general, they observe that for these two sets of data, the gaps that existed in 1989 widened by 1993. And while these two factors, income and education, are highly correlative, the net differences are still significant. In other words, while there are strong relationships between income and education (one third of the income gap can be attributed to education), education (and other variables) cannot completely account for the fact that the wealthy own more computers and have greater access to computer networks than the poor. Income and education considered as separate variables are significant contributors to access. Taken together, income and education form the foundation for a profile of those who fall into subordinate class positions with respect to access to computer technologies and institutions that require such accesses (e.g., "good" schools and jobs). Furthermore, other variables cannot account for the fact that over time, these access gaps have widened, not shrunk.

For nearly every other demographic category that Anderson et al. looked at, the numbers were similar. Racial and ethnic disparities are significant (although they did not widen between 1989 and 1993). Asian Americans tend to own more computers (37 percent in 1993) than do non-Hispanic Whites (31 percent), non-Hispanic Blacks and Native Americans (13 percent each), and Hispanics (12 percent). Interestingly, while Asian Americans have a higher percentage of computer ownership, non-Hispanic Whites actually have a higher percentage of network use (13 percent to 10 percent in 1993). Hispanics, non-Hispanic Blacks, and Native Americans all fall below 10 percent for network use. The only surprise in the Rand analysis of Census data was the category of "Sex." Their numbers show that while in 1989, controlling for other variables, men were more likely to have computers, the gap closed by 1993 (28 percent to 26 percent). Network use data is also nearly identical in 1993 (12 percent men, 11 percent women). Anderson et al. account for the similarity by suggesting that men use computers more at home, women at work.

More recent numbers suggest similar patterns, these taken from the second NTIA report on access "Falling Through the Net II" (1997). The data and definitions used in the "Falling" report are similar but not identical to those used in the Rand report. Like the Rand report, this NTIA report used Census Bureau data. There is one significant difference, however. The Rand report defined computer access in terms of personal ownership plus that access afforded by school or work. In contrast, the 1997 NTIA report focuses on personal computer ownership in the home. While there are likely other differences in the specific questions asked in each data collection, both the Rand and NTIA reports are looking at similar phenomena with a similar data source; therefore, I don't think the differences are significant for my purposes here. Still, readers should be aware of the differences.

With this recent data collection and analysis, one can see changes in access from roughly 1989 (earliest Rand use of Census data) to 1997 (most recent NTIA use of Census data).[6] The NTIA concludes that overall, "Americans have increasingly embraced the Information Age through electronic access in their homes" (p. 2). Echoing the earlier conclusions of the Rand report, however, the NTIA (1997) reports that "the 'digital divide' between certain groups of Americans has increased between 1994 and 1997 so that there is now an even greater disparity in penetration levels among some groups" (p. 2). In particular, there are increasing disparities between upper and lower income groups (see Figure 4–3) and between African-Americans, Hispanics and Caucasians. The NTIA suggests that these numbers reflect general, national trends. More people own computers and have network access now than they did in previous years, and this is true across income levels. Like with all the numbers I present here, however, those at higher income levels have had a significantly higher increase in computer ownership and online access, resulting in an ever growing gap.

The numbers for educational attainment tell a similar story (see Figure 4–4). While there are some interesting differences between these 1997 numbers and the Rand numbers from 1993, the trends more or less hold true, particularly the magnitude of computer ownership and online access for those with more education. Both the relative differences between levels of educational attainment and the relative magnitude of their increases have expanded over time. Moreso now than in 1993, those with higher levels of education are even more likely to own computers and have network access than those with lower levels of education.

The numbers on race/origin (as the NTIA characterizes it) complete the picture (see Figure 4–5). While the "other, not Hispanic" category is an odd and ultimately ineffective category encompassing, for example, both Native Americans (with horrifically poor levels of computer access) and Asian Americans (who account for the high levels in that category), ownership of computers has increased most significantly for minority groups since 1994 (according to their 1994–1997 comparison). However, the NTIA writes that the "digital divide" between communities of color and whites has increased from 1994 to 1997, exacerbating the divide that already existed. Indeed, as Figure 4–5 shows, whites are twice as likely

Figure 4-3
Percent of US Households with a Computer
and Online Service by Income, 1997

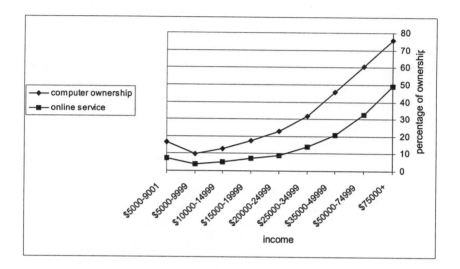

Figure 4-4
Percent of US Households with a Computer
and Online Service by Education, 1997

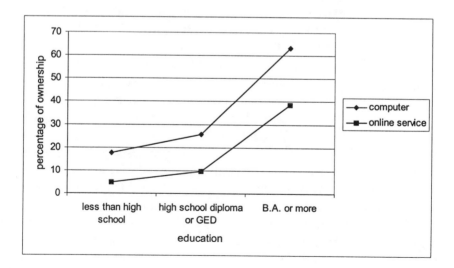

to own a computer and nearly three times as likely to be able to access online services than either blacks or hispanics. Concluding their analysis, the NTIA creates profiles of the "least connected": (1) the rural poor; (2) rural and central city minorities; (3) young households; and (4) female-headed households.

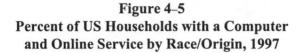

Figure 4–5
Percent of US Households with a Computer
and Online Service by Race/Origin, 1997

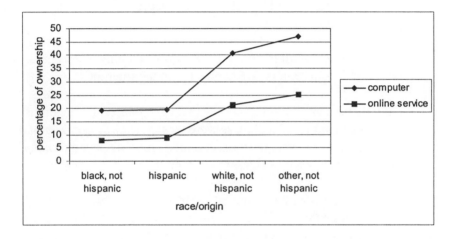

The picture that this data helps paint is not pretty. In a sense it seems irrelevant to talk about how electronic discourse in a medium like e-mail can hide markers of race, class, or gender or that network use may allow a group or individual more easily to cross lines of social stratification. Given this data, it is unlikely—and increasingly so—that individuals of lower income, education, and people of color are online to begin with. Groups and individuals who fit the Rand (1995) and NTIA (1997) profiles of those without access form a fluid, multiple, and complex class position of the technopoor.[7] For visible socio-economic reasons—most power-fully income and education—the technopoor's relation to institutional accesses to computer technologies is one of hierarchical exclusion. Understanding this disturbing trend, an earlier NTIA (1995) report argues that "public institutions will play a critical role in assuring public access to the economic and social benefits of the Information Age, especially for those who do not have computers at home" (p. 3). And the later NTIA (1997) report reasserts this argument: "Because it may take time before these groups become connected at home, it is still essential that schools, libraries, and other community access centers ... provide computer access in order to connect significant portions of our population" (p. 4). But as Piller's (1992) look at computer technologies in schools shows, the gaps within public schools are severe and widening. And more recent National Center for Education Statistics (NCES) numbers seem to suggest the same. The NCES finds the following:

- Only 35 percent of public schools have access to the Internet (49 percent to some kind of wide area network)

- Only 3 percent of all instructional rooms (including classrooms, labs, and media centers) are connected to the Internet

- Only 40 percent of public schools that have telecommunications capabilities indicated that these were located in classrooms (broad cast and cable TV were the most common types of telecommunications systems located in classrooms)

- Smaller schools with enrollments of less that 300 students are less likely to be on the Internet than schools with larger enrollments (30 percent for smaller schools; 58 percent for schools with enrollments over 1,000 students) (cited in NTIA report, "Connecting the Nation," pp. 9–10).

Given these numbers, the NTIA writes that "low-income groups and rural areas tend to have less access to information technology at home and in public schools and libraries" (p. 3). In effect, while universal access seems to be a desirable public policy initiative, reliance on market forces and public schools, which are also subject to "the market," have allowed access problems to be exacerbated, not relieved. In addition, neither the "free market" nor public schools addresses the adult population and issues of work and job training.[8]

The notion of a "free market" is a powerful belief system, and therefore I think it is important to take the time to examine this system as it applies to public access because in the case of computing technologies, I'm afraid the notion of free markets has taken on mythic qualities. I'm a bit of a technophile, and as such, I tend to read computer industry and commercial press publications. In these publications, the entrepreneurial and "wild west" character of this industry is palpable. Combined with the deeply embedded "free market" mentality that permeates most of society, much of what people hear about access to computer technologies is dominated by market logic. But let me be more specific. Like Peter Huber, most "industry insiders" would like to let "market forces" take care of making computer resources available to most. Their pragmatic rationale is to keep the government out of the business of "redistributing," as they often phrase it, computer wealth. Redistribution gets in the way of abundance. This position is backed philosophically by market theory and some version of trickle-down distribution: at first only a few get it, but over time and given the space to innovate, technologies will be made available to all (a function of the "logical" decrease in cost and the desire to increase market size). These philosophical and pragmatic positions are commonly backed by the example of the phone, a technology that was first available to a very few but is now "universal."

There are problems first with the example. Hennelly (1996) reports that researchers interested in increasing access to computers for minority students in one central city discovered that "the information technology gap went beyond access to computers and included a troubling increase in the number of poor young urban families living without even the phone service required for computer networking" (p. 42). The NTIA (1997) profile of the least connected also measured phone access. While still relatively high, the young poor, rural poor, and rural and center city communities of color lack phone access at levels well below the national average. In short, the phone may not be the best model for thinking about access and only works if we look at generalized statistical pictures (e.g., national averages) and if we are willing to wait decades for equality. If we are interested in access, we ought to be asking "for whom?" Who are we talking about when we say that people have universal access to phones and computers? And to whom are we speaking when we say "you must wait for the market to make it possible for you to access tomorrow technologies necessary for success today." People like Huber certainly aren't talking to their own children and community when they says this, and I certainly hope they aren't talking to mine. But they are talking to and about someone else's children and community. So when we talk about access, for whom are we concerned? To whom are we committed? Belief in the market as a mechanism for bringing about access falls down in terms of examples and is a theoretical article of faith—do we really have any good examples of "market forces" working on behalf of the poor and powerless? So far, as both the Rand and NTIA numbers suggest, it hasn't worked for those least powerful. And this is the key point: Those who argue that we must have the courage to do nothing that gets in the way of the market are telling Diane that they must wait to have access to the tools and literacies necessary to better her life, and she has no power to disagree. This is unjust. It is significant, therefore, that both the Rand and NTIA reports look to public institutions to help increase access. Access, however, is complex, and dumping machines in a public institution, like a library or a community literacy program, does not solve all access problems.

Next, I turn back to Western District as one type of public institution that may serve as an on-ramp for more general access. But as this example will show, while a promising site, there are significant problems. Using Porter's access framework, I want to use the case of the computers and communications class to outline the promises and problems of community literacy programs as access sites to writing technologies.

Public Institution as On-Ramp: Western District

Western District is just the sort of public institution that both the NTIA and Rand envision as the public gateway necessary for increased access to e-mail and other internetworked technologies. And I agree that institutions like Western District are important public sites. Such programs are a visible public space for simple infrastructural access, but more importantly, they are also spaces in which more complex levels of access can be obtained because of the presence of teachers, structured learning environments, and at least in the case of Western District, relationships with area workplaces that potentially provide access to decent employment. The "Computers and Communication" class was the class with which I spent the most time during my study, attending classes during both the spring and summer sessions of 1996. The purpose of the class, according to Katherine Bell, the teacher, was to help students learn how to communicate through the computer, although she said it was not a writing class (personal interview, 7/25/96).[9] The purpose of the class according to the course materials (a locally assembled book) was to give students knowledge of PC computers with the expectation that upon completion they would be able to enroll in a high school computers course.

The most promising infrastructural access at Western District was that they were using computers as writing technologies.[10] The class had seven to eight working IBM 286 computers linked via a LAN to the computer systems of a larger school corporation. Each classroom had a set of software available to it tailored to meet the needs of the class. The computers and communications class was supposed to have a typing tutorial program, a tutorial for Word Perfect 5.1, the software for Word Perfect 5.1, Microsoft Works, Print Shop, and a writing skills program. However, only the tutorials, Word Perfect 5.1, and the writing skills program worked (Works, for instance, was not really available because the machines could not run Windows). Students extensively used all of the available programs. In the spring session, there was one computer for each student (about eight), but with increasing enrollments in the summer session (about twelve students), computer availability became a problem.

Infrastructural access, however, means more than providing the technological infrastructure. Infrastructural access also deals with issues of systems design and decision-making—how is hard and software configured and who participates in those decisions?—and begins the process of design-related decision-making that runs through Porter's framework. When one looks at Western District through this expanded sense of infrastructural access, one begins to see serious problems. For late 1996, the technology in this classroom was out of date. The only aspect of the classroom that was current was the existence of the Local Area Network (LAN) that tied Western District to computing services across the school corporation. However, the machines that Western District had were so small and slow, and the technical support so bad, that Western District in effect did not have access to the technology and knowledge necessary to function effectively. The LAN was down so often that Western District did not have the same level of access as the rest of the school corporation. The small and slow machines had other concrete effects. The machines were too small to run Windows, so entire generations of word processing/publishing software was not available to students. Thus, students were forced to learn commands and function keys for a version of WordPerfect 5.1 that made difficult some of the page layout activities students wanted to do (see discussion of the curriculum below). In addition, Katherine, the teacher, was forced to spend a significant amount of time teaching the technology. Some students became frustrated and quit, while the few who could preferred to do the work on computers they had at home.

The problems Katherine and her students had with the technology were related, at least in part, to their lack of access to decision-making about the technologies. As Katherine told me numerous times, she wanted and needed newer machines and better software because she knew that businesses in the area were demanding skills she could not teach in this class. Katherine also wanted consistent access to the LAN. But her interactions with the technology staff of the school corporation were frustrating. She often waited weeks for repairs, she never knew when technicians would show up, and they rarely told her what changes they were making to her classroom. At one point they came and removed the floppy drive from her computer, effectively making it a dead terminal (fieldnotes and personal interview, 7/25/96). So while a program like Western District is promising because of the presence of machines for student use, at significant infrastructural levels, access is still denied to students because the users of the technology, both teachers and students, are denied access to technological decision-making.

The second access issue in Porter's framework is literacy. Literacy takes on added significance when discussing computers as writing technologies because literacy concerns how to use the computer as a *writing* technology. In keeping with a focus on design, the issue of literacy also focuses on whether or not student/user needs drive decision-making. In the computers and communications class, new students began the course with Unit 1 of the curriculum, while returning students began with Unit 3 (some students took the class for multiple sessions, which was possible because of the self-paced nature of the course and Katherine's willingness to give returning students new projects). The curriculum was written by a former secretary at Western District based on an outline given to her by the former director. No teacher who taught the class had a hand in writing the curriculum (Katherine Bell, personal interview, 7/25/96). The first three units of the curriculum dealt with the computers themselves, covering topics like:

- what is a computer (and various types of computers)

- how does a computer work (covering issues like input, memory, and output units)

- what is programming (an overview of what programming is and the languages used, including a rudimentary lesson on BASIC) (all information in this paragraph taken from the Western District Adult Basic Education unpaginated curriculum, "Computer Information Course").

Unit 3 dealt with the input/output issues introduced in earlier lessons, but this unit also asked students to begin using an input device by loading, learning, and running the typing tutorial program. From this point on, much of a student's time was spent exclusively at the computer, both because they wanted to be there and because the curriculum demanded it. Students began by learning the keyboard, setting and meeting typing goals, and as the semester progressed, producing documents.

Students would work through the curriculum at their own pace, producing the letters and memos as they learned the technology. Writing, for Katherine, is a "mirror of the soul," and therefore, Katherine had students write paragraphs, letters, and essays which were deeply personal (all information from interview, 7/25/96). However, Katherine was quick to point out that essays were also a part of the GED and therefore an "absolute necessity" for the class. While Katherine included personally expressive writing in the class, the class also was devoted to genres of writing that I consider "professional writing": memos, letters, and resumes. The curriculum framed these genres as templates and supplied all the content for the documents. In many ways, the writing in the computers and communication class did not vary from the writing done in other language classes at the program. All was geared toward GED preparation. What students learned about memos, for example, was how to create a template using Word Perfect. In class, time was spent dealing exclusively with technical matters related to the computer (function keys and creating templates) or to technical elements of writing (correctness). Often, then, time was spent learning to use the technology, not how to write with the technology. In terms of access, the class provided some important literacies. Students did, in fact, learn something about computers, how to use certain applications, and how to write more effectively. But I think there are some structural limits to the literacies taught in an ABE course such as this. As *structural* limits, they can be addressed through issues of curricular design.

One can seriously question curricular decisions in the computers course from a number of perspectives. First of all, some of the students in the class already had a high school degree or the equivalent. They had little need to learn GED writing. Secondly, most of the students were taking the class to try and find better work, seeing the computer as a "skill" they could use to better themselves. The relationships between work, writing, and a community program such as this are too complex to delineate here. But my sense is that students were learning little that was likely to help in the workplace. As Dautermann and Sullivan (1996) argue, "workplace literacy programs . . . have not responded by connecting writing, reading, and technology. Instead they have focused on a basic skills set they identify as functional literacy . . . generally emphasizing forms, instructions (sometimes with graphics), and memos" (p. xi). Their characterization fits the situation at Western District. In many ways the curriculum fell short of maximizing the computer as a writing technology because it was designed by people working within a functional literacy framework without any consideration of technology. Instead, curriculum design that might increase the literacy accesses of students would include teachers, students, and if necessary, outside resources, like computers and writing specialists, who could help design more appropriate curricula.

While there were problems with the curriculum at Western District, there were significant student projects that seemed to foster access to different computer and writing literacies. One such example was part of an extra-curricular class project in which two students, Carol Thomas and Tina Marua, produced documents typical of a university-based technical writing course. I met Carol during my observations of the class, and at one point in the session, Carol asked me to proofread a cover letter she had written to her family's optometrist. She went to this doctor because he advertised at her husband's union hall. Carol and Tina decided that his advertising fliers were poorly done, and therefore, in need of revision. Their primary criticism was that the fliers were ineffective because they were hand-written and tough to read. They rewrote the fliers, with most of their writing coming in the form of document layout. After completing their work, they wrote a cover letter and submitted the fliers to their optometrist. He, in turn, wrote them a note of thanks with the message that he would use them the next time he advertised. Such an approach to writing and learning is one of the promises that I saw of dedicated computers and writing classes. The students were able to connect writing to their professional and personal needs outside the classroom. None of Carol and Tina's work would have been possible without the computer as a writing technology. But the difficulty for systematic curricular design changes is to see projects like theirs not as a exception but as the "rule" of what literacy access should mean in community settings.

The third aspect of access within Porter's framework is community acceptance. At Western District, this was the least relevant issue because there were no electronic communities within which the students needed acceptance. Western District, like many programs that serve people who are relatively poor, women, and/or of color had no access to Wide Area Networks or the Internet. Because the people who attend programs like

Western District often do not have jobs that allow them access at work, these adults are shut out of *inter*networked writing. Katherine told me that using the Internet might not be a possibility for her class. She said that she was promised e-mail for the class in 1997, but she was unsure whether this meant local area e-mail or an Internet-based system. Besides, she told me, she did not know how to use such technologies (again, training for teachers is an often forgotten issue). During my time in the computers and communication class, students would bring in disks they had received in the mail from commercial vendors promising Internet access and try to use them on the machines at Western District. They did not work, of course, but the exercise illustrated how much students wanted internetworked access. At least at this public institution, these individuals were denied access. Acceptance was an issue for the "haves."

Western District as an example of a site for access to computer literacies presents both exciting possibilities and disturbing problems. It is clear that when confronted with computers and writing issues in non-school settings, access becomes a central intellectual, ethical, and political issue. This is even more true if access entails inquiry into the decision-making processes that establish the meaning and value of literacy. Currently, there are fundamental problems with access to computer technologies that will affect every aspect of public life. As the NTIA (1995) report notes,

> as computers and advanced telecommunications are now essential tools in the workplace, it will become increasingly important that individuals obtain the necessary training and education to become computer literate and to be able to 'navigate' information networks. . . . It is estimated that 60 percent of the new jobs in the year 2010 will require skills possessed by only 22 percent of workers today. (p. 7)

As I have tried to illustrate through the Western District case, the quandary posed by the government numbers hides important issues, namely (1) the complexity of access; (2) the use of the computer as a writing technology; and (3) the reality that many citizens do not get the necessary education at school and therefore must look to other institutions to provide that training. Computers and writing specialists have significant experience and expertise to offer both public policy debates and those working within community-based institutions. We can work through professional organizations to help place complex notions of access and writing on the table for public policy discussions. Research in non-school sites can help provide complex pictures of writing with computers in both workplace and non-workplace settings. Such work could be useful for new curricula in schools, but hopefully, researchers will work with participants to try to help workers and students in non-school settings become better writers, workers, and citizens. And of course, teachers and writers both within traditional school settings and public forums can help highlight the importance of access to writing technologies. Work on access in non-school settings might prevent future Dianes from missing something, and such work will likely enrich literacy theory. Clearly community literacy institutions are key locations for helping people gain access to resources, knowledge, literacies, and institutions. But they won't necessarily fulfill this mission if we don't design them to be the on-ramps they can be.

Chapter 5

Community and Community Literacies

"contrary to the laws of physics, we can stand straight ...
only when our center of gravity is outside ourselves."
(Gustavo Gutiérrez, 1988, p. 118)

The concept of "community" is difficult to grasp. As it is used in discussions of ethics, politics, philosophy, public planning, and even writing studies, the concept has been thoroughly examined. This process has been generally positive but nonetheless threatens to destabilize a potentially useful term. In discussions of community literacy, however, the concept of community has not been subjected to much critical scrutiny. This despite its obvious importance. In this chapter, I look carefully at the concept of community and then at a framework for seeing and understanding community literacies. I attempt to work at the intersection of those who see community as terribly problematic and those who see community as powerful and indispensable. My work at this intersection will focus on developing a critical yet useful concept of community. A working understanding of communities—how they are formed, how they operate, their relations to other systems—is essential for meaningful work in community literacy to continue.

If this chapter is to have a thesis, it would be something like this: Communities and institutions are interrelated and constructed. They, in turn, give literacies meaning and value. My ability to make this argument is important for what happens next. If communities and institutions are interrelated, constructed, and the source of meaning and value for community literacies, then to change the meaning and value of literacies means to change particular intersections of communities and institutions. This, of course, is the larger argument of the book, and subsequent chapters will take up these issues of design and institutional change. The point here is to focus on communities and institutions and their literacies, to focus on the extent to which literacies practiced in a particular community literacy institution are indeed local literacies or just transplanted generalized literacy practices. So there are two issues of concern in this chapter: developing a certain understanding of communities and institutions, and developing a framework for how to look for local literacies within specific communities and institutions.

Finding the "Community" in Community Literacy: Theories, Problems, and Possibilities

The concept of "community" within rhetoric and composition has had currency for some time. An extension of older, linguistic notions of speech communities and contemporary discussions of audience, notions of community—in this case "discourse community"—have been an important development. Previous to this, those who discussed audience in rhetoric and composition were limited to real, more-or-less immediately present audiences (like teachers and classmates in a university classroom), or the closely related yet more textual/ideal audiences addressed or invoked (see Ede and Lunsford, 1990, for a discussion of these audience constructions). With the infusion of poststructuralism into audience discussions, particularly the notion of intertextuality, textual constructions of audience became more social (see Porter, 1986). And with the rise of social epistemic rhetorics driven in part by social constructionist theory, the notion of audience as coherent collectivity (a "community" held together by shared beliefs and languages) was asserted (see Bruffee, 1984, for an often cited and disputed overview of social construction; Porter, 1992, for an extended discussion of audience; Berlin, 1996, Chapter 5, for a useful discussion of social-epistemic rhetoric). The development of more social, communal notions of audience-as-community were also aided by developments in reader response theory (e.g., Fish, 1980) and the philosophy of science (e.g., Kuhn, 1980). Although the theory of the discourse community that resulted was subsequently critiqued (see Harris, 1989), the discourse community has nonetheless remained a central component of audience theory in rhetoric and composition. Therefore, some idea of "community" should be familiar to many. Furthermore, the way in which rhetoric and composition has conceptualized the discourse community—in the sense that it is *constructed*—is important for my discussion here.

More recently, composition studies has begun to look outside the university community to other sites of reading and writing. The most significant articulation of community literacy within rhetoric and composition is Peck et al.'s (1995) article "Community Literacy." The article describes activity at Pittsburgh's Community Literacy Center and the interactions between individuals at that center and researchers from Carnegie Mellon. The article defines community literacy as "literate acts that could yoke community action with intercultural education, strategic thinking and problem solving, and with observation-based research and theory building" (p. 200). This description of community literacy leaves undefined and unproblematized the meaning of "community." Community simply exists. And if one drops the word "community" from the quotation, it could just as easily describe a classroom at Carnegie as a community literacy program. My point here is two-fold: First, this definition of community literacy fails to deal adequately with its most difficult and important term, "community." Second, because this is a definition focused on cognitive processes and research methodology, it is narrow and excludes a wider range of community literacy practices. In short, this article, while opening up spaces that make work like mine possible, does not define community in a meaningful way, yet ironically manages to define "community literacy" within composition.

The problem of course is the difficulty of defining community. Communitarian Amitai Etzioni (1995) admits this very fact, acknowledging the difficulty communitarians have had with this task.[1] He writes that communities are "webs of social relations that encompass shared meanings and above all shared values" (p. 24). As examples, he mentions families, villages, and neighborhoods, but he also extends his definition to encompass "well-integrated national societies" and communities, like professional communities, not connected in any way by geography. In fact, he writes, "People are at one and the same time members of several communities" and that it is best to conceptualize communities as "nested" (p. 25). Also attempting to define community, Fowler (1995, pp. 88–95) discusses three types of communities: communities of ideas (centered around intellectual concepts or schools of thought); communities of crisis (e.g., ethnicity, race, tribe, neighborhood); and communities of memory (nostalgia about shared values). Fowler moves toward a definition of community based on the shortcomings of his taxonomy but never quite gets there.

What I take from my reading of recent communitarian attempts to define community is that it is relatively easy to name small, homogenous communities, like tight cultural or family groups, particularly when they are situated within a shared space. The task becomes more difficult when confronted with a contemporary heterogeneous society. In such a context, sociologists like Cohen (1985) argue that community is constructed symbolically as a system of values, norms, and moral codes that provide boundaries and identity (p. 9). For Cohen, the term "community" is relational. One locates community by recognizing boundary construction. He writes that the construction of symbolic boundaries is an oppositional act. Boundaries are constructed in relation to some "other," not to something fixed or absolute (p. 58). While some boundaries may certainly be material or biological, most are symbolic—constructed through the communication of shared symbols and meanings. In other words, they are rhetorical. Cohen writes, "the boundary may be perceived in rather different terms, not only by people on opposite sides of it, but also by people on the same side" (p. 12; see also Sibley [1995] for a thoughtful discussion of boundaries).

Any discussion of community, therefore, must deal with the issue of how they are constructed and with the issue of boundaries. In fact, "community" is a contested term because of these boundaries and the inclusions and exclusions they entail. Indeed, for some, community is a dangerous concept because of the risk of domination. Political theory is perhaps where notions of community have been most vigorously contested. Iris Marion Young (1990), for example, expresses the fears of many theorists by writing that the boundaries of community eradicate difference and submit minorities to the whims and potential violence of the majority (much of the communitarian wrangling with definitions is a response to these very critiques). Ultimately, then, community is a concept loaded with possibility yet fraught with problems.

The possibilities for community as a concept and as the location for meaningful civic practice are important because meaningful participatory design practices must be situated within a community. Furthermore, institutions absent community-based design run the risk of decontextualized practice; they run the risk of dominating those they are meant to serve. The tension between community as the location for meaningful collective activity and community as homogeneous and silencing will never go away, and I think this is probably good. In other words, the theory of design I am pursuing is dependent upon working with others to design institutions that meet local needs. These "others," this "local" are the community to which this design stance is committed. Yet the critical rhetoric I am pursuing is equally committed to "difference," to naming those differences that mark one as less powerful. So I want to have my cake and eat it too; I want to walk that difficult line between community and difference. In fact, I want to suggest that the commitment to others is a commitment to collective action *and* difference. I see no other way.

Community Versus Institution

In order for my design strategy to work, it is necessary to consider communities and institutions as concepts that can work together. This is difficult because objections to institutions and institutional change are often raised from the perspective of "community." John McKnight (1995), community activist, university professor, and co-director or the Asset-Based Community Development Institute at Northwestern University, sees institutions as coercive, violent, and illegitimate. In contrast to the institution, McKnight poses the community as the proper place of collective action. By community, McKnight means "the social place used by family, friends, neighbors, neighborhood associations, clubs, civic groups, local enterprises, churches, ethnic associations, synagogues, local unions, local government, and local media" (p. 164). Communities, unlike institutions, are informal, unmanaged, associational in nature, and driven by consent. Consent is an important concept for McKnight; part of his critique of institutions and their failures stems from the lack of consent many individuals give to such institutions. His evidence comes from the ways people tend to avoid institutions: schools (truancy), government agencies (delinquency), and medical facilities (absence/avoidance) being some of his examples. In effect, institutions cannot be changed because they are homogenous and monolithic and lack communal qualities of care. In contrast to the coercive qualities of institutions, communities:

- are interdependent
- recognize their fallibility and
  are not ideal constructions
- include everyone
- are democratic
- can respond quickly to local needs

- allow greater creativity
- are individualized
- continually reform and rethink themselves
- create forums for citizenship
- care

While a good example of a critique of institutions from a community-based perspective, some of the entities that he describes above as community—churches, enterprises, civic groups—are what I would call institutions. McKnight partitions institutions and communities much differently than I do, and he does so because his view of community is idealized and nostalgic. Institutions are everywhere, exist on a number of levels, and cannot be avoided. We cannot locate community *outside* all social institutions because human associations themselves become institutionalized. Therefore, to see institutions as monoliths that cannot be changed, as McKnight does, is politically problematic because it is dystopic (akin to Feenberg's [1991] portrayal of "substantive" approaches to technology—our only hope is God). Institutions are visible spaces *within* which people interact and are a location for individual and collective action. As Sullivan (1995) writes, institutions are "the chief sources of individual identity and meaning" (p. 176). Young (1990) underlines the importance of institutions as public space by calling them the locations where "strangers" can be together and experience a collective sense of belonging (p. 237). So who is correct?

My problems with McKnight shouldn't conceal my basic agreement with his critique. Institutions can cause harm and be completely removed from the people with whom they work. I don't read McKnight as objecting to institutions *per se* but rather to the ways in which they are designed. This is the point at which the tension between community and institution can become productive. My argument is this: First, as communitarians and sociologists tell us, *communities are constructed* and can be conceived in terms of any number of issues: race, ethnicity, spatiality, ideas, or other affinities. In addition, the primary means by which communities are constructed are rhetorical, through the symbols that represent the values, morals, codes, and ideologies of a given community. Second, like communities, institutions are constructed. Therefore, the issue is how to construct communities and their related institutions in a meaningful way such that one reinforces the other. This is an extremely difficult task. However, the dual construction of community and institution is necessary so that institutions—an unavoidable and powerful part of the social fabric—can be ethical spaces within which people feel like they belong and through which they feel they can act. When this is the case, community has been constructed within an institution, and conversely, institutional processes reinforce the always ongoing processes of community construction. So rather than providing yet another definition of community, I argue that those of us concerned with community literacies *should focus on the procedures by which communities are constructed* and the related social institutions that result. As DeRienzo (1995) writes, "If a community is a collection of people united around common goals, then institutions are those vehicles created *by the community* to achieve shared purposes ... (p. 11, his emphasis). To make this argument more concrete, I want to present two cases of how community and related institutions are constructed.

Looking for Community: Two Cases

The United Way is a vast network of local volunteers and charities dedicated to helping local organizations and communities help themselves. Along with the national umbrella organization, each local United Way raises a significant amount of money that it then uses to support various local projects. Currently there are about 2,000 United Way organizations around the country.

The United Way of Metro Atlanta serves a significant geographic area and population. My association with the United Way began recently (fall 1998) and is linked to our service learning efforts at Georgia State. We have been trying to incorporate service learning into our developing professional writing curriculum. Right now, service learning in professional writing takes the form of working with community-based non-profits to help them solve writing-related organizational problems. These service learning projects take place in our business writing and technical writing classes, and we are currently exploring ways in which we can provide service to small neighborhood-based organizations funded by a new United Way grant program. This new grant program is designed to help those organizations not currently receiving United Way funding, particularly grassroots organizations that can help address concerns related to neighborhood crime and violence.[2]

I look to the United Way for an example of constructing communities because they have a history of such work and can provide some useful insights. My contact at the United Way is Alvin Lindsey, a coordinator of community-based networks. What follows is based largely on an interview I conducted with Mr. Lindsey about his work.[3] His job as a coordinator of community-based networks came about as a result of taking a more asset-based development approach to community building (the concept of asset-based community development is important, and I will return to it shortly). Mr. Lindsey's role is to go into communities and talk to people, associations, and organizations in order to build relationships. Community-building starts with such relationships, and because Mr. Lindsey is known and invited into many of the communities with which he has contact, his job is to nurture these relationships and create new ones around a set of issues and concerns. The United Way can then offer financial and non-financial investments to neighborhood-based networks. Financial investments take the form of cash grants, but Mr. Lindsey emphasized that the "non-financial" supports such as space, time, expertise, and technical assistance are just as important. The United Way goal is to support good ideas that come from community networks in order to strengthen those networks and the communities in which they are situated.

In general, then, Mr. Lindsey and others at the United Way work with a neighborhood-based notion of community defined in terms of territory and common interests. In cities like Atlanta, it is relatively easy to define a community in terms of physical space. Outside cities with well-defined geographies, defining communities in terms of neighborhoods becomes much more difficult. Both inside and outside cities, however, establishing common interests, a second component of community, is critical work. There are some "communities," Mr. Lindsey noted, where no networks exist, where people do not know each other, how to build networks, or the power that they have to transform their local contexts. And so, even given defined spatial communities, networks are tough to construct because finding common ground can be difficult. Mr. Lindsey frankly called it a "miracle" when communities are built around a common idea, interest, desire, or affinity, for while any number of people and organizations may want to address the same concern, they each may have their own way to do it. It is tough to find both a common interest and a common procedure, and this is the crux of community building for Mr. Lindsey and the United Way: nurturing networks of people in such a way that they can come together, at least for brief periods of time, to act collectively. Mr. Lindsey and the United Way have had some success despite the difficulties. They provided assistance to a small group of working mothers trying to meet new Temporary Assistance to Working Families (TANF) requirements.[4] The group was able to put into practice community-based ideas about how to best take care of issues such as childcare and transportation given the new TANF welfare-to-work requirements. In another case, the United Way has been assisting a small group called New Leaf Services. New Leaf provides a car, insurance, and maintenance to individuals making welfare to work transitions. After one year, given that the individual has maintained work, he or she can then buy the car for one dollar.[5] Both programs are grassroots efforts, and both have been successful.

Community building such as this takes place on a foundation of assets and relationships. In some cases, it takes good, long-term, and interpersonal relationships to convince people that they have assets to begin with. Thus community-building starts with relationships. Mr. Lindsey stressed to me that he only goes into a community when invited. Community members must decide that there is an issue to address and ask for help. And even once Mr. Lindsey or others have been called in to help, members of the community "decide the plan of engagement." Mr. Lindsey emphasized, and I think this is a crucial point, that community-building doesn't happen without an infrastructure, and he sees his role and the role of the United Way as providing part of that necessary infrastructure. By an infrastructure, Mr. Lindsey meant that there must exist an environment where it is possible to talk about differences, where diversity is appreciated and valued, and where people feel comfortable sharing the gifts that they bring. Without such an infrastructure, community-building is unlikely to happen. Spontaneous, organic, Romantic communities are rare. Communities must be built.

In my conversation with Mr. Lindsey, he referenced asset-based community development as a model for their work. Asset-based community development is an approach to community development that positions itself in stark contrast to current social service practice. The "traditional path" to community development, what Kretzmann and McKnight (1993) call a deficit model, is an approach that focuses exclusively on needs. Kretzmann and McKnight argue that such a focus on needs and problems fails to lead to community building. They describe the deficit approach in the following way:

> Public, private and non-profit human service systems, often supported by university research and foundation funding, translate the programs [deficiency oriented programs] into local activities that teach people the nature and extent of their problems, and the value of services as the answer to their problems. As a result, many lower income urban neighborhoods are now environments of service where behaviors are affected because residents come to believe that their well-being depends upon being a client. They begin to see themselves as people with special needs that can only be met by outsiders. They become consumers of services, with no incentive to be producers. Consumers of services focus vast amounts of creativity and intelligence on the survival-motivated challenge of

> outwitting the "system," or on finding ways—in the informal or
> even illegal economy—to bypass the system entirely. (p. 2)

Kretzmann and McKnight's work is a devastating critique of most
contemporary social service models, and its effectiveness is one reason
why organizations like the United Way are looking for new ways to work
in and with various communities. In the deficit models as they describe
them, people cannot construct communities or design institutions because
as "clients," they are given no agency and credit for the expertise that
arises from their lived experiences. The language of business that is used
here (and in use in an increasing number of institutions, particularly
schools) shapes relationships that mitigate productivity. Kretzmann and
McKnight want citizens, not consumers; they want people who are active,
productive, and creative, not those who passively receive the goodwill of
others or are allowed an extremely limited number of choices.

The alternative to predominant deficit models is called "capacity-
focused development" or asset-based development. Kretzmann and
McKnight look to this model because of their experience in communities
in Chicago and other cities. They argue that community change only
happens when local people invest themselves and their resources in the
effort. In other words, communities are built from the bottom up, from the
inside out, not from the top down or outside in. Asset-based development:

- Begins with the assets present in the community and then turns to
  address problems by utilizing those assets

- Focuses (internally) on local consensus-building and problem-
  solving

- Is relationship driven (individuals, associations, institutions).

While asset-based development begins with assets instead of deficits, this
doesn't meant that problems don't exist and that asking people in a given
community what they need isn't important. Kretzmann and McKnight
insist, however, that the use of outside assets to address needs will only
be utilized effectively if the community is actively addressing problems.
The process is complex. As Mr. Lindsey noted, if one is "outside" a given
community, this approach to community building begins with an invitation to help. Once that invitation to help has been extended, then a
collaborative process of problem and asset identification and problem

solving can begin. Of necessity is a local desire to change and the development of local assets before any outside assistance can be useful.

Kretzmann and McKnight work with a notion of community, like Mr. Lindsey's, that is based on specific urban experiences. In the case of Kretzmann and McKnight, their urban experience is Chicago, a city with even more and more clearly defined urban neighborhoods than Atlanta. So "community" is nearly synonymous with "neighborhood." Furthermore, Kretzmann and McKnight seem to assume that communities exist. Even though their book is a manual on community building, they spend no time contemplating the possibility of the lack of a community or the difficulty of the concept. I raise these issues to suggest that the work of Kretzmann and McKnight has problems. At the same time, however, Kretzmann and McKnight provide a model of community and community building that is useful.

Figure 5–1
Community Assets Map

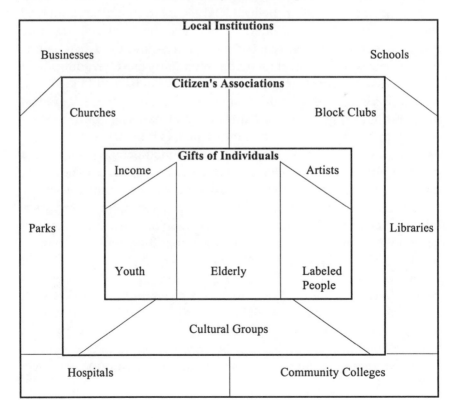

Early in their book, they draw a community asset map that is meant to be developed in order to create a picture of a given community's assets (see Figure 5–1). This map lays out the range of assets every community likely has and stands as a literal map for how community-builders should go about creating inventories of community assets and building relationships and networks. But the map is also a model for how a community can be constructed; it has significant heuristic potential. According to this map, a community is composed of three elements: individuals, associations, and institutions. The focus on individuals in the construction of community allows community builders to examine the individual strengths in a community, hopefully looking for and emphasizing issues of diversity and difference as assets. The move to consider associations allows community builders to look for loose institutional associations that may be deeply rooted in a given community and therefore open to local concerns and action. Finally, this model of community emphasizes the role of institutions in a community, like a community-based literacy program. Institutions have an important role to play because they are more powerful than either individuals or looser institutional associations, and they are often tied into larger institutional systems and therefore can serve as an interface between the local and the more global. Faced with the prospect of community-building, a map such as this is a heuristic for conceptualizing community and then going about the processes of constructing it. Indeed, Mr. Lindsey and the United Way utilize maps just like this that enable them to keep track of local networks as they grow and that allow them to match people and issues in a given community. A community, then, is not best seen as a pre-existing, clearly coherent group of like minded people occupying a discrete physical space. This can be the case, but more than likely, community must be constructed, and when it is, community is usefully seen as some connection of individuals, loose institutionalized associations, and stronger institutionalized associations, all linked by some idea, issue, or vision. Community building must encompass asset mapping of individuals, associations, and institutions. To build a community, people must (1) map the relationships among assets; (2) build new relationships; (3) mobilize assets (new and already known); (4) convene as broad as possible a group to build a vision and a plan; and (5) leverage assets and relationships to solve problems (Kretzmann and McKnight, 1993, p. 345). In other words, community building names strengths, names problems, builds a collectivity, and acts collectively.

Operation P.E.A.C.E.

The Bedford Pines Community is an area of subsidized living units located in Atlanta's Old Fourth Ward, a part of downtown with a long and prestigious history. Unlike many subsidized living communities in urban areas, Bedford Pines is not one or two large apartment buildings, and it doesn't have the dense, planned appearance of other government housing units. In fact, the area has much of the architectural charm that is the neighborhood's legacy. The street that runs through the heart of Bedford Pines, Boulevard Avenue, was once known as "Bishops Row" because of the number of African Methodist Episcopal bishops who once lived on the street. A couple of miles south of Bedford Pines, Boulevard intersects with Auburn and Edgewood avenues, once the heart of the African American commercial district and the home of Ebeneezer Baptist Church and Martin Luther King Jr.. The Old Fourth Ward is indeed an important place in the powerful history of Atlanta's African-American community, making the story of the Bedford Pines community all the more poignant.

The decline of the Bedford Pines community began, ironically, after the civil rights victories of the 1950s and 1960s. With the passage of civil rights legislation and the promise of a desegregated society, some of the more affluent and mobile in the Old Fourth Ward moved out of the community, resulting in the fragmentation of old communities held together by generations of family and neighbors living in close proximity. Soon after, Wingate Management, a property management company, began buying and rehabilitating apartment buildings in the area. When Ms. Edna Moffet came to the Bedford Pines community in 1983 as an assistant property manager, Wingate Management had just completed their purchasing and rehabilitation project. But Ms. Moffet's arrival corresponded with more than the end of a project phase, it corresponded with the beginning of Atlanta's crack problems.

Ms. Moffet is the source of my material here and the woman who has been the driving force behind P.E.A.C.E. (Positive Education Always Creates Elevation), a grassroots community-based organization formed in the Bedford Pines Community. I have worked with Ms. Moffet twice on service learning projects in professional writing, and she has been instrumental in helping me learn how to manage such projects success-fully. But she is also an expert, I think, in community-building, and it is in her capacity as a community-builder that I tell her story and the story of P.E.A.C.E.

To counter the disastrous effects of crack on the Bedford Pines community, Ms. Moffet, in her capacity as an assistant property manager, tried numerous times to start citizen/community groups. She utilized events like health and job fairs, but she was unsuccessful. However, it was the loss of JoJo, a particularly bright and promising young man, that was the turning point for Ms. Moffet's community-building efforts. Kids, particularly young boys, have always been the focus of drug dealers' recruiting efforts. Easily influenced and rarely arrested and seriously prosecuted, young children often begin as lookouts and then move up in organizations. JoJo followed this route and eventually lost his life. His loss was particularly difficult for Ms. Moffet and motivated her to try a new community-building tactic. She turned to the college students who lived in Bedford Pines and called them to serve. And with that, they launched P.E.A.C.E.

Bedford Pines attracted a large number of college students for two reasons: (1) there were a large number of studio units, and (2) the subsidized rent made paying for college much easier. Ms. Moffet went to those college students with a simple challenge: this community helps make your education possible, so you must give back to the community. They met in the laundry room in one apartment building and decided to offer after-school tutoring and mentoring for school age students as a direct alternative to the recruitment efforts on the street. When they announced the after school program to the Bedford Pines community, they filled the program within two hours (twenty five children). Within three months, they had outgrown the small space they had in the laundry area. And the following summer when they announced their summer academy, 100 children applied for fifty spots.

Almost immediately, the community accepted and embraced the efforts of the college students, a marked contrast to Ms. Moffet's initial efforts. But why? Ms. Moffet believes they earned the trust of the community by convincing them that they had a sincere, long-term interest in them. This was made possible by the fact that the community-building efforts of P.E.A.C.E. began on the inside. The program is community-based and community-built. After the initial tutoring and summer programs, Ms. Moffet and the college students went door-to-door and used the phone to contact every member of the community in order to conduct a needs assessment survey. Based on this survey, they began to plan the expansion of P.E.A.C.E.'s services in the areas of literacy/education and programs for seniors, who were often too scared to leave their apartments. All these efforts were part of the larger plan to eliminate drugs and reduce crime by raising hope and expectations. In addition, the residents of Bedford Pines, along with homeowners in the community, worked to close a liquor store in the area that was also a location for drug transactions. It took three months, but the store was closed. These early successes and attempts to reach out and ask the community what they wanted and needed were key moments in P.E.A.C.E.'s community-building efforts.

P.E.A.C.E. has since grown substantially, and as they have grown, they have made connections to area institutions in order to strengthen their efforts. Wingate Management aided the construction of a community reach out center. Located in the basement of two apartment buildings (the old laundry room areas), the center has offices, classrooms (including a computer classroom), meeting rooms, and a kitchen area. P.E.A.C.E. has also been the recipient of grants and awards from the US Department of Housing and Urban Development (they are a model program), the US Department of Labor, the Atlanta Metropolitan Community Foundation, and has received support from other private and public organizations. Georgia State University has supplied work study students and interns, and faculty from Georgia State have donated time and talent as well. In terms of programming, P.E.A.C.E. continues to offer its after school and summer programs and now offers G.E.D. classes. They have graduated six people, and each is currently employed. P.E.A.C.E. has also started a computer literacy program, a teens in business program (in which teens run a thrift store and learn legitimate business skills), a seniors club (with activities such as a walking club, a garden club, and a quilting club), a Narcotics Anonymous chapter, and a dedicated security patrol. Most importantly, perhaps, is the growing number of people who participate in P.E.A.C.E. activities. Once someone has benefited from a P.E.A.C.E. program, they are expected to give back by volunteering or contributing in some way. Seniors, for example, make it a goal to bring one new person to each senior's club meeting, thereby expanding "the community."

P.E.A.C.E. is a thriving and exciting organization that is having success in building and transforming a community. And like the United Way/asset-based development model, I think there is something worth learning from P.E.A.C.E.. First is the belief that communities must be built. For Ms. Moffet, communities form the foundation of society and are organized around institutions like local businesses, churches, living units. Like many of the communities I have discussed in this chapter, Bedford Pines has a strong spatial component to it, but the construction of community entails more than space; it entails a symbolic construction around some affinity. In the case of Bedford Pines, the affinity was the vision of a community free of drugs and crime and a community in which children could grow up free of the temptations of the street. The second lesson from P.E.A.C.E. is the fact that their community-building efforts are grassroots; they begin inside the community and rely first on the assets of the community. Community-building, then, is first and foremost a long-term effort built on relationships of trust. Mr. Lindsey mentioned this in terms of community-building efforts related to the United Way, and no case illustrates the importance of strong long-term relationships more clearly than the example of P.E.A.C.E.. As Ms. Moffet phrased it, they needed to persuade a tentative and fearful community that they were sincere and that they would be around for the long haul. Once others in the community knew that P.E.A.C.E.'s risk was long term, they were willing to risk themselves as well. Furthermore, P.E.A.C.E. provided the community with a place to talk about fears, needs, differences, and visions, a space that Ms. Moffet thought essential to their community-building efforts. The third lesson of P.E.A.C.E. is the relationship between institutions and community-building. Quite unlike the antagonism that some see between community-based action and institutions, P.E.A.C.E. simply could not have expanded as quickly and successfully as it expanded without the assistance of "outside" institutions. P.E.A.C.E. is itself an institution, and there is a clear relationship between this community-based institution and institutions outside the Bedford Pines community. P.E.A.C.E. in my mind is an excellent example of the necessity of community-building, the success of community-building, and the relationship between communities and institutions.

Local Literacies: Writing the Everyday, Writing and Work

If both communities and institutions are constructed, then the literacies given meaning and value at a local community literacy institution are similarly constructed. This book is a glimpse at how one institution gives certain literacies meaning and value, yet as I have argued, the literacies at Western District are to a significant extent abstracted from the local community; they reflect more clearly the values of larger and more powerful institutional players than the students or workers or even teachers. In addition to the lack of local community and institution building, another reason for the lack of significant local participation in constructing literacies is the difficulty of understanding how to look at/for community literacies. And so I offer here a framework of issues and perspectives for doing so, focusing briefly on "everyday" literacies and more significantly on work and workplace literacies.

The most recent book by David Barton, the result of a long collaboration with researcher Mary Hamilton (1998), takes an extended look at what they call "local" or "vernacular" literacies. The goal of their large-scale ethnographic project is to uncover the often silent and hidden literate practices of everyday life, to "offer an alternative public discourse which foregrounds the role of literacy as a communal resource contributing to the quality of local life" (p. xvi). In their book, they take a look at writing in one community, Lancaster, England. They examine Lancaster from an historical perspective, and then they take a detailed look at the literate practices of individuals in one working class neighborhood.[6] In this look at the neighborhood, they profile the everyday literate practices of four individuals, and based on these cases and other data, begin to paint a picture of the vernacular literacies of Lancaster: they examine practices in the home, the relations between the home and school, and the network of literate practices associated with local organizations. Based on these analyses, they begin to from a theory of "vernacular" or local, everyday literacies.

According to Barton and Hamilton, vernacular literacies are those "not regulated by the formal rules and procedures of dominant social institutions and which have their origin in everyday life" (p. 247). Vernacular literacies are learned informally, tied directly to use, and encompass a wider range of practices than allowable in a structured institution like a school. In this way, they are typically less dominant (e.g., literacies from different cultures or utilizing different languages and/or registers), self-generated, voluntary, and creative. Their concept of vernacular literacies is important because it focuses on the reading and writing that is valued by individuals and communities, not necessarily by schools and workplaces. The importance of this should be clear to anyone who has spent time in a community literacy program. People will come to a community literacy program because they want to be able to read the Bible. Others will come because they want to write letters to family members or be able to better help their children or grandchildren with their homework. Still others want to learn English more proficiently for work and family life, or they want to be able to use a computer. The list of reasons that people come is literally endless, and any community literacy program that serves a given community must keep its ears open in order to listen to these needs.

For Barton and Hamilton these everyday literacies are just as sophisticated and important as those directly warranted by dominant institutions, and in their book they go so far as to develop a theory of vernacular knowledge—an everyday epistemology if you will—to accompany their notion of vernacular literacies. Everyday reading and writing practices imply a way of knowing and being in and with the world that is powerful and far too often ignored or diminished in the face of more dominant ways of knowing and practicing literacy. Their work is a fantastic argument for the variety, the depth, and the sophistication of everyday literacies. I won't repeat it here. My point is that those participating in the construction of community-based programs must be open to seeing and understanding the everyday literacies of their communities and local institutions. They are not only personally and communally meaningful, they are also a powerful currency of social interaction, status, and well-being. Vernacular literacies are powerful and practiced widely, and even the most seemingly mundane practices (like reading a favorite book) are of the utmost importance to people, and therefore, should be important to program designers.

Work and Workplace Literacies

Recall the work order I used in the first chapter to frame this project. It was an artifact given to me by a woman associated with a community literacy program. That program taught reading and narrative writing but ignored work. Western District focuses on work but not workers. These tensions are representative of relationships between work and community literacy programs more generally. Some programs choose not to see the importance of work or don't know what to do with it once it is visible. Other programs focus on work but only in the most generalized ways. We can do better.

In my conversations with students at Western District, I learned that many of them were attending classes for reasons related to work. For some, this desire was as simple as getting a GED so that they could apply for better jobs; for others this desire was as complicated as looking for elusive "computer skills" so that they could get better, "cleaner" work.[7] Work was important to many of these people, and it is an important consideration for any community-based literacy program. In my discussion here I emphasize two issues that I would like to see more clearly foregrounded in workplace literacy discussions: the importance of work itself and the need to move beyond the functional/critical binary that marks many discussions of workplace literacy.

I noted in the preface to this book that researchers in professional writing are concerned with the relationships between writing and work, and I am no exception. I also noted that much of the research in professional writing focuses on professional workers—engineers, bankers, and the like—and ignores the relationships between writing and work in a number of other workplaces. In fact, much of this research would not see an engineer as a professional *worker*. Instead, the engineer, if described in any other way, would be seen as a professional, a member of a different class than a mere worker. This work and class distinction is important: workers whom we prepare for the professions are more highly regarded by most of society (including teachers) because their work is more highly regarded, and this regard is reflected in the sophisticated literacy curriculum to which they are given access; workers whom we prepare for "mere work" are simply not as highly regarded because our perceptions of the work they do isn't highly regarded, and this too is reflected in the more basic literacy curriculum designed for them. Recent changes in work and specific workplaces, however, mean that we ought to rethink the class divisions in our educational practices, and these complicated relationships between work and literacy profoundly affect community-based literacy programs.

There are many formulations of the "changing nature of work" thesis. Perhaps the most well-known is former Labor Secretary Robert Reich's (1992) book *The Work of Nations*. All of them make a similar argument: first-world economies are moving from agriculture and manufacturing to service and information-based production, and these changes are having a deep and in some cases catastrophic affect on job availability and the nature of the work that remains. Bernhardt and Farmer (1998), for example, list the following workplace trends:

- a shift from a manufacturing economy to service, information, and knowledge economies;

- a re-engineering or restructuring of the workplace to meet demands for higher productivity and quality;

- the arrival of new technologies in the workplace and an accelerated speed of change in the workplace and the marketplace; and

- changes in workforce demographics, including a gradually aging workforce; a shrinking labor pool; increases in the representation of immigrants, minorities, and women with families; and significant numbers of contingent or part-time workers (p. 57)

These changes impact significantly the skills required for these changing workplaces. Again as Bernhardt and Farmer see it, "many changes underway in the workplace require high-level communication skills . . . the need for strong communication skills is inextricably linked to such higher order thinking skills as problem solving, critical thinking, systems analysis, and resource management" (p. 56). Indeed, there is no more influential source arguing for the need for higher-level skills than the US Department of Labor's (1991) own report on "necessary skills" for the workplace (commonly known as the SCANS report). Not only have the findings from this report been pervasive in recent scholarship on workplace literacy, but they have had an equally powerful effect on community-based programs. When I was first planning the research described in this book, officials associated with Adult Basic Education in Indiana insisted that I become familiar with the SCANS report and said that it was driving adult-basic education throughout the country.

The five competencies that form the core of the SCANS "necessary skills" are anything but basic. Workers must be able to (1) allocate resources such as time, money, and staff; (2) possess sophisticated interpersonal skills such as working on teams and working with people with different backgrounds; (3) acquire and use information, which covers research and writing; (4) understand social, organizational, and technological systems, and (5) use and adapt technologies. These five competencies are built on a foundation of reading, writing, and computational skills as well as sophisticated thinking abilities and sound personal qualities (material taken from Garay, 1998, but it is easily found in the report itself). The sum of these skills and abilities is the superworker— who wouldn't want to possess these qualities and work with people who have them? While many people have noted problems with the SCANS recommendations—sophisticated literacies packaged within an old, functional, skills-based paradigm (see Garay, 1998)—these new competencies make the case for changes in the workplace that are coming (if they haven't happened already). As Bernhardt and Farmer (1998) suggest, "these skills are just as necessary in traditional manufacturing environments as they are in the knowledge or information sectors" (p. 65).[8]

There are two serious questions that remain (at least) even if one accepts all that I have written about the changing nature of work and workplaces, particularly if one is interested in community-based programs and the people served by them. The first question concerns the availability of jobs themselves and the training necessary for those jobs, and the second question deals with what, exactly, we mean by workplace literacies. With the restructuring of work has come the restructuring of workplaces. And many observers have noted the destructive effects these processes have had on job availability. Aronowitz and DiFazio (1994), for example, present an extended and sobering analysis of the factors decimating the job market for both traditional production and professional workers (technological innovation, investment patterns, and globalization; see also Castells, 1999). In addition to questions about job availability are concerns about our ability as a society to retrain displaced workers. As Jeremy Rifkin (1995) characterizes it, "the few good jobs that are becoming available in the new high-tech global economy are in the knowledge sector. It is naïve to believe that large numbers of unskilled and skilled blue and white collar workers will be retrained to be physicists, computer scientists ... and the like" (p. 36).

While Rifkin's characterization may be too stark, his point is worth remembering, and he helps make the connection between more abstract, global economic movements and the concerns of a community-based literacy program. People come to such programs for work-related training, which raises questions as to what kind of training a community-based program might provide given changes in work and the economy. Dautermann and Sullivan (1996) note that the old notion that a job can be broken down into discrete step and that those steps can be matched with specific skills is quickly disappearing (if it ever existed at all). Yet at Western District, this was the structure of work-related curricula, and my reading suggests this is widespread (for an important exception, see Soifer et.al, 1990). Sally Robinson (1998), the former director of a community-based adult education program and long-time workplace literacy teacher and researcher further emphasizes that the old notions of "basic skills"—discrete, functional, technocratic literacies—are no longer appropriate. Accordingly, she has developed a new basics for the workplace. I want to share what those new basics look like in terms of reading and writing:

> In the traditional community-based program, [reading] skills were taught in the context of short stories, poems, articles, and novels. Students were taught to read from the beginning to the end of a piece of writing. In the workplace, however, almost all reading is technical. To meet ISO 9000 requirements, employees must be able to read, understand, and perform their jobs according to long, frequently changing documents .... They must also be able to locate specific information in indexes, matrices, notices, manuals and equipment specifications. (p. 110)

> The *kinds* of writing workers do is different from the creative writing, essays, and story summaries done in the community-based program. In the workplace, employees need to [be] able to get their ideas down on paper quickly and organize their writing into different formats for different purposes and audiences. Today's workers need to be able to write memos, business letters, reports, procedural directions, meeting minutes, peer evaluations, and proposals, among other things. (p. 111-112)

The basics described here sound more like a university classroom than a community-based literacy program, and this is precisely the point. We should think of workplace literacies as encompassing sophisticated reading and writing practices, the kind we might teach to our "professional workers." When we begin to walk down this path, another "literacy binary" begins to fall away as well—the boundary between "functional" and "critical" literacies. As Dautermann and Sullivan (1996) again note, "workplace literacy efforts have existed separately from efforts to understand critical literacies," a separation that further alienates, minimizes, and disempowers literacy education for workers. This alienation is unacceptable. And so what we have is a situation in which the literacy needs of workers are sophisticated and far outpacing both people's conceptualization of work and workplace literacy and the ability of community-based programs to provide appropriate educational opportunities.

One way to work through the problems presented here is to look to work in technical and professional writing (and conversely, for researchers in technical and professional writing to look at community contexts). But first some hard work needs to be done to rearticulate the unhelpful binary of functional-critical literacy. In many ways, discussions about literacy have revolved around and sometimes centered on the issue of functionality. Within academic circles at least, the functional serves as the negative of what literacy should be. But many have not moved much beyond some equation of functional literacy (bad) versus "new definition" (good), and because of this, have not displaced the power of functional notions of literacy (see Dautermann & Sullivan, 1996, for a discussion of the functional/critical binary). Yet despite repeated critiques of functional literacies as limited, the power of functionality resides in its often "common sense" usefulness, and those who champion functional literacies do so because such notions of literacy help people *do* things better. The failure to displace functional literacy is the result of the failure, I think, to see literacies as institutionally situated and *necessarily* functional. The task is not to displace functionality but to rearticulate it, to make it useful to the institutions that warrant functional literacies and more generally powerful to the workers and students who must acquire a new literacy in order to function within new institutional settings.

Functional literacy definitions are actually quite commonplace. In chapter 2 I listed the few embedded within the federal and state legislation that make programs like Western District possible. Functional literacy definitions, like those in the legislation cited in chapter 2, emphasize what Scribner (1988) calls the "survival or pragmatic" value of literacy (p. 75). Brian Street (1984) notes this power on a more global scale when discussing his work with UNESCO. For that organization, and for many others world-wide, literacy is often tied to a particular development or economic *telos*. That is, functional literacy becomes that level of literacy necessary to sustain economic development at a certain, pre-defined level. The meaning and value of literacy, when tied to development, becomes a function of measurement tools.

In Western District's contact with workplaces and workers, they used assessment exams to test workers and prescribe a program of instruction. In addition, the state of Indiana often did a "literacy task analysis" of the workplace, a procedure which again breaks down actions required of workers into their subskills (see Mikulecky et al., 1992). David Jolliffe (1997) also notes the commonplace use of technocratic instruments to assess job and worker skills even though, as the practitioners he spoke with stated, they often have little to do with what is asked of workers. In short, in a variety of workplace and classroom practices, functional literacy is "the ability to competently read required, work related materials ..." and only sometimes the ability to write simple documents (like form-filling), an ability that does not require "a high level of sophistication" (Rush, Moe, & Storlie, 1986, p. 1; Diehl, 1980, p. 50). Such notions of literacy are developed in response to the real needs of workers and organizations who have the need to quickly and efficiently train people to be better at their jobs. Thus, standardized approaches to needs assessment (a literacy task analysis), operationalizing those needs (naming literacy skills), and testing attainment (standardized assessments) help define literacy in ways common throughout social institutions because they are warranted by powerful institutions and are believed to be tied to material gain for companies, communities, and nations. Therefore, functional/ technocratic literacies are institutionally powerful and ideologically pervasive, making them difficult to displace with alternative notions of literacy.

Most critics of functionality focus on its limits, and obviously, I agree. This is precisely the argument Collins (1989) makes by writing that many functional definitions of literacy are driven by business and encompass a view of education "more explicitly oriented to the demands of capitalist rationality and the values of the market ..." (p. 27). She postulates that the interest in literacy in both schools and workplaces on the part of the business community is part of an increased interest in the socialization of students into more docile workers. From a critical literacy perspective, functional literacy

> has led to an increase in "functional" exercises, such as reading classified advertisements, filling out job and credit applications, and so on ... [which] presents as legitimate educational knowledge information which is artificially simplified, linear, mechanistic, and essentially powerless. (DeCastell & Luke, 1988, p. 172)

Such an approach to literacy is driven, scholars argue, by a "vulgar pragmatism" that seeks to unproblematically instruct students in the "neutral" skills needed in order to attain economic prosperity (Carlson, 1993, p. 217). This proposition is warranted by one powerful assumption: a functional relationship should exist between the needs of the labor force and the curriculum (p. 217). However, critical theorists argue the equation is backward. It is not the lack of functional literacy skills causing economic strain for both workers and organizations, it is a problem "deep in the logic of capitalism, and in economic restructuring and lesser adjustments made imperative by the quest for capital accumulation. . ." which is driving the "literacy crisis" (Lankshear & McLaren, 1993, pp. 29–30). The solution, they argue, is not "fixing" individuals according to a mechanistic, skills-based approach to literacy, but rather, the solution can be found in addressing the structural economic causes of current literacy and employment crises. As part of such structural change, students cannot be given access only to functional/technocratic literacies, which Carlson (1993) argues prepares people only for entry-level positions and Stuckey (1991) similarly argues is part of the "violence" of limited, socially stratified literacies. Rather, students and workers must be given access to critical literacies, part of what Giroux calls a "cultural politics" and Freire "critical consciousness." Critical literacies give students and workers an opportunity for education as a "practice of freedom," or a reflection on one's place in the world and an examination of ways to change it (Freire, 1992, p. 69).

I agree with Freire (1995) when he argues that only someone who is "grossly materialistic" could "reduce adult literacy learning to a purely technical action" (p. 399). So when Freire writes that "the worker learning the trade of machinist, mechanic, or stonemason has the right and the need to learn it as well as possible ..." (p. 131), he is walking a thin yet important line connecting functionality to the necessity for critical consciousness as a condition for greater justice and democracy and better workers and workplaces. While not explicitly framed in this way, my critique of critical literacy theorists for the tendency to generalize and abstract people and institutions (see chapter 2) is tied to their tendency to ignore the very real and material needs that people in community literacy programs have to attain functional proficiency. In the most general sense, the critical literacy critique of functional/technocratic literacy stems from the desire for "something more." Yet the desire for something more cannot ignore the power and importance of functionality. And frankly, critical theorists too often have ignored what people say they want and need. While I position myself close to many critical literacy theorists because of their concern for a literacy designed to enable individuals to increase their access to structures of power, I have a problem with such positions because they have not adequately worked through—made a part of critical literacy—the importance of functionality. Three examples from Western District can be used to problematize critical literacy positions in terms of what students and workers "should" learn and what can be empowering.

Prompts: People and Practices at Western District
While people choose to come to community-based literacy programs, some are forced to attend as well. Some have been kicked out of traditional schools; others have been ordered to attend as part of sentencing; and increasing numbers of students attend as part of welfare-reform programs. My point is to highlight the diversity of people who come to such programs and their motivations in order to emphasize once again the importance of local contexts. With this in mind, the stories and examples I turn to are not extraordinary; in fact, they are quite mundane. They are deliberately chosen to be everyday occurrences at Western District involving people with whom I had regular contact. The prompts reveal a range of what I call functional desires and needs on the part of students and workers at Western District that pose problems for current critical positionings of functional literacy. The prompts also pose problems for traditional functional notions because they question the common *telos* of

functionality: work. My ultimate concern in posing these stories and examples is to see if a critical functional literacy, the rearticulation toward which I am heading, can take seriously the needs and experiences of the people I represent in this section.

Selden and Gertrude. Selden and Gertrude are a couple who attended one of the GED preparation classes I observed at the Western District site. Selden and Gertrude were both in their late fifties and able to attend classes during the day because neither of them currently worked. Gertrude had gone to school into her senior year in high school but never finished. She left school to work in order to supplement income lost because of a strike at her father's place of employment. Over her lifetime, Gertrude worked for a television manufacturer and at a nursing home in addition to raising three children. Selden never learned to read in school. Selden left school his first year of high school and immediately began working. At about this time, he also met Gertrude and they married. Over his long working career, Selden worked in numerous machine shops and was currently on disability because of a bad back. As Selden said to me during one of our conversations, he could not read words very well, but give him any picture and he could make an object. He was proud of his ability with blueprints (although he insisted he couldn't "read"). He was also proud of his ability to craft metal which was "art" and not the mere "piecework" produced by many of his recent co-workers. Gertrude had not worked for a number of years, due in part to a series of small strokes which had "erased" some of her memories and abilities.

Selden and Gertrude were attending classes at Western District for personal and pragmatic reasons. Gertrude wanted to relearn how to read so she could read the long novels that she once enjoyed:

> I always looked at books, and I just looked at them and I'd think some of these days I can read this when I was ... and I said I'll be able to read this again. So I always loved to read, 'cause reading always, I've always just ... you read that and you just transfer you to someplace else, you know, or different people and different times, different things. Maybe you can't go there but you can read about it, and that way you, so you can go there by reading. (personal interview, 6/12/96)

Selden wanted to learn how to read so he could assume ownership of his late brother's computer. Selden loved computers and was promised his brother's computer if he would learn to read. Therefore, as Selden told me, he wanted to learn some new words, especially their correct spelling. The best part of the classes for Gertrude was the opportunity to renew some things she had forgotten as well as the new things she had learned. Her examples were new spelling rules. The best part for Selden was the teaching, which was more attentive and invigorating than any of his previous experiences.

Selden and Gertrude were attending the Western District program for personal reasons. They were not there to attain a better job or a GED. Furthermore, they were satisfied with what they were learning and the ways they were learning it. Both could recite their current grade levels on language exams (a common ability program wide), and both considered literacy the ability to communicate with others. Communicative ability is achieved by knowing words, how to spell those words correctly, and how to punctuate sentences appropriately. They were immersed in a technocratic curricula learning functional literacies, but for these students, it was what they wanted, and perhaps, needed. Clearly it was the only way they knew how to think about literacy and literacy instruction.

The case of Selden and Gertrude presents a few problems for both functional and critical literacy theories. Their training was functional and meaningful to them, yet it was not driven by the reasons proponents of functional literacy posit—to better prepare individuals for workplace or provide necessary life skills (e.g., consumer reading and math). Their training was a function of the institution in which they were situated; functional literacy *was* literacy training at Western District. How does critical literacy theory deal with an example like Selden and Gertrude? In many respects, critical literacy theory simply does not deal with students like Selden and Gertrude, preferring to theorize more abstractly. How, then, does a theorist or a program deal with Selden and Gertrude if the purpose of literacy is critical consciousness and the student just wants to learn how to read a book so he can get a computer; how does a program resolve this (potential? actual? theoretical?) conflict? Programs and teachers cannot force critical consciousness after all, nor can they minimize personal and/or functional needs. This, I'm afraid, is the problem with which we are left given the typical functional/critical binary: a limited domain for the functional (which prevents asking the question "functional for what?") and a critical domain either completely removed or at odds with functional or personal desires. The conflict cannot be resolved if one takes an "either/or" position with respect to functionality and critical literacies. And the conflict cannot be resolved if one simply ignores the wishes of the student. The difficulty is how to take seriously and simultaneously individual needs, the powerful pragmatism of functional literacy, and a critical literacy that helps avoid continuing or imposing social stratification.

Carol Thomas. Carol Thomas was arguably the most advanced student in the computers and communication class at Western District (see chapter 4 for more on this class). She had progressed through most of her lessons and often worked on individual projects in order to push herself, and she also helped other students. Carol earned her GED some fifteen years ago and was attending these classes for personal reasons. Carol did not work and originally came to classes at Western District to help comfort a friend who was ordered to attend classes by a local court. Carol showed up that first day but her friend did not. Carol kept coming to class because she was interested in computers and was investigating the possibility of enrolling in classes at the local university extension campus.

In the computers and communication class, students often produced a set of what I would call "professional writing" documents, some to help them attain new jobs, some simply to learn how to make templates (memos, letters, resumes). The focus of the class was learning the computers, not producing the documents. So I was surprised when Carol came to me in class and asked for help with a project she and another student (Tina) were working on. They had taken handwritten fliers produced by their eye doctor and independent of any guidance or instruction, decided that they were sloppy and difficult to read. They then laid out new fliers on the computer and produced a set of new promotional documents. Carol wanted me to help her with a cover letter to the doctor so they could send the documents to him. Later I learned he planned to use the documents in the future.

Again, this example presents problems for the relationship between functional and other literacies. The class was not broken down into a set of testable skills as many other classes were at Western District. The class allowed students to do things better, but it did not teach what I would call traditionally functional literacy. Still, DeCastell and Luke (1988) would see the types of documents produced in this class as "mechanistic" and "powerless" (p. 172). Similarly, other critical approaches would not recognize this course as "empowering." But I see this class as allowing spaces for empowerment. By providing the class, Western District provided a space—physical, intellectual, emotional—for students to learn and work. Within this space, Carol and Tina learned about the analysis and production of documents, and their experiences gave them positive contact with real audiences. Is it possible that a class that deals more clearly and rhetorically with certain types of professional writing could teach literacies that are both functional and critical? This question challenges critical literacy as the only model for a "true" empowering literacy. Most critical theorists would not recognize professional writing as a site for their work. But can professional writing provide a model for teaching a set of written literacies that enhance employment and people's ability to act powerfully in the world? If so, how is this not "functional"? And if functional, how is this not potentially "critical" and "empowering"?

These prompts are levers for moving positions typically at odds with each other into a third space. This space is the location of a literacy that is necessarily functional and critical; a literacy that is concerned with *doing* and *moving*. Such a notion of literacy can work toward a more dynamic and sophisticated sense of functionality. Others are doing this as well.

Collins' (1989), for example, writes that workplace notions of functional literacy are responses to the general interest of business to control the educational process, both within and outside their own organizations. She poses the question of whether or not "worker literacy [can] be an opportunity to develop a more critical, creative, and militant workforce?" (p. 27). Will workplace literacy serve the interests of capital accumulation in the hands of a few, or will it "be the path to genuine upward mobility, self-actualization, and economic democracy for US workers?" (p. 27). Instead of leaving this tension where it is, however, Collins admits something important and rare for a critical literacy scholar. She writes that it is not just business that is interested in more sophisticated levels of workplace literacy, but that:

> Working-class parents and low-wage workers know that something different must be done, and political progressives know that a system of economic democracy, no less than one of corporate capitalism, needs workers who can read, write, compute, and problem solve. (p. 28)

As a solution, Collins begins by invoking Freire's position of "cultural action for freedom," but more interestingly, she points to a solution that changes the institutional structure for literacy training. Her solution is to make unions responsible for literacy training, thereby altering the power arrangements from a hierarchy (business responsible for employees) to a partnership (business and union together) in an attempt to make the power relations more symmetrical.

In another article (Collins, Balmuth, & Jean, 1989), Collins and her colleagues detail the effects of relocating literacy learning. The context is a program called the Consortium for Worker Education, an arrangement created with unions to create Workplace Literacy Centers across the state of New York. The goal was to fill a niche "created by the shift from an industrial to a high tech service economy and a changing urban work force, more heavily female, non-English-speaking, poorly educated, and either unskilled or with few marketable skills" (p. 457). The goals of the program were (1) job retention, (2) job upgrading, (3) re-employment, (4) problem-solving skills, and (5) "the ability to take greater control over one's life and environment" (p. 457). The union was seen to be an appropriate institutional structure for such a program because unions could help workers attain many of the goals of the program, especially job upgrading.

From my perspective, there are two key aspects to this program. First, the program saw institutional location as essential for the success of the program. The program designers saw that the institutional context within which they worked would determine the nature and success of that work; thus, they sought to change the institutional arrangement of the program by moving it into a union context. Second, they recognized the importance of functionality but gave it new meaning. They understood that "retention rates are maximized when education addresses real needs, benefiting the adult learner in specific ways" (Collins et al., 1989, p. 457). And they understood, as Carlson (1993) also argues, that "some relationship should exist between schoolwork and work in other important institutional sites in society, since education serves to initiate individuals into the productive work of building culture and objectifying experience" (Carlson, 1993, p. 238). For Carlson, the relationship between work and literacy should enhance workers' participation in a wide range of substantive issues. Collins et al. (1989) pose the problem (and solution) in the following question:

> What kind of education will allow people to enhance their job and earning prospects; preserve their rights and dignity as workers; increase the productivity of U.S. businesses; enhance the efficiency of public services; and become self-actualized citizens? (p. 458)

This quotation embodies many tensions that pose real problems for workplace literacy, and more generally problems that show up in other literacy studies. But the quotation is also productive because the tension that is the most significant problem (functional versus critical literacy) is also the source of the solution. A notion of literacy that is useful for the variety of people, practices, and institutional arrangements found in community literacy contexts must be flexible and powerful enough to be both functional and critical, to allow workers and students to learn what is necessary to meet their needs and give them the ability to *move*—to change their positions within the workplaces where they currently are or to gain access to new institutions. The work of these workplace literacy scholars points to a rearticulation of functionality that works through old oppositions and contains new possibilities.

Clearly I think the typical ways we think about functional literacy and the relationships between functional and critical literacies are limiting. Moreover, I think these ways of viewing functional and critical literacies are particularly problematic for community-based literacy programs. Community-based programs, after all, often are the places where people go for the functional training they need to better their lives. Functional literacies defined as mechanistic basic skills are inadequate for the workplace, and a more sophisticated literacy training absent a critical edge is inadequate for the world.

And so it is important that those of us interested in community-based literacy practices and programs be careful about the ways we talk about them. We cannot assume the existence of community, and we can never assume that a community-based program is empowering. Communities and institutions must be built, and the systems that result must be able to see the pervasiveness and relevance of what I've called everyday and work literacies. In seeing these literacies, however, program designers need to work outside the categories typically constructed for work literacies in particular because functional-critical literacy for work and everyday life cannot take place anywhere; the system must be designed to allow it. If we can't see communities and institutions as constructed and mutually reinforcing, and if we can't therefore see the meaning and value of literacy as situated within these communities/institutions, then local people and places are largely inaccessible as sources for alternative literacies and new design practices. If this is the case, community-based programs will fail to be the major institutions of literate behavior in American life that I think they can be, and in many communities, must be.

Chapter 6

Participatory Institutional Design

"A bad designer is to that extent a bad citizen" (Vachel Lindsay, 1968[1])

A critical rhetoric for the design of community-based literacy programs is a procedure for making decisions that is situated and nomadic, committed to participatory decision-making, and gives preference to the less powerful. In this chapter, I explore participatory procedures in an attempt to justify why they are so important as an alternative way to establish the meaning and value of literacy. I argue for participation in terms of its ethical and political suitability and its pragmatic power by focusing on power, difference, and the expertise of participants, particularly those commonly thought to lack such expertise. The purpose of this chapter is to show the relevance and usefulness of participatory design for the construction of community-based literacy programs.

Most theoretical discussions of participation come from political theory but also can be found in treatments of participatory design (e.g., in human computer interaction or urban planning), public policy decision-making (e.g., risk communication), and participatory action research (widely interdisciplinary and discussed in chapter 7). In nearly all theoretical discussions of participation, scholars debate the type, quality, and nature of participation. Laird (1993), for example, divides democratic political theory into two camps, pluralism (or representative and interest group democracy) and direct participation (or "strong democracy" as

119

Barber [1984; 1996] has articulated it). Despite significant differences, each approach to democratic practice posits that citizens have the right to directly influence decisions that affect their lives. This means that citizens must be able to understand their own interests and how they affect public questions and be able to have *substantive* influence on decision-making processes (p. 344). For reasons I will discuss below, I am going to assume that people know their own interests and how their lives intersect with the lives of others in order to focus on why individuals and communities *should* have the ability to affect public decision-making. The need to make this argument is significant and reflects not only the reality that much public decision-making is not participatory but also the feeling, held by many "experts," that decision-making processes shouldn't be participatory (see Simmons, 2000).

The justification of participation from an ethical and political stand-point must address the nature of participatory processes themselves. Participation doesn't mean the same thing always and everywhere. The type of participation in which I am interested is localized direct participa-tion, not pluralist or representative participation. Because I'm interested in situated participation, more abstract theorizing is less useful than an examination of deliberative processes and procedures (see, for example, Habermas, 1990; Benhabib, 1992; Benhabib, 1996). According to phi-losopher Seyla Benhabib (1996), deliberative approaches to democratic processes are "a necessary condition for attaining legitimacy and rational-ity with regard to collective decision-making processes in a polity ..." (p. 69). Legitimacy and rationality, of course, are key criteria, for democratic theorists are never interested in illegitimate exercises of power (e.g., violence or dictatorship) and irrational decision-making (e.g., mob rule). Thus the "necessary condition" that must be met in a democratic polity is some procedure for coming to decisions that are equally in the interests of all, and this is possible only if decision-making processes are "in principle open to appropriate public processes of deliberation by free and equal citizens" (p. 69). I will soon get to the pragmatic problems of freedom and equality, but for now it is important to note that deliberative theories of democracy are general arguments for how citizens can participate in making decisions about their lives without explicit or implicit exclusions, coercion, violence, or other asymmetrical exercises of power.

Freedom and equality are guaranteed in a deliberative democracy through some version of a discourse ethic many trace to Habermas (1990). According to this ethic, certain procedural norms must be in place for decision-making processes to be legitimate. These norms, or rules, include statements that declare that all have the same right to initiate speech acts, to question, and to argue (even about the rules themselves), just to provide a few brief examples (see Benhabib, 1996, p. 70 for a good overview). So if the procedures of discourse are ethical, then the decisions will be just. For all the complexity involved, the justification of partici- pation can be rather simply stated: *only* those decisions that have been freely arrived at through open and equal processes and which are in the interests of all are legitimate in a democratic polity. That is, if we are interested in decision-making processes that avoid violence, coercion, and authoritative controls, then the processes must be procedurally sound, and they must allow those affected to participate; this deliberative model provides a process for doing it. To be politically viable in contemporary democratic societies and to be ethically just requires some form of direct participation.

To justify participation, however, is more difficult because the pragmatics of participation are complex. Deliberative democracy opens a door by providing the most general political and ethical justification for direct participation, but it doesn't work well as a practice because it is a highly idealized system that assumes freedom, equality, and the ability to participate in real discursive situations; it cannot account for asymmetries of power because all of the conditions that must obtain for decisions to be legitimate rarely do. Still, I want to keep the above principles intact as a horizon while I try to work through some of the more difficult issues in order to come to a more convincing conclusion about why direct partici- pation in decision-making about the design of community-based pro- grams makes for "good" design.

To work through issues of power, difference, and the pragmatics of actual decision-making processes, I return first to the work of Iris Marion Young (1990), who recognizes the importance of identifying oppressive relations of power within institutions and framing less oppressive pro- cesses as a response. Young argues that those who conceptualize justice do so primarily in terms of distribution. Deliberative notions of democ- racy and justice are important because they focus on a wider range of issues. She claims that:

> instead of focusing on distribution, a conception of justice should
> begin with the concepts of domination and oppression. Such a shift
> brings out issues of decision making, division of labor, and culture
> that bear on social justice but are often ignored in philosophical
> discussions. (p. 3)

Her problem with distributive approaches to justice is that they fail to adequately conceptualize power as a function of relations, and they therefore tend to commodify such relations, to make them objects or goods to be granted or taken away.

To focus on distributive justice is to limit the range of politics through a narrow understanding of power that also serves to limit public space. As Young writes, "the distributive paradigm of justice tends to reflect and reinforce this depoliticized public life, by failing to bring issues of decision making power, for example, into explicit public discussion. Democratic decision making processes, I argue, are an important element and condition of social [and institutional] justice" (p. 10). So for Young, justice means "the elimination of institutionalized domination and op-pression," by which she means "structured" domination and oppression in the sense of large scale social institutions. But this is also true for institutions of smaller scope and scale.

Young's focus on nonmaterial relations and processes situates her firmly within the realm of rhetoric. For Young, rights refer more to doing than to having; thus, the ability to do, to act, to participate, to write is necessary for less dominating and oppressive social relations. The ability to participate allows one to exercise rights, and this space can be institutionally given or taken away. As Sullivan (1995) argues, institu-tions make certain practices possible and others impossible, yet at the same time individuals can also change institutional orders. Similarly, Young argues that:

> only a social theory that takes process [design] seriously . . . can understand the relation between social structures and action. Individuals are not primarily receivers of goods or carriers of properties, but actors with meanings and purposes, who act with, against, or in relation to one another. We act with knowledge of existing institutions, rules, and the structural consequences of a multiplicity of actions, and those structures are enacted and reproduced through the confluence of our actions [the ways we institutionally structure our interactions]. (pp. 28–29)

Institutional procedures are obvious and important locations for indi-vidual and collective action. And so these procedures must be taken seriously if one is interested in just institutional orders. Young writes that institutional context "should be understood in a broader sense than 'mode of production.' It includes any structures or practices, the rules and norms that guide them, and the language and symbols that mediate social interactions within them, in institutions of state, family, and civil society, as well as the workplace" (p. 22). Western District as a literacy institution operates as the type of "institutional context" that Young describes. Western District was created and operates by a set of norms, rules, and mediating discourse practices. The issue for Young, and indeed my interest here as well, is not taking for granted any pattern of decision-making or model of institutional order. Since institutional systems are places where literacy is given meaning and value, I want to contest and challenge institutional structures in order to revise what literacy can mean and how learning literacies can more meaningfully allow individuals to change their lives.

While understanding power and its function in institutional systems is one part of Young's contribution to a theory of institutional design, her take on "difference" is another. As I noted in my discussion of community, political theorists like Young have been the most effective critics of community in the name of difference. Young is bothered by notions of community because they can deny difference and lead to exclusions, oppression, and enforced homogeneity. In contrast, she argues for a "group-differentiated participatory public" as a way to prioritize difference (p. 95). She writes, "A politics of difference argues . . . that equality as the participation and inclusion of all groups sometimes requires different treatment for oppressed or disadvantaged groups" (p. 158), a position at the very core of a liberation theological argument for a "preferential option for the poor." Young's principle here is to avoid communities or institutions that silence, marginalize, and oppress others, and so participatory practices must provide "different treatment" for disadvantaged groups. The reasons for preferential treatment are rather simple in principle yet terribly complex in practice. Recall that the ethical and political justification of democratic processes depends on there being free and equal participation. Once we acknowledge that decision-making processes aren't free and equal—and they never are—then it is necessary to think carefully about how they can approach that ideal.

The argument for a "preferential option" that informs my thinking here comes from liberation theologies in the Roman Catholic tradition and South American context (e.g., Gutiérrez, 1988; Dussel, 1988). Within this context, a preferential option for "the poor" is justified through Biblical interpretation and the lived experience of domination and oppression. We must give preference to the poor, in other words, because God demands it and our brothers and sisters cry for it. Within the context of a religious community, such an argument is powerful and persuasive. Because the contexts of community literacy program design are not religious, such an argument doesn't work as well.

So what does work? Within the context of deliberative democratic theory, to give preference to Others is a way to ensure equality.[2] Disadvantaged groups should be given special treatment within decision-making processes, either because they have never been represented before and the difference they represent has been either dominated and/or oppressed or because they have special knowledge and insight to contribute (see below). Of course, to provide a space for difference doesn't mean that those normally silenced will be able to participate equally. To participate equally is to possess certain institutional literacies. I prefer to think of them in terms of access (as in chapter 4). In the sense in which access is important for institutional design, infrastructural access means access to the processes of decision-making within an institution, literacy means the discursive means to participate effectively, and acceptance refers to a "listening stance." Access means not only "a place at the table," it means the rhetorical ability to participate effectively and the structured requirement to listen to what others say.

Without a doubt, the space within institutional processes for those normally excluded but just as normally affected is a key to my understanding of institutional design. We all know that not everyone is free and equal and not everyone can participate. So what do we do? We put in place procedures that provide access to those normally excluded (yes, in some cases, perhaps many, this is benevolence on the part of the more powerful). We also must put in place ways to teach others the literacies necessary to participate. And we must listen. To listen is to act in solidarity with Others; it is to create, as I argued in chapter 5, a community in the most important sense—solidarity and commitment around a set of shared goals and/or values. Here I hope the connections between community and difference are clear; they are linked by a certain type of participatory decision-making. As Benhabib (1992) notes, one cannot know the mind and life of others without the voice of another. Actual discourse between others is required for ethical institutional design, and it is required as well to build community.

While I hope my ethical and political justification of participation in terms of power and difference is persuasive, perhaps the most convincing argument for participation is its pragmatic power. In this sense, participation in decision-making is "good" because participants in any given institutional context possess knowledge about that system that constitutes a form of expertise. Decision-making processes that rely on such insights stand a good chance of being better than those that don't, and by better I mean that those processes will likely culminate in sound and acceptable decisions. The claim I have just made is based on insights gleaned from usability. Usability refers to a range of research that studies how real people in real situations ("users") interact with products such as instructional manuals, technologies (like computers or computer interfaces), and any number of consumer goods. The assumption of usability is that humans should be integral to product design. In the course of numerous studies across industries and disciplines, usability researchers have discovered the considerable knowledge and expertise that users possess and have come to rely on that expertise in order to carry out effective design. In its most radical manifestations, use and user-driven design in workplaces has championed greater worker control and democracy in the workplace itself, a form of institutional design (e.g., Ehn, 1988).

What does it mean to say that users are "productive," that they are "experts," and therefore that they have something invaluable to offer design processes if allowed to participate? And even if I can answer that question, what do users of texts and artifacts have to do with those who take classes at or work for a community-based literacy center? I'll take the second question first because it is easier to deal with but no less important to the argument of this chapter. I am simply asking readers to follow this line of thinking in order to understand that the users of a computer interface are much like students in a classroom, or workers on a shop floor, or citizens in a democracy: they all occupy subordinate positions with respect to powerful and often related systems that affect nearly every aspect of daily life. While subordinate, users, students, workers, citizens have some power with respect to how these systems operate. While the nature of that power depends on the situation, it will always be linked to the ability to produce knowledge about a system. Usability researchers have been at the forefront of understanding that users possess and produce knowledge about the systems they use. In this case, my focus is on the "users" of community-based literacy programs and what they offer in terms of participatory design.

In his book on user-centered technologies, Robert Johnson (1998) argues that users generate knowledge about the technologies and systems they use, and therefore, that they should be integral to design. This knowledge can come in the form of adapting technologies to new and changing systems, or it can come in more explicit design situations. Regardless, Johnson asserts that user knowledge and understanding is unique and a function of certain identities and experiences. Johnson writes that "user-centered approaches should rethink the user as being an active participant in the social order that designs, develops, and implements technologies" because users experience systems much differently than "designers" or "experts," people who may not experience them at all (p. 64).[3] This is why user knowledge constitutes a form of expertise. But it is an expertise that is wasted when traditional hierarchies of knowledge are thoughtlessly maintained (e.g., expert/novice), particularly in situations in which they may not apply.

Johnson's concern is that highly structured systems of power/knowledge do not allow us to consider that users might have something important to say about the effectiveness of a technology, or closer to home, that students, workers, and teachers might have something crucial to say about how to define literacy and construct a community-based program to meet specific needs. In such a situation, those who are the users of a system help determine the parameters of the problem to be addressed, frame the questions that must be asked and answered, help decide the information that needs to be gathered, help interpret that information once collected, and therefore participate substantively in decision-making. One objection to participatory decision-making such as this is that users lack the expertise that specialists possess and therefore cannot possibly participate meaningfully in complex decision-making processes. While it is true that there are considerable barriers to creating the shared language and knowledge necessary for meaningful participatory processes, they are not impossible to overcome. My argument is that reinforcing the power of a narrow "knowledge elite" by ignoring users not only runs the risk of perpetuating a system of domination (see Sohng, 1995), but it also runs the risk of producing truly useless knowledge (see Deshler & Ewert, 1995). Both are risks I wish to avoid, and one way to avoid such risks is to take seriously the argument of Johnson and others and trust an alternative epistemological history that understands and respects the expertise of users. This is what it means to say that users are productive: It means to assert that they participate in and experience systems in unique ways and that their understanding of such systems is essential for designing "good" systems. Good design, then, is participatory in truly fundamental ways, beginning with problem posing itself and moving through phases of research, analysis, implementation, and evaluation. A participatory process that takes the process itself seriously, understands that such processes are structured by relations of power, and that makes space for difference stands a good chance of avoiding domination and oppression. Such a process seeks to produce with participants truly useful knowledge.

Participatory Institutional Design

As sociologist Dorothy Smith (1987) sees institutions, they are a local manifestation of more general social relations, a nodal point in what I would call a rhetorical relationship between general social processes and local practices. She sees institutions similarly to both Barton (1994) and Street (1995), particularly the ideological function of institutions. Vincent Leitch (1992) writes that institutions authorize ways of "speaking, writing, reading, and acting" by means of systems of codes (policies, rules, regulations) and rewards or punishments. According to this view of institutions, an institution is a well-established, rhetorically constructed design, a bureaucratic and organizational site where people live and work and where they interact with others inside and outside the institution. But just as importantly, according to this view, institutions can be changed. Institutions are fundamentally constructed out of the discourses that make them possible and the discourses by which they operate. Individuals can change institutions, then, (1) because institutions are rhetorically constructed, (2) because their construction and operation is a function of specific procedures, (3) because key processes can be places of interaction and difference, and (4) because such places are potentially unstable and open to change.

So how does one do this? Institutional critique and (re)design—a set of pragmatic mechanisms for change—is part of the answer.[4] I will discuss this methodology in general here, and in chapter 7 I will discuss specific tactics that can be utilized to foster institutional change. As a methodology, institutional critique focuses on making institutions visible and then looking for spaces within institutional systems where change is possible. Institutional critique works through two general mechanisms, postmodern mapping and boundary critique, but there can be empirical components as well, like an institutional case. Postmodern mapping, which I use most clearly in chapters 2 and 3, is used to make visible perspectives, positions, and values, and does this by charting changes over time. These maps are tentative and always partial, but they are useful in helping to make visible institutions in terms of the discourses and ideologies that make them possible. Boundary interrogation is a similarly important mechanism. Boundary interrogation seeks to locate spaces of difference within the institution that mark places for change. Sibley (1995) calls these places "zones of ambiguity," those spaces in which there is change, difference, or a clash of values and meanings; these zones of difference are places for change because of the instability that difference often brings (p. 33). Zones of ambiguity within institutions can often be found within processes of decision-making. It is within these processes that people within an institutional space, talk, listen, act, and confront differences.

Institutional critique seeks to enable institutional change, then, by locating gaps or fissures where resistance and change are possible. The key and unique function of institutional critique is that it provides the means to recognize and construct institutions (its methodological focus), and it insists that institutions can be changed (its action focus). The action focus can be thought of in terms of design, which is yet another discipline interested in process.[5] Mitchell (1988), writing from within design studies, argues that the "static object" or "product" approach to design "must be abandoned for new process-oriented and observer/user-dependent design tasks such as the design of computer software" (p. 209). He links this necessary move with a shift from "hardware" and "software" ages toward a "human" age that locates human needs and actions at the center of developmental processes. In effect, design is process:

> The designer's role in the post-mechanical era is to make the design process equally accessible to everyone. In order to realize this programme, design, like the avant garde of art before it, must abandon aesthetics and become instead a socially oriented process in which, like the new scientists, we are all both spectators and actors. (p. 214)

Following Mitchell, I want to think about design as a form of rhetorical action within institutions that focuses on process. To do this, I will look to two sources, Scandinavian work-oriented design (Ehn, 1988; Bødker, 1991) and an example drawn from my own work.

Ehn (1988) sees design as part of larger human activities that create worlds, and the role of design specifically as "a *process* of changing practice" (p. 82, my emphasis). From his perspective, the processes of design should enable emancipatory technical and social change (pp. 82–102); design is an attempt to change an oppressive situation. Design as a process of changing practice begins with a theory of knowledge. Within this framework, there is theoretical knowledge (expert driven) understanding (a product of knowing and/or knowing how), and insight. Insight is ultimately the most valued because it entails the active production of knowledge. These types of knowledge are procedural, and worker/user actions are particularly valued. Note here the clear connections between Ehn's epistemology and that of Johnson (1998). In both cases, useful knowledge is created in the day-to-day experiences associated with use and the subject positions occupied by users. These subjects positions are unique with respect to the technological systems within which users are situated. User knowledge constitutes a form of expertise that is deeply connected to the day-to-day use and experience of technological systems.

Design processes such as Ehn's cannot proceed without expert knowledge, critical reflection, and insight, and because no single group of people can generate all three types of knowledge, design processes must rely on the collective resources of multiple people and interests. From Ehn, then, there are three points to understand: (1) design concerns the processes of developing and changing institutional systems; (2) the key to work-oriented or collective resource design is the participation of users (workers, students) in decision-making processes; and (3) such an approach to design has as its driving force and goal the ideal of democracy. Design as a process of change must necessarily be involved in changing institutions. Design is a form of institutional rhetorical action.

Such a design stance, of course, enacts an ethic. For Ehn, the democratic ideal that drives design processes is based on the right of individuals to participate in decisions that affect their lives. Such an ethic focuses on worker need and use as the starting point for change. This is, of course, difficult because it alters typical relations of power. As Bødker (1991) writes, while need often drives design, "this need is not necessarily the common need of the group of users and other involved parties. Most often, computer applications [for example] are designed to fulfill the needs of managers of the use organization. Design takes place within organizational frames that tie groups with different interests together by means of power and resources" (p. 42). Bødker's point is that design decisions are not always made on the basis of rationality.[6] Rather, "the needs of the most powerful parties often drive design in a direction away from seeing and designing the product as an artifact" (p. 43). The most powerful party involved in the design of community literacy institutions, particularly when those institutions receive government funding, is the government itself. This happens through a number of complex mechanisms, some explicit (legislation) and other more implicit (assessment). This is not to say that government and other powerful institutions are bad.

My point is only to reinforce Bødker's assertion that design isn't a purely rational exercise. Design is a process of creating a reality, and those interests more powerful—often because of their ability to construct more persuasive knowledge—get to create their reality.

Let me turn to an example of an attempt to intervene in an institutional design. This example comes from an action research project that attempted to solve complicated problems associated with HIV/AIDS policy-making (see Grabill, 2000, for a full account). Most government funded HIV/AIDS services are funded through the Ryan White C.A.R.E. Act, a piece of legislation that has a progressive provision: those affected by HIV/AIDS must participate in local policy decision-making. This is, of course, difficult to achieve for a number of reasons.

Federal Ryan White money is granted to a local government. In Atlanta, that government is Fulton County. The local government, in turn, sets up a Ryan White Planning Council (RWPC) composed of elected officials, administrative professionals who deal with HIV/AIDS issues, other concerned professionals like doctors, researchers, and service providers, and individuals affected by HIV/AIDS. The RWPC, largely through its various committees, carries out the policy-making work associated with HIV/AIDS services in Atlanta, a monumental task that covers everything from research to housing, including key decisions about which local social service agencies will receive federal funds. In order to meet both the spirit and the letter of federal rules associated with Ryan White money, clients must be involved in these decision-making processes. Meaningful client involvement, however, has long been a problem, and those associated with the RWPC are concerned about client involvement in two related ways: (1) that they meet the letter of the law and maintain and document a certain level of client involvement; (2) that they meet the spirit of the law and good practice by generating meaningful involvement with clients, particularly those clients who are most often silent in the process—the powerless.

I became involved in this project through my relationship with a key player, Ko Hassan, and my involvement grew from that.[7] As an action research project, the goal was to achieve two deeply interconnected goals: (1) to document client involvement for use in reports to the government; (2) to improve client involvement generally to create better policy-making procedures. Therefore, I came to this project as a technical writer associated with an ad hoc group of HIV/AIDS educators and clients who want to improve client involvement (our ad hoc status is represented by the dotted-line circle in the corner of Figure 6–1). We worked for one year on an ad hoc basis with the knowledge and blessing of the RWPC.

Figure 6–1
Ryan White Funding/Administrative Structure: Atlanta

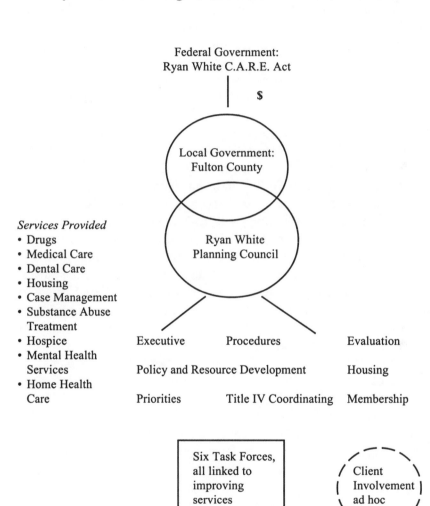

The goal of the project was to solve problems with those most affected by those problems, and to do so necessitated changing the institutional system of policy-making. Furthermore, I saw that the mechanism for this change was writing—documentation in this case. Let me explain more carefully. With a few exceptions, what "counts" as client involvement is membership on the RWPC, participation in RWPC committee work, and attendance at council meetings. Not only is documenting this form of client involvement a rather simple process, but this form of client involvement is severely limited and self-selects those who can and will participate through constraints such as meeting days and time, ability to make and participate in committee work, and the literacies necessary to understand and participate in rather sophisticated processes. So the argument we began to make is that we needed to rethink what client involvement can mean: we needed to work outside the metaphor and practice of "the meeting."

During my time with this project, two things happened that constitute, in my mind, institutional change. The first and perhaps most significant change is that our work moved from ad hoc to task force status (the seventh task force, see Figure 6–2). Within a bureaucracy, this is significant. Whereas previously our work and recommendations were useful for conversation and consideration, with task force status our work and recommendations became part of the public record and required action at meetings. Through our research and our speaking and writing within the institution, we managed to persuade others to give our work more power. There is no question that we were given power, but there is also no question that the power "given" to us was a function of our ability to persuade others that it was necessary. Understanding the rhetorical processes by which the institution operated, we used them and wrote our way to a new space within the institution. The possibility now exists that client involvement will become a standing committee and part of the day-to-day work of the Council.

The second change concerns what we have done with the client meetings over the last year. Where once they were heuristic and much more fluid, they are now focused forums for improving client involve-ment, and significantly, client involvement activities themselves. This is a subtle move, yet important. Our meetings, which were always located in a different part of the city and often at variable times, connected those of us who met regularly with a wider spectrum of those affected by HIV/AIDS. In this little way, we have changed the processes of client involvement, although we have yet to impact in any significant way how policy is made.

I provide this example not only because it shows that institutional change can happen but also because it makes visible some key issues,

Figure 6–2
Changed Ryan White Funding/Administrative Structure: Atlanta

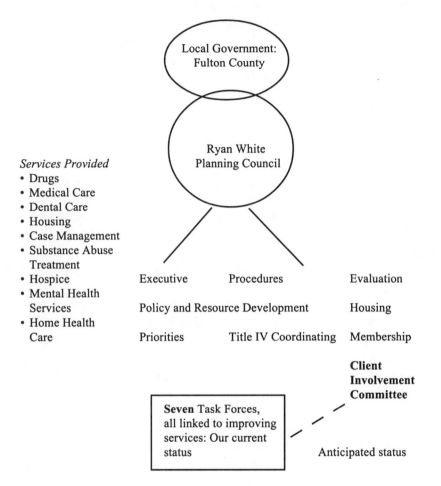

Services Provided
- Drugs
- Medical Care
- Dental Care
- Housing
- Case Management
- Substance Abuse
  Treatment
- Hospice
- Mental Health
  Services
- Home Health
  Care

particularly the rhetorical processes by which institutions operate and the necessity of making visible and understanding relations of power in the design of institutions. This example also illustrates how difficult significant institutional change is. We certainly didn't achieve it. And it also underlines how mundane decision-making processes are and the work required to intervene. The mundane, however, is a critical site of activity precisely because it seems so common, so obvious, and because it is often invisible; the transparent procedures of the mundane are the locations of the most significant exercises of power.

Design Problems and Possibilities

In order to interrogate this theory of institutional design and change, let me turn to some concrete examples of design problems and possibilities. The example that illustrates bad design comes from the case of Western District and focuses on the program located at Rosewater Publishing. The example that illustrates good design comes from a book on program design (Auerbach et al., 1996) and deals with three community-based programs in the Boston area.

The Problem of Rosewater Publishing

I discussed Rosewater publishing in chapter 3 in terms of the ethics of decision-making. The workplace literacy program at Rosewater Publishing was initiated by a grant through the Indiana Department of Workforce Development, took place at Rosewater, and was staffed by Western District. In chapter 3, my discussion of Rosewater centered on whose interests lay at the heart of its design. I want to pick up on that discussion here in order to focus more specifically on design, and as an analytical tool, I want to return as well to the work of Iris Marion Young (1990).

Domination and oppression are key terms in Young's work because they are a flexible way to talk about injustice. For Young, domination occurs when people are systematically excluded from "participating in determining their actions or the conditions of their actions" (p. 31). In certain ways, many people experience dominating systems, usually at work or school. Oppression, however, is a qualitatively different experience that results from these same institutional relations and processes. An oppressed group need not have an oppressing group; oppression is structural and relational as well as material, and often the result of "humane" practices and intentions. In Young's schema, oppression has "five faces," and it is a useful heuristic for looking at Rosewater Publishing.

> *Exploitation.* An oppression that is the function of the transfer of the benefits of labor from one social group to another. Central to exploitation is the problem that people are "exercising their capacities" under a system devised and implemented by others—workers or others here do not have a say (pp. 49–50). Young extends this economic analysis to include issues like sexual and racial exploitation. The classic example is the Marxist argument that owners of capital exploit workers by extracting profit from their labor. This is done by controlling workers to maximize profits.

Marginalization. An oppression connected to those who cannot or will not be utilized (e.g., by a system of labor). This often refers to the unemployed or the underemployed, the "unemployable" or others cast aside by systems. The homeless who panhandle for money outside my building at Georgia State University, for example, are the most visible example of those marginal to society; they are visibly cast aside. There are other marginalizations that are less visible but just as harmful.

Powerlessness. An oppression that is the result of a lack of participation: "The powerless are those over whom power is exercised without their exercising it; the powerless are situated so that they must take orders and rarely have the right to give them. ... The powerless have little or no work autonomy, exercise little creativity or judgment in their work, have no technical expertise or authority, express themselves awkwardly, especially in public or bureaucratic settings, and do not command respect" (pp. 56–57). The situation of the workers at Rosewater Publishing is a good example of this oppression.

Cultural Imperialism. An oppression that is a function of the "universalization of a dominant group's experience and culture, and its establishment as the norm" (p. 59). It is this form of oppression that makes arguments over "cultural literacy" so important. Proposed English-only laws in the United States are an example of cultural imperialism, or the forceful establishment of a language and culture to the exclusion of others.

Violence. An oppression that is often the most visible, but violence is oppressive not only in terms of the actual act, but also in terms of its threat.

The purpose of the Rosewater Publishing program was to "identify the gaps between job tasks and performance and basic skills, and to deliver an instructional program that reduces or eliminates that gap" (Western District Adult Basic Education, "Workplace Literacy Grant Proposal," p. 6). The program was funded through a state grant, which was written collaboratively by the director of Western District and the CEO of Rosewater Publishing, with a "literacy task analysis" done by the Indiana Department of Workforce Development. While students/workers were to be a part of an advisory panel to help develop the program, none of the students I spoke with were ever part of the decision making (group interviews, 7/03/96 and 7/17/96). The original grant plan proposed four classes, two classes geared toward basic skills development/GED preparation, and one class each on better communication skills and personal qualities, described to me by Judy Rooney as a "business ethics" course dealing with issues like showing up on time. The latter two classes were particularly important to Rosewater management (Judy Rooney, personal interview, 5/13/96).

There were significant problems with the Rosewater programs, problems I detail in the third chapter, and these problems were acknowledged by all with whom I spoke.[8] The question I pose here is whether or not (or in what ways) the students/workers I spent time with were oppressed, and what then could be done about it. This is a question of institutional design and change. My concern is with the powerlessness of the students/workers within the decision-making processes used to develop and implement the literacy classes at Rosewater. The seven women with whom I spent time were in no way granted access to decision-making and felt at the whim of management. To a woman, they had bitter feelings for the management at Rosewater. The reaction of the women to the interruptions of their class is the clearest example. They felt that they had been promised uninterrupted time to work, yet they were continually interrupted by management using the office where class was held. Their anger, I think, was a function of their inability to do anything about the interruptions or much else connected with their education. What the students/workers at Rosewater could do was resist, and they did. The two classes that management was most excited about, the communications and personal qualities classes, had low enrollments for the first four week session and failed to draw any students for later offerings. The basic skills/GED classes were the only ones that were successful, but only the more experienced workers were taking the classes, and they were taking classes only for personal reasons (group interviews, 7/03/96 and 7/17/96).

The teachers from Western District felt that the program at Rosewater was going to fail. The problems at Rosewater Publishing were a function of a design that oppressed workers at Rosewater. But to redesign the program in ways I have been suggesting in this chapter is problematic. I have argued that "just" and "democratic" institutions, like a community literacy institution, must grant to those least powerful special access to decision-making processes. But how can this happen, particularly when the institution in question, like Rosewater Publishing, does not have a history of worker participation?

Tough question. Let me begin first with the design problems. They start with the ways in which literacy is conceptualized. Program designers used a standardized methodology that abstracted local work-related literacies into general categories of skills. From the very beginning and based on expert analyses, program designers knew the necessary literacies. Therefore, worker participation, despite its space within the initial grant application, was unnecessary. The result was classes defined by management, and this message that was not lost on the workers. Finally, one cannot separate the workplace literacy program from the workplace itself, and Rosewater was a workplace in which workers played no role in work-related decision-making. In addition, they were given no incentive to attend the classes themselves—no advancement, no pay, not even time off for GED examinations—and so both the workplace and the workplace literacy program were dominating systems (at least). Workers/students were left with two options, then, to resist or adapt. They resisted by avoiding those classes that were clearly management classes and that had no connection to their personal lives, and similarly, their adaptation strategy was to take and change those classes they wanted into spaces that allowed them to achieve something personally meaningful. The failure of the Rosewater program is disturbing because a well-designed literacy program could have made a difference to more workers and perhaps resulted in changes in the workplace itself. But a participatory workplace literacy program cannot continue to co-exist with an oppressive workplace. This is why understanding the relationships between literacies and institutional systems is so important. One cannot change one without changing the other. All else is smoke and mirrors.

Participatory Program Design
My second case is an example of an effectively designed program as described by the participants in that program (Auerbach et al., 1996), and I intend it as a positive contrast to the missed opportunities represented by Rosewater. One of the most difficult issues in participatory design relates to how to involve students, workers, and others in the community in the design and conduct of a community-based program. Auerbach and the others who write about their multi-site ESL program in the Boston area provide one example of how to do this. The program was based on a collaboration between the University of Massachusetts at Boston and a number of sites administered through the Boston Adult Literacy Fund. The sites focused on distinct communities and participants. The Harborside Community Center is located in East Boston, and at the time of the program, it served a large Central American Population; the Haitian Multi-Service Center is located in Dorchester, and as the name implies,

served Haitian immigrants and refugees; the Jackson-Mann Community School is located in Allston and served a diverse group of people.

As the authors note, instruction at each site was designed "to meet specific needs of the surrounding communities," and this is really the key to the programs, not just in terms of their content but also in terms of their design and operation. Their model of program design, which they call "from the community to the community," has a few key features. The first feature is the training of community members to be mentors and interns, and this feature is the focus of my narrative here. Other necessary features include adult learners participating in setting learning goals, identifying needs, and choosing activities (practices common to Western District as well), participatory teacher, mentor, and intern training, and significant collaboration between the communities served and their outside partners (recall here the asset-based development model presented in chapter 5). As the authors of this program and book note, there is nothing new about the idea of participatory literacy learning and program development. What is new is its effective practice.

The guidebook from which I am taking the story of the Boston area programs is full of material relevant to participatory design. Here I am going to focus on one practice as an example of how to involve community members in fundamental program activities, and therefore, in the initial and continued design of a program. As an ESL program, one of their key issues was using literacy teachers from the communities they served, a practice particularly important given the particular language practices associated with distinct cultural communities. Using teachers from the community has also proven to improve learning and overall program effectiveness (see pp. 16–18). Such a practice need not be limited to ESL programs. Each community will have its unique characteristics and assets, and once mapped, those assets can then be targeted to address particular needs. Many of those assets will be the people themselves, and like the Boston area programs, these people can be incorporated into a program in substantive and meaningful ways.

To illustrate more concretely, let me focus on two positions within each of the programs and how they function: the mentor and the intern. Each site had an adult education coordinator who was a university faculty member and who was responsible for coordination between the university, the local programs, and project funders. They were also responsible for university-based training that was provided to mentors and interns. Each site also had a mentor and two interns. As I describe below, those who held these positions were largely responsible for the day-to-day educational practices of the programs. Mentors are described in the following way:

> [Mentors are] key in the day-to-day implementation of the project. They provide role models for students and Interns, facilitate interactions between Interns, and address any tensions that arise. They are the link between the university-based and site-based training, guiding the process of translating what has been done in the workshops into practice. (p. 25)

The mentors played a key role in each program. Mentors were chosen by each site, and those who were chosen were usually people who already had a relationship with the program and strong ties to the community. In addition, each mentor had experience teaching introductory level ESL classes. While the activities of the mentors varied somewhat from program to program, in general they were responsible for:

- modeling or demonstrating a particular kind of activity or task

- observing Interns and giving feedback or making suggestions

- designing activities for the Interns to do

- relegating specific responsibilities to Interns

- planning lessons with the Interns

- assisting with materials development (e.g., typing up a language experience story and suggesting how it might be used)

- facilitating the resolution of tensions between Interns. (p. 61)

The mentors clearly had significant teaching responsibilities as well as the responsibility to help train interns. They also worked with program coordinators and rotating curriculum specialists. In the stories that the mentors tell about themselves and their work, they stress their own experiences as learners and as members of the communities they serve. These experiences were key in how they approached the classroom and the people who utilized the program. Their experiences constitute an expertise about language learning and the community itself that is unique and indispensable, expertise the "outside" staff and curricular "experts" could not possibly possess. They brought issues and perspectives to bear that were essential, and only a participatory design process allows such people "into" the institution and gives them the space to make it their own. Their work and their example was central to each program's success.

The interns, in this respect, played a similar role. Interns fit one of four profiles: former teachers or literacy workers; advanced ESL students; bilingual undergraduate students; and/or community and parent leaders. Like the mentors, most of the interns came from the communities the programs served. Like the mentors, the interns had primary teaching responsibilities in the classroom, although because they were less experienced, they worked closely with and were trained by mentors. Still, their function in a collaborative program was essential because they were closer to students in language experience than were the mentors. In fact, many interns were recent "graduates" of the programs themselves, so like the mentors, they had a world of experiences to share and empathy to give to students. And like the mentors, their experiences and perspectives constituted a kind of expertise about the specific communities in which they lived, and therefore, about the type of program that would best serve those communities. Again, only a participatory design process creates a space for such local expertise and community participation and then provides the training and support people need to contribute. According to the accounts in the book, the programs were wildly successful, and the success can be directly attributed to their design and conduct. I cite these example programs because I think they illustrate sound participatory principles and show that participatory design can result in effective programs. But I cite these programs as well because they are an example of situated design, design that first and foremost maps the community in which the program is situated for both assets and needs and utilizes the assets of the community in the programs themselves. Participatory design can work, and these two contrasting examples show that students and others most in need benefit from participatory design done well.

Chapter 7

Next Steps: Tactics for Change

> "Research and experience in both the UK and the USA
> ... is suggesting that, whatever governments may say,
> the only long-term way of dealing with the defined
> 'problem' of literacy levels is to change the institutions
> themselves. Some radical literacy teachers, however,
> despairing of achieving such a goal, have opted in the
> short term for changing the 'victims'" (Brian Street,
> 1984, pp. 215–216).

Who can change institutions? This is a vexing question. In this book, I assume that members of communities, whomever they may be, can help change institutions. And because of my argument for a preferential option for those less powerful, I'm even assuming that those who are often the least effective as agents for change do indeed have some power. I hope I'm not waxing too utopic. Without question, however, my argument requires an agent with considerable power. An insider.[1] And while I reconfigure the inside/outside binary to privilege those inside communities, we all know that it is those inside *institutions* who hold more power than those outside, and so I'm left with a problem of agency.

With respect to my project, I anticipate at least two major critiques of agency, both of which, in part, I am sympathetic to: (1) a critique of the possibility of institutional change, and (2) a critique of my localized politics, which is both a political and an epistemological critique. The first objection insists that one cannot change institutions, that they are intractable and oppressive bureaucracies insensitive to difference. This might be true, and in some cases, probably is. Generally speaking, the argument that institutions cannot be changed comes from two directions. The liberal-individualist objection is based on the argument that individual agency can only happen (or be maximized) free from social constraints, and therefore, outside institutions (Sullivan, 1995, p. 171). It is based on a social theory that sees the individual as the fundamental element of society and any proper institutional arrangements the function of voluntary associations. Any non-voluntary organization or obligation is seen as coercive. In a sense, then, objections from this perspective not only doubt one's ability to change institutions—the individual is relatively powerless in the face of institutional bureaucracy—they call into question the impulse to change them at all.

In addition to the critique from a liberal-individualist perspective, there are those who view social institutions as inherently dystopic. One way of reading Foucault suggests this. Goffman's (1961) "total institution" and Giddens's (1984) "structuration theory" are other views of institutions that render largely impossible institutional agency. Goffman's (1961) institution "refers to a more or less isolated, cloistered, and private organization that is certainly oppressive in its practices (such as a prison)" (Porter, et. al., 2000, p. 633). He writes, "A total institution may be defined as a place of residence and work where a large number of like-situated individuals, cut off from the wider society for an appreciable period of time, together lead an enclosed, formally administered round of life" (p. xiii). Agency simply isn't possible according to this view of institutions. Giddens as well offers little in the way of hope for individuals within institutions, for his discussion is so abstract that it is impossible to locate where and how individuals could change institutional systems (Porter, et. al., 2000, p. 633). These various objections to institutional agency, however, are dependent upon a certain understanding of institutions and their relationship to both individuals and the social. I hope that I have dealt with these objections in the preceding chapters by offering an understanding of institutions that is more situated and dynamic. In terms of who, *specifically*, changes institutions, however, I am less sanguine. This will remain a real concern.

The second objection to my view of agency comes from the left and asserts that localized politics are incapable of real social change. Perhaps the strongest version of this critique is Teresa Ebert's (1996) attack on ludic feminist postmodernism, and I think it is important to explore in some depth the contours of Ebert's position. Ebert sees the problems of

Theory connected to (the problem of) ludic postmodernism. From the ludic perspective, Theory is totalizing, and for many feminists, "masculinist, abstract, elitist, phallogocentric, and a form of instrumental reason" (p. 16). Instead, ludics and ludic feminists, in Ebert's view, prefer a more local, contingent, and undecidable theory affirming the "play of difference" (p. 16). For Ebert, there are ultimately two choices that are not simple alternatives. Theory as play (ludic) and Theory as explanatory critique (critique aimed toward the material base of social formations). A resistance to Theory as explanatory critique is a resistance to a "coherent understanding of capitalism" and to the subsequent change of the "actually existing" world (p. 17). While the type of agency I am suggesting is not in any way ludic, it is nonetheless a localized politics. In the following quotation, Ebert describes, in some respects, my project:

> This antitheory theory seems, on the surface, to be progressive: it opposes the totalitarianism of reason and instead advocates reform through local communities of resistance (rape counseling centers, prisoners' coalitions, support of battered women). But in actuality it is a postmodern fatalism that reifies the existing world and, in so doing, protects the material interests of the powerful and the propertied classes. Rape is not a local issue and has everything to do with the global socioeconomics of capitalist patriarchy: without the transformation of those structures according to the critique-al knowledges produced by theory, rape will not be brought to an end. (pp. 17–18)

Ebert continues by arguing for Theory as an embodiment of both practice and coherent understanding. She writes that theory is best understood "not in an idealist way (theory as metalanguage) but as a materialist explanatory critique of the ways in which meanings are materially determined by the operation of relations of capital and wage labor..." (p. 18). Furthermore, theory is an "historical site of social struggle over how reality is represented.... Theory, in short, is a political practice, not simply a rationalist and ahistorical abstraction or discursive play" (p. 18).

While I can understand Ebert's investment in the power of Theory, I find such positions problematic for two reasons. First, as an argument for a practice, Ebert's Theory as understanding-and-practice is unpersuasive. Second, and most importantly, her glorification of Theory rests on a binary between Theory (good) and theory (bad)—or macro versus micro—that relies on a simplistic understanding of the spatial (a key dynamic of any institution). This is a binary that can and should be taken apart.

Ebert's argument that Theory is a form of practice is a problem on its face and using her own example. She critiques local institutions like rape crisis centers—or at least the intellectual work that supports and/or looks favorably toward them—for a fatalistic politics that reifies current conditions. Her solution, it seems, is to confront rape in a given community with an explanation, perhaps published in an academic journal or through a university press, of the violence of labor processes that generate surplus value and the position of women within these processes that makes rape possible. It may be true that Ebert's explanatory critique can make sense of why women are subject to systematic violence in contemporary society, but her explanatory critique is no solution for the local problems and rings hollow despite her arguments to the contrary. Rape is also a local and personal issue, and the resources of the university institution that she is a part of may help other institutions in her area. Support for such institutions as a part of intellectual work can help improve the lives of individuals in her community, and to reject theory that supports such political practices undermines the credibility of Ebert's own claims. One function of the practice of theory should be to foster more effective and indeed emancipatory practice in local situations. In short, while I can understand Ebert's tactical positioning of explanatory critique, her argument for Theory as a practice—as the only "good" type of practice—is unnecessarily limited.

The stronger critique of theorizing and institutional agency rests on an unhelpful macro/micro binary. Doreen Massey (1994), a feminist geographer, takes on this very issue while fighting similar battles with Marxist geographers. She writes that "it seems to me important to establish the inherent dynamism of the spatial . . . such a view directly relates spatiality to the social and to power" (p. 4). This connection of the spatial to the social, or perhaps more properly, this reconceptualization of the social as also inherently spatial is important for studies of writing and adds a dynamic missing from Ebert's largely historical critique of postmodernism. Massey continues:

> "The spatial" then, it is argued here, can be seen as constructed out of the multiplicity of social relations across all spatial scales, from the global reach of finance and telecommunications, through the geography of the tentacles of national political power, to the social relations within the town, the settlement, the household, and the workplace. (p. 4)

What she is talking about here as "spatial scales" is what I have been trying to suggest with my invocation of macro and micro institutions. Both ends of the scale are important to understand and constitute, as Soja (1996) would assert, locations of political struggle. The concept of spatial scales is useful for conceptualizing the spatial in meaningful ways and enacting a politics and ethics with reference to space. Massey writes:

> there has been a continuation of the tendency to identify "places" as necessarily sites of nostalgia, of the opting-out from Progress and History. There was within the discipline of geography a fiercely negative reaction, on the part of some Marxist geographers in particular, to the move to include within the compass of radical geography a focus on "locality studies." (p. 5)

The distinction between space and place is a resistance on the part of Marxists to the local as politically effectual, but this perception, at least in geography, rests on what Massey suggests is a view of place (micro) as singular, fixed, and bounded. In contrast, space (macro) is viewed as dynamic, open, and unbounded. Massey argues, however, that if "the spatial is thought of in the context of space-time and as formed out of social interrelations at all scales, then one view of place is as a particular articulation of those relations, a particular moment in those networks of social relations and understandings" (p. 5). In such a view, the space/place, macro/micro, global/local binaries that fuel such arguments of political position and strategy are undermined, as the two are interrelated. Changes in the relations of local spaces necessarily affect the global. This interrelation constitutes a "third space" of analysis and activity. Massey continues, "if each is part of the construction of the other then it becomes more difficult to maintain such simple contrasts" (p. 9).

Massey's position is similar to Dorothy Smith's (1987) feminist critique of sociology. In particular, she counters the abstraction of sociology with a notion of the "everyday as problematic." She sees the relationship between the local and the general not as a function of methodology but as a "property of social organization." (p. 157). What she means is that the "case" is not a particular instance of anything general (methodologically), but rather it is "a point of entry, the locus of an experiencing subject or subjects, into a larger social and economic process" (p. 157). The point, then, is not to generalize from the particular but to stay rooted in the local in order to investigate how subjects experience relations of social organization. Understanding local institutions is essential because the local always bears marks of the global. More importantly, perhaps, is the possibility that understanding the experience of local institutions can point the way toward change. So while I understand and am sympathetic to the traditional Marxist view of agency and change, its attack on micropolitics is unfortunate and intellectually based on a binary that views change as historical and exclusively global. In contrast, the local is a concrete place for agency that is not necessarily removed from more global issues. Each is part of the construction of the other. This assertion of the local highlights the importance of spatiality for understanding social institutions and change. To change Western District is to change, perhaps, adult education in the State of Indiana. Each occupies a different position on the spatial scale but each is related. Thus, it is not only possible to act within institutions, as some of the locality studies within geography show, it is *necessary* as a site of power to act within such institutions.

With this in mind, I want to move to a discussion of concrete tactics that can be used by teachers, researchers, and students within universities to create avenues for institutional change. I frame them in terms of research, teaching, and service not because I am resigned to the same old categories of university work but precisely because these are the categories that matter. They are powerful frames of reference that can be twisted into more productive community-based work.

Action Research

Research can change things. Research can also be one way in which outsiders like those of us based in universities can work with those inside particular communities or literacy programs. In this discussion, I see research as more than a way to generate understandings of particular phenomena or situations. Research can be a tactic for institutional change.[2]

There are important methodological traditions that see change as one purpose of research. I won't gloss them all here, but those that have been important to me are feminist approaches like those of Stanley and Wise (1993) and Patricia Sullivan (e.g., Hawisher & Sullivan, 1998). Sullivan's work, of course, is central to the articulation of critical research practices that I rely on here (in Sullivan & Porter, 1997). Postcritical research like that of Lather (1991) is also useful for thinking about how research should change conditions for research participants. Ellen Cushman's (1998) book is an example of activist research and is based on a study in which emancipation was a goal. Research methodologies linked to specific feminisms and empirical methodologies that come out of a critical theory tradition most clearly foster a view of research as interested, partial, and powerful, and argue that the researcher ought to incorporate into study design the impulse to help others.

For my purposes here, I look to one tradition, if I can call it that: participatory action research. Participatory action research is interdisciplinary and proponents write different histories for their work, so it may be impossible to think of it as a singular tradition (see Greenwood & Levin, 1998). Some call it participatory action research, others action research. Some who use the phrase action research assume that everyone knows they require fundamental and meaningful participation from participants, while others argue that there is a difference between participatory and other action research approaches. Some work with corporate organizations, while others work to organize farmers. Action researchers work on nearly every continent, and can be found in most academic disciplines. While I won't attempt to capture the complexity of action research, I can provide my own reading of its applicability as a tactic for fostering participatory design and institutional change.

The Western District study that forms the core of this book was not designed as an action research project, although I wanted my work to enable change to take place at Western District. Subsequently, I have begun to think about my work in terms of university-community collaborations and frame it methodologically with action research principles. I have discussed one of those studies already in this book (the Ryan White Planning Council project). I am currently working on a collaborative project with the goal to provide to community-based organizations the same data used by government and private organizations to make public policy and planning decisions. This move to "democratize data," as it is phrased in the urban planning literature, takes the form of a Web site on top of a Geographic Information Systems architecture (see Sawicki & Craig, 1996). Our process involves participatory design of the interface and some of the underlying functions, and the goal is to solve problems related to access to information. This project involves community literacy programs as access sites to sophisticated networked computer technologies.

Action research is fundamentally a philosophical position about how research should be done, a position articulated best in the various definitions of it. Greenwood and Levin (1998) write that action research:

> is social research carried out by a team encompassing a professional action researcher and members of an organization or com-

munity seeking to improve their situation. AR promotes broad
participation in the research process and supports action leading to
a more just or satisfying situation for the stakeholders. (p. 4)

Action research demands the codefinition of problems, the cogeneration
of knowledge, and collaborative action. It is concerned with local or
community-based action, it is participatory, and it seeks to solve problems
as articulated by those most in need. It can work within the model of
community building that I discuss in this book, and it accounts for the role
of outsiders and insiders in solving complex, local problems. It is, or can
be, critical rhetorical research.

Wadsworth (1998) argues that participatory action research shouldn't
be seen as an unusual or variant form of social research. It is just social
research that is conscious of its commitments, its partiality, and the
actions that result. It is self-conscious research, or as Sullivan and Porter
(1997) argue, research that understands its rhetorical, ethical, and political situatedness and explicitly works through those issues to clearly
articulate the purpose of research and those who are to benefit from it. The
bottom line for action researchers is change that is made possible through
the knowledge generated and the participation that it fosters. Greenwood
and Levin position action research at the center of the larger world of
research. In their view, action research is positioned between traditional
academic research and local activism, which is focused on change but has
little authority and power. In an attempt to avoid the positivism/relativism
binary and the values implied, Greenwood and Levin position action
research at the midway point or center between these two research values.
I don't disagree that action research can be located where it is, but let's
look at another way to think about action research (see Figure 7–1).

My map dispenses with the suggestion that little to no authority
resides in communities themselves. As I tried to argue with my discussion
of user knowledge, there is considerable expertise and therefore authority
within communities. Users, participants, communities are productive. I
also created a horizontal continuum to more clearly express the differences between Theory and rhetoric that I have played with throughout this
project. Particularly in terms of research methodology, understanding
research as rhetorical is important and really where Greenwood and Levin
are going with their notion of research and knowledge as interpretive and
communicative. Finally, I locate action research all over the map, moving
and not sutured in a single place. In my mind, action research facilitates
a move between the university and community. Action

Figure 7–1
A Map of Action Research from a Critical Rhetoric Perspective

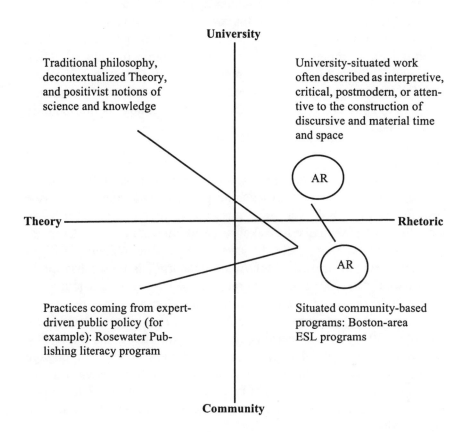

University

Traditional philosophy, decontextualized Theory, and positivist notions of science and knowledge

University-situated work often described as interpretive, critical, postmodern, or attentive to the construction of discursive and material time and space

AR

Theory ——————————————— Rhetoric

AR

Practices coming from expert-driven public policy (for example): Rosewater Publishing literacy program

Situated community-based programs: Boston-area ESL programs

Community

research can affect both traditional notions of research and community-based practices that might be based on such research.

I go to these lengths to position action research because of the status given research within the university. Because research is taken seriously, it is necessary to see action research as an argument about how research ought to be conceived and conducted, and so it needs to be seen within the larger context of research within the university. How one actually conducts an action research project will vary widely. It looks differently according to the needs driving the research and the disciplines within which the researchers are situated. Action research is a tactic for institutional change and design, however, because it provides a way to be involved with community-based work and do the work of the university at the same time. It can also be a sound and powerful methodological framework for helping to solve community problems and generate useful knowledge. It is a tactic, finally, for enabling institutional change to the extent that research can make institutions visible and uncover those boundaries and ambiguities where change is possible. In doing so, action research as a way to change community-literacy institutions can help redefine the meaning and value of literacy and provide access and voice to the powerless. Research as a tactic for change is limited only by our vision.

Service Learning
"Service learning" or "community service learning" are terms that describe an amazing variety of teaching practices and contexts. Service learning courses and even programs can be found in schools K-16. Composition in particular has taken a recent interest in service learning. There are books (e.g., Adler-Kassner, Crooks, and Watters, 1997), a listserv (Service-learn; see <http://www.ncte.org/lists/> for subscription information), and special interest groups as well as regular sessions at the Conference on College Composition and Communication (see, in particular, the programs for Phoenix, 1997; Chicago, 1998; and Atlanta, 1999). Service learning constitutes another general tactic by which university-based writing teachers and researchers can engage communities and community-based institutions. Service learning allows us to take another powerful category of our work—teaching— and turn it into a new category that benefits both the university and the community.

In general, service learning involves integrating school or community-based service with representative academic experiences in ways that should benefit those served and the students involved. For many service learning proponents, particularly those working in schools, service learning is connected to civic education. The purpose, therefore, is not to teach the benefits of charity or self-sacrifice but rather to "work alongside those in need, recognizing our common purpose, and enabling those being served to become more empowered in the process" (Wade, 1997, p. 14). The principle of working alongside others is important for structuring effective service learning. In addition, it is essential in my mind that service learning should benefit first those most in need (a preferential option) and then others, and so those who should be the primary beneficiaries are individuals and/or community-based groups with which university-based teachers and students work. Service learning, then, needs to be designed carefully so that it is intellectually and curricularly sound and therefore worthwhile for students; it also needs to be designed, of course, with those served so that it is meaningful service. As a tactic for enabling institutional change, service learning gets university-based teachers into the community within the context of primary work activities. In addition, such a teaching practice makes available to communities in need a significant array of talent and energy that can be a powerful outside asset for solving problems. I think this effort becomes even more powerful if service learning is integrated into research as well (more on this below), but there is no question in my mind that well-designed and committed service learning activities can change things. Let me be more specific.

Ellen Cushman (1999) provides a good example of service learning in composition. Within the context of a writing class, Cushman's students approach community contexts as researchers. Immediately, then, she frames her student's experiences as research as well as service and learning. Her students use fieldwork methods to inquire into the reading and writing practices of particular people in particular situations (a YMCA literacy program in Cushman's case). About her program, Cushman writes "when activist fieldwork is a cornerstone of the course, students and community residents can develop reciprocal and dialogic relations with each other; their relationship is a mutually beneficial ..." (p. 330). Later Cushman writes that student work serves as a supplement to her own work. In this way, the line between research and teaching blurs, and both help people improve their own lives. Within a framework such as this, teaching can become a tactic for intervening in community contexts. Framed appropriately, service learning teaching can be a way to participate in the design of community-based literacy programs.

My own service learning work is not directly involved with community-based literacy programs but will hopefully serve as an example of community-based service learning work. I should say a word here about why my work recently hasn't involved community-literacy programs even though I profess enough interest and concern about them to write a book. The answer, really, is quite simple. In the two years that I have been in Atlanta, I haven't gotten to know enough people in the city to be involved in such a project. In addition, most of my teaching has been in professional writing, so that has also been the focus of my service learning efforts. The two efforts—community literacy and community-based professional writing—are clearly connected, but the connections take time to develop. In terms of *design*, one should see the efforts I will describe here as building the relationships necessary for effective university-community collaboration and the possibility for good community-based program design.

My service learning teaching has been part of a larger project of incorporating community service learning into a professional writing program at Georgia State University. In this respect, my colleagues and I have determined that community-based work can be a compelling and sophisticated way to teach professional writing. Such community based work is also a meaningful part of Georgia State's mission. Service learning in business and technical writing takes the form of working with community-based non-profits to help them determine and solve organizational problems. Nearly all such problems involve writing, and so these are excellent writing projects for our students.[3] Through Georgia State's Office of Community Service Learning and through my own contacts, I began developing five to seven projects each semester for each business or technical writing class I teach. Unlike many service learning initiatives, these projects are first set up by me, including the initial contact, site visits, co-determination of problems and project viability, and rough schedules. There are two reasons for this. First, the projects are too complicated for students to find, conceive, and complete within the time frame I give them (a little less than two-thirds of a semester), and part of my responsibility for these projects entails ensuring that they make sense for both community partners and students, and that neither is exploited. The second reason is one of institutional design. I want the relationship to be institutional in nature, to be between community-based non-profits and the professional writing program, not just between those organizations and individual students. There are lots of reasons for this, but they come down to building solid and long-term relationships between our program at GSU and various communities around the university. In my mind, this is an enactment of a critical rhetoric of design along the same lines as the design practices pursued by the United Way and operation P.E.A.C.E.. We are here for the long haul, and we are committed, in various ways, to positive change in the communities we work with. The ways in which that change gets articulated varies and is driven by those community-based organizations who constitute the insiders.[4]

I hope it is possible to see how community service learning can work as a tactic for institutional change. Service learning allows students and teachers to move into community contexts in structured, meaningful, and potentially long-term ways in order to solve problems. My goal is to create long-term relationships and therefore increase the likelihood that working between university and community contexts can provide committed outside assets to communities who need them. Most promising have been those projects in which my students and I have both been participants. In both cases—working with the Ryan White Planning Council and with the community-based database project—I have framed my involvement in terms of research and involved students through service learning projects. In this articulation of community-based work, my relationship with a project is long-term, a research study, and a part of my teaching. Students not only get to work on service learning projects, but they also get to participate in meaningful ways in my research, which some, thankfully, find interesting. I see this as more than just research or service learning; I see it as a localized rearticulation of research, teaching, and service. I hope it is possible to see in my discussion here a number of tactics that can be used to engage in community-based work and institutional critique and design. I have tried to be pragmatic, yet I hope I have opened up the possible as well.

Public Policy

Recently I sat in an auditorium listening to a slick presentation by two scholars from The Center for Strategic and International Studies, one of those "non-partisan" Washington think-tanks. Their talk was fascinating, mostly because it was imaginative and smart. They were discussing seven revolutions that will shape the world that we will see in 2025. At one point, they discussed the state of education in the US and trotted out the same tired set of test score numbers to bemoan the sorry state of "our" schools (I'm sure the schools their kids attend are just fine). My frustration stemmed from the fact that they played fast-and-loose with the numbers by comparing students and phenomena that aren't the same and concluding that low test scores on a science exam mean the end of civilization as we know it. Their discussion demonstrated none of the nuanced care that I thought they had showed throughout most of their presentation. The audience, as impressed as I was with their talk, cheered them on. And given the fact that the public discourse on schools is overwhelmingly negative, we were an easy crowd. I became depressed, however, when I thought about the fact that the audience—the Georgia Executive Women's Network and their guests, like me—is extremely well-educated, well-connected, and very powerful. They were owners of their own businesses, directors of foundations, major executives with major companies, and even a university president. They shape public policy, both directly and indirectly. They are an important audience, and yet we—and here I mean English and literacy teachers and researchers—rarely get to talk to them. That auditorium was a space in which policy gets made—granted, very subtly and not immediately—but it gets made. We ought to be making it too.

This is precisely one of Cindy Selfe's (1999) points in a recent article about paying attention to technological literacies. In her article, Selfe is critical of the current discourse on the role of computers in education. In terms of policy and local practices, Selfe argues, educators are buying technology at record levels because they already have bought a set of myths about literacy and computer technologies. She characterizes the current climate as one that is dangerously uncritical because people are not paying attention to technology. In the current climate, we run the risk of perpetuating historical violences of literacy. I agree with her, and I want to use the argument she makes as an example of the types of analyses and actions necessary in order to see public policy action as a tactic for institutional change. In this respect, the tactics covered in this section are closest to the type of institutional change Street (1984) calls for in the epigraph to this chapter.

Early in her article, Selfe (1999) makes a claim similar to arguments I have made throughout this book, namely that powerful policy and procedure documents that are institutionally created, both with and without the input of English professionals, have a profound affect on how we understand literacy and technology (p. 416). While Selfe takes care to point out that English and literacy professionals do, in fact, partici-pate in public policy decision-making, we don't do it nearly enough, and this is the point I wish to underline. To do so, I quote Selfe at length:

> Since 1996, although our professional standards documents now … assume the necessity of computer use by communicators in the 21st century, they do not provide adequate guidance about how to get teachers and students thinking critically about such use. Moreover, in a curious way, neither the CCCC, nor the NCTE, nor the MLA, nor the IRA—as far as I can tell—have ever published a single word about our own professional stance on this particular nationwide technology project: not one statement about how we think such literacy monies should be spent in English composition programs; not one statement about what kinds of literacy and

technology efforts should be funded in connection with this project or how excellence should be gauged in these efforts; not one statement about the serious need for professional development and support for teachers that must be addressed within the context of this particular national literacy project.

Nor have these organizations articulated any official or direct response to the project's goals or the ways in which schools and teachers are already enacting these goals within the classroom. And this is true despite the fact that so many literacy educators in a range of situations—including all English and Language Arts teachers in primary, secondary, and college/university class-rooms—have been broadly affected by the technology-literacy linkage for the past decade and will continue to be so involved well into the next century. (p. 419)

The silence of many professional organizations on the issue of technological literacy is remarkable, but it is matched by the silence of such organization on literacy issues outside the classroom. Granted, the organizations named by Selfe are primarily concerned with schools and so I'm not quibbling with their focus. In the future, however, I would indeed like that focus to be expanded to meet the reality that community literacies impact the classroom and play a role in the larger perceptions that people these days don't read and write as well as they used to and that the workforce is poorly prepared for the 21st century. This is true whether we think about family literacy issues or workplace related literacies. Both issues are addressed every day by community literacy programs.

Selfe's point is that such professional organizations are how English and literacy professionals act collectively on national and international scenes, and therefore, a loud and clear voice is essential if we are to participate in public policy decision-making. Without a doubt, organizations like NCTE have been active politically. My concerns are with issues that currently aren't on the table, like community literacies, and with arguing to this audience that participation in national and international organizations is an essential tactic for institutional change. But public policy action should not be seen exclusively in terms of macro level issues. There are certainly more local public policy tactics that are equally important, and I'm going to steal a few more ideas from Selfe to illustrate the point:

- Working on curriculum committees, standards documents, and assessment programs (pp. 430–431)

- Working in school districts and systems that are "poor" or whose students are relatively powerless in relation to other school districts or systems and the larger community (p. 433)

- Working for school board elections, serving on local committees for either school districts or literacy organizations (p. 433)

- Working to develop with others (as an outside asset) in-service and pre-service training programs (p. 433)

These are just a few specifics that I think fall under the rubric of public policy tactics for institutional change. For English and literacy professionals to be effective as public policy participants, we must do work other than that carried out by our professional organizations. Local involvement in community planning and more global involvement in state-level decisions about the meaning and value of literacy and the programs that result are essential. Granted, this work is difficult, often thankless, and requires thick skin and patience, but I see no way around public policy decision-making as a key tactic for changing the meaning and value of literacy. I want to see an English teacher talking to an auditorium full of executives and other decision-makers.

Changing Western District

The study of Western District that forms the core of this book was never designed as an institutional critique, and for this and other reasons, my goal as a researcher was never to change Western District as an institution (by myself and without invitation, that is an arrogant goal that I want no part of). I certainly wanted to leave Western District a better place than when I found it, and this is perhaps the most significant limitation of the study for me: I'm not sure my work had any effect at all. At times and in some classes, I probably helped some students. After she expressed an interest in my help, I offered to work on curriculum with one teacher in particular. The director of the program wanted me to write something for them related to writing instruction, but when I tried to follow up with both, they never returned my calls or letters. They lost interest in me. For these and other methodological reasons, I would never hold up my study of Western District as a model for critical research. So my discussion about changing Western District here is tentative and should be read that way.

It is part of a larger argument about literacy and change. As a community literacy program, Western District doesn't necessarily need to change. There are processes at Western District that I have neither the experience nor expertise to understand. Furthermore, the students with whom I spoke liked the program—even the students at Rosewater Publishing—and I found the teachers at Western District to be as creative, caring, and engaging as I find most teachers to be. The power of the Western District case for me is its complexity. There are no clear good or bad guys, and so in the speculative way in which I highlight ways to change Western District as an institution, there are no clear and unproblematic possibilities. To close, I look at two spaces within Western District, the Adult Learning Plan and the curriculum for the computers and communications class, as examples of possible locations for institutional change at Western District.

The Adult Learning Plan (ALP) is one of the most important zones of ambiguity within Western District. Western District is an institution with fairly tight but not malicious controls. By that I mean that in terms of the meaning and value of literacy, the decisions are made quite clearly at levels above the students. Indeed, above Western District itself. Control over the meaning and value of literacy is exercised through assessment practices. They are tied to funding and therefore mandated, and they are used to track student progress through the program. But the ALP is a moment in the larger processes of Western District in which differences exist and must be confronted. The most significant difference that the ALP allows into decision-making processes is the students themselves, and they, of course, bring an array of differences. The ALP itself also constitutes a significantly different process—at no other time are students allowed a structured, institutionally warranted say in their education. These differences may seem mundane and insignificant—indeed, in practice they proved to be—but if we are speculating about ways to change an institution like Western District, then the differences in process represented by the ALP are significant.

The Adult Learning Plan, as I discussed in chapter 2, was designed to:

- enhance learner ownership of his/her learning plan and generate enthusiasm and commitment

- provide a "roadmap" for decisions

- provide a tool to chart progress

- serve as a tool for better communication among everyone in the program

- provide documentation of learner gains for referral to other agencies or funding agencies (taken from Division of Adult Education, "Purposes of Adult Learning Plan," p. 1).

The ALP is intended as the primary means of collaboration between the institution and the individual student, providing that student with the means to participate in planning their own education. However, as my description of its use suggests (see section on "Eligibility, Assessment, and Placement of Students," chapter 2), there is very little collaboration, and students do not participate in the design of the decision-making processes. If we think of the problems of the ALP in terms of Ehn's focus on process, then students, in this case, would have to have a voice in the design of the ALP itself as well as a greater role in how it is used at Western District. Currently, the ALP is developed at the state level and guides an intake process that consists of fill-in-the-blank forms and standardized assessments. The results of these assessments become the source of student placement. From there, student curricula is similarly shaped by assessments and future choices constrained by that initial placement.

So how could the Adult Learning Plan be used differently? Following Ehn's (1988) insight that for processes to be participatory, the tools used to facilitate those processes should be similarly designed, I would begin with the Adult Learning Plan itself. I would first be interested in why anyone thought the ALP would be a good tool to facilitate collaboration and student ownership of the learning process, and I would want to know when and where this had been successful. These questions are necessary in order to understand how to start thinking about the participatory design of the ALP itself. Such questions might focus on student attitudes about collaboration in developing an educational plan, their sense of when they would find this helpful, their preferred mode of collaboration (e.g., face-to-face or small group), the person(s) with whom they would like to collaborate (their teacher and/or their peers?), the range of options and decisions possible, and the role of the ALP document itself. In terms of the ALP process, I would focus on the nature of the collaboration and look for ways to expand the process and the authority attached to it (in part by way of an argument for the expertise of user/student knowledge). Right now, the ALP is a tracking document and process, but what if it allowed students to propose changes in the curriculum like new classes or skills they want to learn? What if the ALP allowed students and workers more evaluative roles, and what if, as part of an enhanced ALP process, students played a role in curriculum planning itself?

Good design is a systematic, long-term process; it is a structured part of an institution. The changes in the ALP process that I envision are complicated and long-term. Yet both teachers and students can participate in long-term institutional processes. Teachers can rely on their expertise and knowledge, and they can do so over time. A large number of students over many years can also similarly contribute what they know to the development and implementation of an Adult Learning Plan. Right now the Adult Learning Plan (ALP) is not a tool for participatory dialogue about education because key users in the educational situation at Western District did not participate in its design, and furthermore, have no significant role to play in its use. If the processes of developing and using the ALP were to change, Western District would change.

The second space at Western District is occupied by the curriculum of the computers and communications class (see chapter 4). With this short example, I am again suggesting possibilities but also foregrounding curriculum development as one form of agency for institutional change. As I wrote in chapter 4, I felt this class had a confused identity. For Western District, it was clearly a computer literacy class. Students learned the parts of a computer, an introduction to BASIC, and how to navigate the keyboard. But the bulk of the work in class revolved around the production of what I call "professional writing" documents: letters, memos, resumes, graphic layouts. Within the curriculum, however, the documents were used to teach the computer. The focus was the technology, not what one could do with the technology.

But the computers and communications class was a writing class; in fact, it was a professional writing class. Students completed the curriculum, but they also wrote letters and notes, put together a newspaper for the program (Western District had previously never had a newspaper), and produced promotional fliers for real audiences (see chapter 4). Because many of the students in this class were working toward a better job, they also put together resumes and letters of application. The computer as a writing technology enabled activities not possible elsewhere at Western District.

Curriculum change is one possible way to enable institutional change. In this case, curriculum constitutes an important boundary within an institution like Western District; it has one foot in the classroom and the other in administration. Working with curricula touches on a number of important institutional processes. With the computers and communications class, the first task is to rename it a professional writing class and therefore to change the horizon for what happens within the space of the classroom from learning the computer to learning workplace writing. Using professional writing as a framework for this class makes it possible to provide students with some of the accesses necessary to be successful writers on the job. In addition, making it a writing class allows the introduction of a more sophisticated set of workplace literacies than are currently possible. There would be clear classroom level changes, but to change this class is also to change the programming of Western District, and perhaps more importantly, to change perceptions. Remember that teachers associated with the computers and communication class insisted that it wasn't a writing class. Writing classes at Western District dealt with sentence and paragraph level issues only. They were called *language* classes. To introduce a professional writing class is to introduce an entirely new definition of writing into Western District. This strikes me as a significant change.

In the brief examples I have developed here, I have tried to highlight how my three general tactics might play out. There is room for research (usability and assessment development), teaching, and even some policy making. Clearly the one obvious way to change Western District is the legislation that makes it possible and that provides the most powerful definition of literacy. Less dramatic, however, are the clear connections in Indiana between what happens in a given program and what happens throughout the rest of the state. This is the irony of institutions, and one illustrated so clearly in Foucault's insistence that there can be no domination without freedom. In this case, there can be no tight controls without the possibility of the controls working both ways. The state not only developed and mandated the Adult Learning Plan, but in terms of most assessment and curriculum issues, maintains contact with programs throughout the state. This contact is not always in the form of rule making or other policy pronouncements. More often this contact comes in the form of teaching or curriculum workshops. At these meetings and through other informal contacts, people at the state and at specific programs are always looking for new ways of thinking about and doing their work. In some cases, innovative programs developed at one site are presented to others as a type of "best practices" to be used elsewhere. Thus demonstrated and effective changes in a particular community literacy program like Western District can then be used to argue for changes at increasingly macro (and seemingly abstract) levels of institutional decision-making.

There is no doubt that such interaction happens in Indiana, and there is equally no doubt in my mind that those processes can be used to foster change. In fact, practices change all the time. So it is not a question of change but who participates and how that participation is designed.

Can we change institutions as Street suggests and therefore progressively change literacy values and practices? I think so, but we must first learn how to understand institutional systems and see such systems as inseparable from the literacies they support. A critical rhetoric for the design of community-based literacy programs can help by focusing on participatory decision-making that gives preference to the less powerful and that utilizes the local knowledge produced by those most affected by institutional systems. To offer a literacy theory is to offer a theory of institutions. Conversely, to offer a theory of institutions and institutional design is to offer a theory of literacy. Yet as Street argues, we have too long been limited to changing the "victims" of institutional systems. To change a theory of literacy isn't difficult and changes very little. To change a literacy institution might change everything.

Notes

Chapter 1

1. There is growing evidence that what I call community literacy programs, such as an Adult Basic Education (ABE) program, are increasingly involved with workplace literacy training. In the state of Indiana, for instance, workplace literacy contracts with ABE programs grew by one fifth in 1995. With "welfare reform" and other such initiatives having picked up steam since then, work related education programs have certainly increased.

2. Access to workplace sites was extremely difficult. One promising site became inaccessible because of contract negotiations between the company and the union. Rosewater Publishing became a possibility early in my time at Western District, but it still took me about six months to get permissions and make schedules work.

3. The Adult Education Act (P.L. 100–297, Section 312) provides more specific details about "adult education." Adult education means "services or instruction below the postsecondary level for adults":

1. who are not enrolled in secondary school;

2. who lack sufficient mastery of basic education skills to enable them to function effectively in society or who do not have a certificate of graduation from a school providing secondary education and who have not achieved an equivalent level of education;

3. who are not currently required to be enrolled in school; and

4. whose lack of mastery of basic skills results in an inability to speak, read, or write the English language which constitutes a substantial impairment of their ability to get or retain employment commensurate with their real ability, and thus are in need of programs to help eliminate such inability and raise the level of such individuals with a view to making them less likely to become

163

dependent on others. (qtd. in Division of Adult Education, "Indiana's Adult Education Teacher Handbook," pp. 2-4, 2-5).

4. In fact, most of the documents that I have been using for this study are part of the required state planning and assessment procedures. One of the reasons that so much time and energy at the local level is devoted to recruitment, retention, and assessment procedures is that these three issues determine funding levels, and in some cases, renewal.

5. This money can be used to pay for instructor's salaries, administrative, and support costs up to 15 percent of the entire local ABE budget. It cannot be used for those costs for these budget items which exceed 15 percent of the budget. No more than 5 percent of the Federal money can be deducted for state administrative costs, and 15 percent must be used for special projects and teacher training. The rest of the money is available for instruction. These percentage requirements are regulated by Federal legislation (Division of Adult Education, "Indiana's Adult Education Teacher Handbook," p. 2-11).

Chapter 2

1. The first year composition literature is a literacy literature, but because it is so focused on composition concerns and school contexts, it actually says very little of use in terms of literacy theory for non-academic contexts. As pedagogical theory and practice, and indeed, as a starting place for how teaching writing might proceed in a community literacy program classroom, this literature is important. But for right now, I see this literature as outside the purposes of this chapter.

2. Western District utilizes workplace literacy assessments provided by the state to help name the literacies functioning in a given workplace before that workplace enters into an agreement with Western District for literacy training for workers. This type of practice typically results in lists of skills. This is an excellent example of what Chase (1990) calls a *worksite* literacy program: a program in which reading and writing is conceived of as discrete skills independent of the worksite; in many forms, an outside curriculum is transplanted at the worksite (often an ABE curriculum). Chase contrasts a worksite program with a *workplace* program, in which literacies are situated within a specific workplace and from which an appropriate curriculum is constructed (see Gowen, 1992, for a useful workplace literacy program ethnography that addresses similar issues). Western District has shelves of decontextualized lists of workplace literacy skills, and to varying degrees, relies on this knowledge for establishing adult basic skills education at their workplace programs. While their intent is to situate workplace literacy programs, their methodologies, literacy task analyses matched to packaged curricula, don't achieve this.

3. A starting place for an inquiry into locating such contexts, however, is obvious in any description or presentation of Freire's curricular materials and practices (see *Pedagogy of Hope*, 1995).

4. The 1991 definition of literacy is often repeated, even in interviews with teachers and students (who reflect the sense of the definition but do not consciously refer to it), and constitutes the core of the mission of Western District's program (Western District Adult Basic Education, "Adult Basic Education Center," p. 4).

5. Initial assessments as well as pre and post testing are required for programs which receive Federal funds. Standardization of tests and testing procedures is also necessary. In response to this, the State uses CASAS (Comprehensive Adult Student Assessment System) and TABE (Test of Adult Basic Education) as their standardized instruments, CASAS for initial placement, and TABE for some initial placements as well as all pre and post testing. Pre-testing occurs as part of the intake process, and post-testing must occur quarterly for students who have accumulated 40 hours of instruction (Division of Adult Education, "Indiana's Adult Education Teacher Handbook," p. 2-19).

State policy is clear on what tests are to be given to whom and when:
- the CASAS Appraisal or TABE Locator must be given to determine the appropriate level of pre/post test to be given;
- CASAS-trained programs are mandated to give the CASAS to Level 1 (lowest) learners for development of the Adult Learning Plan (ALP);
- sub-test choice is up to the program (programs will rarely give the whole test, but rather the one students are interested in);
- however, the same sub-tests must be used for subsequent pre and post tests, and the same instruments (generally) must be used.

6. The required elements of IN PACE training are as follows:

1. Locally identify and validate life skill competencies.

2. Provide open entry/open exit enrollment.

3. Provide planned orientation for new students.

4. Determine each student's short- and long-term goals.

5. Conduct entry assessment for placement purposes.

6. Diagnose specific academic and life skill needs.

7. Develop individual educational plans based on student interviews, goals, and assessment results.

8. Use appropriate and varied instructional materials and strategies.

9. Integrate academic and life skills instruction.

10. Conduct periodic monitoring, recording, and reporting of student progress (including pre/post tests).

11. Document students in accessing other support services and transition activities within and outside the program.

12. Counsel students in accessing other support services and transition activities within and outside the program.

13. Develop, implement, and maintain appropriate staff development activities.

7. The ALP is driven by the following principles:
- Begin where student interest and need are greatest.
- Focus on integration of basic and life skills.
  (1.) Provide opportunities for use of basic skills in real life situations.
  (2.) Emphasize basic skills needed to accomplish life skills tasks.
- Provide task area practice in a variety of contexts, e.g., charts and graphs related to science, economics, health, math, English, etc.
- Use a variety of instructional materials: commercially prepared, teacher prepared, real life materials, non-print materials.
- Use a variety of techniques: individualized, small-group, large-group, peer teaching, cooperative learning, computer-assisted instruction.
- Offer students opportunities to use different modalities for learning—visual, auditory, tactile, etc.
- TEACH FOR TRANSFER OF LEARNING TO OTHER SITUATIONS, CONTEXTS, AND CONTENT AREAS! (Division of Adult Education, "Indiana's Adult Education Teacher Handbook," p. 6-5, caps in original)

8. For Ed Cotton this is an important issue. Very few people who enter ABE actually achieve the goal of passing their GED, a goal which is the most often stated reason for attending ABE classes both statewide and at Western District. The reasons for low levels of GED achievement are many, and often related to social and economic stress, movement of students, histories of educational failure, and the long time it takes for a student to learn what is necessary to pass the exam. The ALP was designed to allow success by encouraging students to set and meet short-term goals and perhaps change long-term goals during the relatively finite time they attend ABE classes.

9. There were problems with this approach to language arts instruction in Joanne's class, and these are similar to problems in other classes as well (but not reported in the text of the chapter). I interpreted the problems and frustrations of students in class as related to the worksheet exercises they had to do. The sentence combining exercise, for instance, did not use student sentences, and in fact, did not use complete sentences and clauses at all. The exercise used fragments and phrases of words which were supposed to be part of larger sentences. Instead of focusing on combining the sentences, students puzzled over the incoherent phrases and often would complete and rewrite the sentences in ways that made combining them in the ways the worksheet wanted unnecessary. Similarly, answers to punctuation exercises were presented by Joanne in terms of how they sounded. In other words, students had a long list of rules, but ultimately Joanne often explained correct punctuation in terms of what sounded correct. This also caused considerable confusion because the sentences sounded

different to different students, and thus the rules were of little use to them. In the language class at Rosewater Publishing (which I will discuss later), students often complained that the tests were "rigged" because the test answer key was always the final arbiter of what was correct, even when the exam was wrong because of misleading typographical errors.

Chapter 3

1. The work of socio-cognitive theorists is closely connected here politically, although the map suggests some differences. This work can be characterized in terms of the processes of "negotiation" (Flower's term), or what Brandt (1990) might call the processes of intersubjectivity. While creating meaning, writers and readers—the subject positions available here—negotiate on equal footing the meaning of a text or the action to be taken. Even in Peck et al.'s (1995), Peck's (1996), and Baskins' (1996) account of community literacy practices—practices in which the processes of negotiation are central—there is no discussion of power, and little acknowledgment that power relations can be asymmetrical or that the institution itself plays a role in such power relations. While it is true, as Flower (1994) argues, that the processes of negotiation are intended to enable writers to see how their actions can "exercise tyranny" or effect progressive practices (p. 28), and within the context of community literacy, can deal with difference, conversation, and community building, they fail to significantly account for issues of power and identity. They typically fail to acknowledge the power of institutional systems to constrain relationships or differences of power between groups and individuals involved in negotiations. In terms of ethics, what this means is that the determination of a good is a product of localized negotiations, which is both wonderful for its attention to local conditions and individuals and problematic for its failure to account more fully for the power relations that shape those conditions and individuals.

2. It is important to note the left's general distrust of ethics, making the commentary I am representing here rather significant. As Porter (1998) writes, the left generally, and Marx in particular, conceives ethics as deontological dicta incapable of enabling social change (pp. 3–4). In rhetoric and composition as well, Porter sites similar positions from Berlin, Vitanza, and from within cultural studies more generally (p. 4). While Porter misses important work on ethics within a Marxist framework, most notably that of Cornel West (1991), Porter's argument is that ethics, like power and ideology, is unavoidable, as all social practices have ethical implications. My argument about literacy theory is a version of this—all theoretical positions have ethical implications. Giroux's discussion of ethics and the necessity for articulating an ethics from the left is an important step.

3. Although there is more flexibility in design, the design processes don't differ significantly from what I have described so far. Typically, the arrange-

ment between a workplace and Western District will be written in such a way that another state agency or a contracted university researcher will come into the workplace and conduct a literacy task analysis for certain job positions within the workplace. In my limited experience, the best aspects of these analyses are conceptual—they ideally develop a localized and sophisticated sense of the literate practices of a work site. I'm not sure this actually happens in practice. At their worst, they result, ironically, in a decontextualized set of skills that fit nicely with the preexisting ABE/GED related curricula. Thus, an ABE program like Western District seems the perfect place for an employer to turn in order to address the "illiteracies" of his or her employees.

Chapter 4

1. The term "internetworked writing" means "computer-based electronic writing that makes synchronous or asynchronous links to remote participants or databases. . . . [It] refers to more than simply closed, local-area classroom or corporate systems—but refers more broadly to what we might consider a wider public space (though the exact notion of "public" may vary from technology to technology)" (Porter, 1998, p. 2). Porter's access framework, which I will be using here, refers to internetworked writing, yet my reference is to a whole range of accesses to computers including both local area networking and stand alone computing.

2. In a Rand (Anderson et al., 1995) report that I will discuss throughout this chapter, the authors refer to the possibility of citizen-government interactions such as social services being conducted online. Already individuals can file income taxes online, so the possibility exists that mundane civic interactions may be conducted in an electronic, written environment. Already there is considerable civic information online that enables those who are aware of it and disables those who are unaware. What one doesn't know will always hurt.

3. There is some dispute as to what universal access means. For the authors of the Rand report, universal access means (1) "available at modest individual effort and expense to (almost) everyone in the United States in a form that does not require highly specialized skills" or (2) "accessible in a manner analogous to the level, cost, and ease of use of telephone service or the U. S. Postal Service" (p. 7). This strikes me as a reasonable and pragmatic approach to some aspects of infrastructural access. Of course, not everyone has a phone or a stable address that would allow ready communication through the postal service. The authors of the Rand report recognize this problem with their analogy. E-mail access actually solves some problems of phones and postal mail. Given public sites, individuals need not have a stable place for communication because the "place" is the network. The Rand concept of universal access is a good place to begin because it allows us to ask questions like ones I am asking here, namely, what

would the public spaces look like that might be access locations for the technologically poor, and what resources and expertise are necessary there?

4. The federal government, in the 1995 National Telecommunications and Information Administration report, estimated that 25 percent of American households had computers. David Kline (1996) puts that number at 30 percent, while a Hotwired feature called "Flux" (1995) put the number at 38.5 percent. None of these sources discussed how the numbers were derived, which might account for the rather larger range for a nearly identical time frame.

5. Anderson et al., (1995) caution readers about the strength of the conclusions that can be drawn from their study based on the type of data they used. They used the most complete set of census data available to them at the time (1993) and compared that data with similar 1989 numbers. The census questions concerned computer and network access, but because the purpose of the Census survey was not to gauge computer and network access, the authors caution readers that the data should therefore be seen as suggestive, not conclusive.

6. The data is taken from the Current Population Survey (CPS), a random survey of households conducted monthly by the Bureau of the Census. In the case of the data used in the Rand study, for example, the CPS survey was conducted for the Bureau of Labor Statistics by the Bureau of the Census.

7. By fluid, multiple, and complex, I am following Aronowitz and DiFazio (1994) in suggesting that class is a construction of situated economic, political, and cultural power. Race, ethnicity, and gender matter in a way different from earlier constructions of class. For example, the experience of Hispanic students in a technologically poor school is likely different from that of white students in that same school. Yet both occupy significantly similar places with respect to the larger picture. The point is simultaneously to take seriously issues of race, ethnicity, gender, and class.

8. One of the arguments of Sullivan and Dautermann's (1996) collection is that the study of writing technologies in workplaces has not received much attention even though computer use by most workers is common. Sullivan and Dautermann note that it is likely that a high percentage of these workers use their computers for some writing activity. In fact, workplaces are the most common site for computers and writing experiences for most adults. And as workplaces continue to change (from production to information-based work, for example), it is more and more likely that new workers will need such skills. The question becomes how to train workers displaced from production work or moving from non-computerized service work? And where does such training take place? Adult Basic Education programs across the country are one type of site.

9. There was some legitimate confusion about the identity of the class. Within the context of the ABE program with its heavy emphasis on Graduate Equivalency Degree (GED) exam preparation, "writing" takes place within the context of specific language classes. This is why it was not surprising for

Katherine to say to me that the class was not a writing class. As I observed and participated in these classes, it became obvious that this was a writing class. The curriculum, however, constructs the course as a computers class; there is a significant amount of information devoted to issues like learning the names of computer parts.

10. I'm unsure how common the presence and use of computers as writing technologies is at ABE programs or community literacy centers more generally. I know that at the Community Literacy Center in Pittsburgh (associated with Carnegie Mellon), the use of computer technologies for this purpose has been common for some time. One other public institution often cited as important for increasing access is the public library. I was working through early drafts of this chapter in a branch of an urban public library system. This library had two computers with Web access, fulfilling its purpose as a public access site. However, the library constructed these terminals exclusively as information searching tools, standing them up against the wall, like a card catalog, in a way that demanded the user also stand, making long-term use problematic. Although the library was running a one hour class about the Internet every Tuesday afternoon during a month in late summer, there was only a five item quick reference card attached to terminals for literacy training. In addition, only one terminal in the library could be used for any kind of writing. My point is to emphasize the difference between internetworked access for writing and for other purposes, and therefore, to further emphasize how important it is to find public institutions that construct computer technologies as writing technologies.

Chapter 5

1. Communitarian philosophy is a diverse and engaging approach to questions of meaning and value in contemporary life. Some see it as a counter to the pervasive philosophies of liberalism (e.g., the individualism of the Enlightenment). For others, it is a systematic reordering of how we think about human interactions, focusing on the community as the basic element of society. Communities are what give individuals identity. Communitarianism actually is used to describe diverse political and philosophical positions. Communitarian thinking from Africa, for example, differs from Anglo-American communitarianism. And communitarians speak from different places ideologically, politically, and ethically.

2. Material in this paragraph about the United Way is taken from the "Stronger, Safer Communities" Request for Proposals, fiscal year 2000.

3. The interview took place on December 29, 1998. Before we began, he cautioned me that his comments were his own, not necessarily those of the United Way, and that I needed to keep in mind that he is only one person among many who do this kind of work and therefore that my picture of building community networks is necessarily partial.

4. Temporary Assistance to Working Families (or TANF) replaced Aid to Families with Dependent Children (or AFDC) with the passage of welfare reform under President Clinton.

5. Two groups of business writing students from my Fall 1998 class worked with New Leaf to help solve problems that were inhibiting growth, namely the lack of an annual report to be used to show compliance and generate new donations and the lack of publicity-related materials that could be used to generate financial support and other services (like donated time from body shops and mechanics).

6. Barton and Hamilton use the terms neighborhood and community more or less interchangeably. They too have difficulty with the concept of community. They express their reluctance to use an unanalyzed notion of community and take the time to recount their difficulties in locating community. Ultimately, they write that their sense of community "remains useful for dealing with ... the realm of local social relations which mediates between the private sphere of family and household and the public sphere of impersonal, formal organisations" (pp. 15–16)

7. Those who have ever worked construction or in most traditional manufacturing settings can attest to the desire of some for "clean" work, or work, simply put, in which one stays clean during the work day. Others also want warm work (if they work outside during the winter). This desire can come from health considerations or be borne of the desire for a job with more status and (generally) pay.

8. A group of my business writing students recently completed a feasibility study for a small manufacturer of envelopes in the Atlanta area. One of the students works as an accountant for this company and was concerned about the lack of communication between management and the shop floor. The particular problem dealt with the issue of cost estimates for production jobs, both in terms of sharing those cost estimates with workers and with giving workers feedback after the job about how well they did with respect to the initial job estimates. The communication systems they thought feasible required workers be able to read charts and graphs on a networked computer system that also allowed workers to communicate with management—literacies not required or found on the shop floor a few short years ago, particularly for small firms.

Chapter 6

1. Published in 1968 but originally part of a series of picture-poems given away by the itinerant, populist poet around 1910.

2. I should note that "preference" never means "exclusive" and that the precise meaning of preference—as well as "the poor" and "the Other"— depends on the situation.

3. My favorite example from Johnson's book is the story about traffic flow

problems in Seattle. The quick version is this: Given increasing traffic congestion, planners is Seattle turned to their experts to plan ways to ease congestion.
Using standard methods (a range of counting methods and statistical analyses),
planners implemented a solution that failed. Meanwhile, technical writing
students from the University of Washington asked the users of the system—the
drivers themselves—what they would need to alter their driving patterns and
thus ease congestion. Their solution worked. This example is not only illustra-
tive of what I mean by user knowledge, it also illustrates the kind of collaboration between users and outside researchers that I think can be productive.

4. Much of the material in this section comes directly or indirectly from an
article I have written with Stuart Blythe, Libby Miles, Jim Porter, and Pat
Sullivan (2000) "Institutional Critique: A Rhetorical Methodology for Change."

5. I've turned to design theory because it can provide a language for talking
about change. Design theory exists in many places, and I'm sure that there are
a number of disciplines that would fight over ownership of the term, but I have
looked primarily to design theories in areas like document and information
design and the broad area of technological design (history and philosophy of
technology; computer science/interface design) in an attempt to develop a way
to talk about institutional design. My sense of design is concerned with
rhetorical processes—the processes of making or doing.

6. Ehn and others highlight a problem for design which is relevant to
community literacy practices such as those at Western District. Often the answer
to the question "in whose interests" design happens is related to clients. One
reason for the trade union-design team connections in which Ehn and Bødker
participated was to counter the knowledge production management could
muster via contractual arrangements with researchers and designers. In much
design work, business and industry is the client; work proceeds in line with their
interests (see also Blauvelt, 1994; van Toon, 1994; and for an activist approach
to design, McKee, 1994). Similarly, at Western District, the design of the
institution reflects the interests of the state and business (and their interpretation
of student/worker interest). This is not necessarily an oppressive arrangement.
But in the case of Rosewater Publishing, that argument can be made. The
importance of "the client" does foreground power and the difficulties of
changing institutions.

7. I met Ko Hassan, an adolescent HIV/AIDS educator and active participant in RWPC activities, through a mutual friend and co-worker of his. We
worked together initially on a service learning project in one of my Technical
Writing classes, and through that project I became interested in the problems of
client involvement. Ko has been one of the key people who provides the energy
to this effort to improve client involvement.

8. The only person with whom I didn't speak was the CEO of Rosewater.
I tried a number of times to meet with her to discuss the program, but she never
returned my calls. My conclusions here about failure, then, should be read with
this important lack of perspective in mind.

Chapter 7

1. My critical rhetoric is designed to offer a range of agents by localizing change within participating communities and looking for ways to construct relations of solidarity between participants. Solidarity, a key component of both Latin American theologies of liberation and Freirian pedagogy, is a useful yet underutilized concept. Freire (1992) writes that when one is confronted with the reality of oppression, one should take a position of solidarity, which "requires that one enter into the situation of those with whom one is in solidarity; it is a radical posture ... [and] means fighting at their side [the oppressed] to transform the objective reality which has [oppressed them]" (p. 34). Solidarity is an ethical commitment which enables the articulation of a "we," the construction of a community. A position of solidarity requires that one stop seeing the oppressed in abstract and generalized terms and see them as concrete human beings with real needs. Acts of solidarity help to articulate a "we" in the interests of which the good of community literacy practices can be articulated.

2. Some readers have questioned why I use the term (and concept) of action research instead of activist research. This is a good question. While I might prefer activist research stances, such a stance is not the only way to conduct ethical research or affect institutional change. So I choose a more general term here because I think it is possible to conduct good and productive action research that isn't necessarily activist research in the way some activist researchers understand the concept (e.g., Lather, 1991; Cushman, 1998).

3. To see this, one has to understand that the writing of an organization cannot be separated from the day-to-day procedures of an organization. Quite literally, to write in an organization is to manage, to plan, and to do any number of activities that are part of the processes by which an organization operates. Non-profit organizations, notoriously short staffed, often have clear writing-related needs that are a substantial part of their work. This is a rich environment for learning and often a significant service.

4. We have worked with organizations such as the following:
- Fulton County Victims Witness Assistance
- The American Red Cross
- Atlanta Urban Ministries (they provide a range of social services)
- Campfire Boys and Girls
- The Atlanta Community Toolbank
- The Georgia Justice Project
- P.E.A.C.E. (see chapter 5)
- Cafe 458/Samaritan House (organizations that serve homeless men)
- Ryan White Planning Council (part of the Fulton County government that sets HIV/AIDS care policy for the metro area)
- New Leaf Services (a grassroots organization that provides a car, insurance, and maintenance to women making welfare to work transitions)

References

Adler-Kassner, L., Crooks, R., & Watters, A. (Eds.). (1997). *Writing the community: Concepts and models for service learning in composition.* Urbana, IL: National Council of Teachers of English.

Adult Education Act, 20 U.S.C. § 1201 *et seq.* (1989).

Anderson, G. L., & Irvine, P. (1993). Informing critical literacy with ethnography. In C. Lankshear and P. L. McLaren (Eds.), *Critical literacy: Politics, praxis, and the postmodern* (pp. 81–104). Albany, NY: State University of New York Press.

Anderson, R. H., Bikson, T. K., Law, S. A., & Mitchell, B. M. (1995). *Universal access to e-mail: Feasibility and societal implications.* Santa Monica, CA: Rand.

Aronowitz, S. & DiFazio, W. (1994). *The jobless future: Sci-tech and the dogma of work.* Minneapolis: University of Minnesota Press.

Auerbach, E., Barahona, B., Midy, J., Vaquerano, F., Zambrano, A., & Arnaud, J. (1996). *Adult ESL/Literacy, from the community to the community: A guidebook for participatory literacy training.* Mahwah, NJ: Lawrence Erlbaum.

Barber, B.R. (1996). Foundationalism and democracy. In S. Benhabib (Ed.), *Democracy and difference: Contesting boundaries of the political* (pp. 348-360). Princeton, NJ: Princeton University Press.

Barber, B.R. (1984). *Strong democracy: Participatory politics for a new age.* Princeton, NJ: Princeton University Press.

Barton, D. (1991). The social nature of writing. In D. Barton and R. Ivanič (Eds.), *Writing in the community* (pp. 1–13). Newbury Park, CA: Sage.

Barton, D., & Ivanič, R. (Eds.). (1991). *Writing in the community.* Newbury Park, CA: Sage.

Barton, D. (1994). *Literacy: An introduction to the ecology of written language.* Oxford: Blackwell.

Barton, D., & Hamilton, M. (2000). Literacy practices. In D. Barton, M. Hamilton, and R. Ivanič (Eds.), *Situated literacies: Reading and writing in context* (pp. 7–15). London and New York: Routledge.

Barton, D., & Hamilton, M. (1998). *Local literacies: Reading and writing in one community.* London: Routledge.

Barton, D., Hamilton, M., & Padmore, S. (1992). *Literacy in the community.* (Final report of ESRC Project R 000 23 3149). Lancaster, England: Literacy Research Group.

Baskins, J. (1996, March). *Forgotten partners: Disaffected teenagers and parents writing together at an urban community literacy center.* Paper presented at the Conference on College Composition and Communication, Milwaukee, WI.

Benhabib, S. (1992). *Situating the self: Gender, community and postmodernism in contemporary ethics.* New York: Routledge.

Benhabib, S. (1996). Toward a deliberative model of democratic legitimacy. In S. Benhabib (Ed.), *Democracy and difference: Contesting boundaries of the political* (pp. 67-94). Princeton, NJ: Princeton University Press.

Berlin, J. (1996). *Rhetorics, poetics, and cultures: Refiguring college english studies.* Urbana, IL: National Council of Teachers of English.

Bernhardt, S.A., & Farmer, B.W. (1998). Work in transition: Trends and implications. In M.S. Garay & S.A. Bernhardt (Eds.), *Expanding literacies: English teaching and the new workplace* (pp. 55–80). Albany: State University of New York Press.

Boiarsky, C. (1990). Computers in the classroom: Instruction, the mess, the noise, the writing. In C. Handa (Ed.), *Computers and community: Teaching composition in the twenty-first century* (pp. 47–67). Portsmouth, NH: Boynton/Cook.

Blauvelt, A. (1994). Foreword: The personal is political: The social practices of graphic design. *Visible Language, 28,* 288–294.

Bloom, A. (1987). *The closing of the American mind: How higher education has failed democracy and impoverished the souls of today's students.* New York: Simon and Schuster.

Bloome, D. (1993). Introduction: Making writing visible on the outside. In D. Barton, D. Bloome, D. Sheridan & B. Street (Eds.), *Ordinary people writing* (pp. 4–12). (Working Paper 51). Lancaster: Centre for Language in Social Life.

Bødker, S. (1991). *Through the interface: A human activity approach to user interface design.* Hillsdale, NJ: Lawrence Erlbaum.

Brady, J. (1994). Critical literacy, feminism, and a politics of representation. In P. L. McLaren & C. Lankshear (Eds.), *Politics of Liberation: Paths from Freire* (pp. 142-153). New York: Routledge.

Brandt, D. (1990). *Literacy as involvement: The acts of writers, readers, and texts.* Carbondale: Southern Illinois University Press.

Bruffee, K.A. (1984). Collaborative learning and the 'conversation of mankind.' *College English, 46,* 635–652.

Carlson, D. (1993). Literacy and urban school reform: Beyond vulgar pragmatism. In C. Lankshear & P. L. McLaren (Eds.), *Critical literacy: Politics, praxis, and the postmodern* (pp. 217-245). Albany: State University of New York Press.

Castells, M. (1999). The informational city is a dual city: Can it be reversed? In D.A. Schön, B. Sanyal, & W.J. Mitchell (Eds.), *High technology and low income communities: Prospects for the positive use of advanced information technology* (pp. 25–42). Cambridge, MA: Massachusetts Institute of Technology Press.

Cerf, V., Huber, P., Duggan, E., Gilder, G., Nader, R., Irving, L., Breeden, L., Perelman, L., Robinson, K., Schrader, W., & Weingarten, R. (1995). Universal access: Should we get in line? *Educom Review, 30*(2), 33–37.

Chase, N.D. (1990). Workplace literacy research issues. In. J.R. Nurss (Ed.), *Literacy in the '90's: Research questions and challenges.* Atlanta: Center for the Study of Adult Literacy, Georgia State University.

Cintron, R. (1997). *Angel's town:* Chreo *ways, gang life, and rhetorics of the everyday.* Boston: Beacon Press.

Cohen, A. P. (1985). *The symbolic construction of community.* London: Tavistock.

Collins, S. (1989). Workplace literacy: Corporate tool or worker empowerment. *Social Policy, 20*(1), 26–30.

Collins, S. D., Balmuth, M., & Jean, P. (1989). So we can use our own names, and write the laws by which we live. *Harvard Educational Review, 59,* 454–469.

Conference on College Composition and Communication. (1997). Just teaching, just writing: Reflection and responsibility. (Conference program. Phoenix). Urbana, IL: National Council of Teachers of English.

Conference on College Composition and Communication. (1998). Ideas, historias y cuentos: Breaking with precedent. (Conference program. Chicago). Urbana, IL: National Council of Teachers of English.

Conference on College Composition and Communication. (1999). Visible students, visible teachers. (Conference program. Atlanta). Urbana, IL: National Council of Teachers of English.

Cook-Gumperz, J. (1986). *The social construction of literacy.* New York: Cambridge University Press.

Cooper, M. M., & Selfe, C. L. (1990) Computer conferences and learning: Authority, resistance, and internally persuasive discourse. *College English, 52,* 847–869.

Cushman, E. (1998). *The struggle and the tools: Oral and literate strategies in an inner city community.* Albany: State University of New York Press.

Cushman, E. (1999). The public intellectual, service learning, and activist research. *College English, 61,* 328–336.

Dautermann, J., & Sullivan, P. (1996). Introduction: Issues of written literacy and electronic literacy in workplace settings. In P. Sullivan & J. Dautermann (Eds.), *Electronic literacies in the workplace: Technologies of writing* (pp. vii–xxxii). Urbana, IL: National Council of Teachers of English.

Davies, P. (1994). Long term unemployment and literacy: A case study of the restart interview. In M. Hamilton, D. Barton, & R. Ivanič (Eds.), *Worlds of literacy* (pp. 41–51). Clevedon, England: Multilingual Matters Ltd.

DeCastell, S., & Luke, A. (1988). Defining "Literacy" in North American schools. In E. R. Kintgen, B. M. Kroll, & M. Rose (Eds.), *Perspectives on literacy* (pp. 159–174). Carbondale: Southern Illinois University Press.

DeRienzo, H. (1995). Beyond the melting pot: Preserving culture, building community. *National Civic Review, 84*(1), 5–15.

Deshler, D., & Ewert, M. (1995). Participatory action research: Traditions and major assumptions. *PARnet*. [Online]. Available: <http://www.PARnet.org/parchive/docs/deshler_95/> [January 5, 1999].

Diehl, W. A. (1980). *Functional literacy as a variable construct: An examination of attitudes, behaviors, and strategies related to occupational literacy.* Unpublished doctoral dissertation, Indiana University.

Division of Adult Education, Indiana Department of Education. (1995–1996). *Indiana's adult education teacher handbook.* Indianapolis: Author.

Division of Adult Education, Indiana Department of Education. (1993). *Policy on ABE/GED standardized testing for federally-funded adult basic education programs.* Indianapolis: Author.

Division of Adult Education, Indiana Department of Education. (1996). *Purpose of the adult learning plan for adult basic education programs.* Indianapolis: Author.

Division of Adult Education, Indiana Department of Education. (1995). *The adult education handbook for Indiana providers funded by the Indiana department of education.* Indianapolis: Author.

Dussel, E. (1988). *Ethics and community.* (Robert R. Barr, Trans.). Maryknoll, NY: Orbis Books.

Ebert, T. L. (1996). *Ludic feminism and after: Postmodernism, desire, and labor in late capitalism.* Ann Arbor: The University of Michigan Press.

Ede, L., & Lunsford, A. (1990). *Singular texts/plural authors: Perspectives on collaborative writing.* Carbondale, IL: Southern Illinois University Press.

Ehn, P. (1988). *Work-oriented design of computer artifacts.* Stockholm: Arbetslivscentrum.

Elshtain, J. B. (1995). The communitarian individual. In A. Etzioni (Ed.), *New communitarian thinking: Persons, virtues, institutions, and communities* (pp. 99-109). Charlottesville: The University Press of Virginia.

Etzioni, A. (1995). Old chestnuts and new spurs. In A. Etzioni (Ed.), *New communitarian thinking: Persons, virtues, institutions, and communities* (pp. 16-34). Charlottesville: The University Press of Virginia.

Faigley, L. (1992). *Fragments of rationality: Postmodernity and the subject of composition.* Pittsburgh: University of Pittsburgh Press.

Feenberg, A. (1991). *Critical theory of technology.* New York: Oxford University Press.

Fish, S. E. (1980). *Is there a text in this class? The authority of interpretive communities.* Cambridge, MA: Harvard University Press.

Flesch, R. F. (1955). *Why Johnny can't read—and what you can do about it.* New York: Harper & Row.

Flower, L. (1994). *The construction of negotiated meaning: A social cognitive theory of writing.* Carbondale: Southern Illinois University Press.

Foucault, M. (1979). *Discipline and punish: The birth of the prison.* (A. Sheridan, Trans.). New York: Vintage Books.

Foucault, M. (1984). Space, knowledge, and power. In Paul Rabinow (Ed.), *The Foucault reader* (pp. 239–256). New York: Pantheon.

Foucault, M. (1991). The ethic of care for the self as a practice of freedom. In J. Bernauer & D. Rasmussen (Eds.), *The final Foucault* (J. D. Gauthier, S. J., Trans.). (pp. 1–20). Cambridge, MA: The MIT Press.

Fowler, R. B. (1995). Community: Reflections on definition. In A. Etzioni (Ed.), *New communitarian thinking: Persons, virtues, institutions, and communities* (pp. 88–98). Charlottesville: The University Press of Virginia.

Freebody, P. (1992). Assembling reading and writing: How institutions construct literate competencies. *The Australian Council for Adult Lit-*

eracy Conference: The Right to Literacy, the Rhetoric, the Romance, the Reality. (pp. 59–75). Victoria, Australia: Australian Council for Adult Literacy.

Freire, P. (1992). *Pedagogy of the oppressed.* (M. B. Ramos, Trans.) New York: Continuum.

Freire, P. (1995). *Pedagogy of hope.* (R. R. Barr, Trans.) New York: Continuum.

Garay, M.S. (1998). Of work and English. In M.S. Garay & S.A. Bernhardt (Eds.), *Expanding literacies: English teaching and the new workplace* (pp. 3–20). Albany: State University of New York Press.

Gee, J.P. (2000). The New Literacy Studies: From "socially situated" to the work of the social. In D. Barton, Mary Hamilton, and Roz Ivani (Eds.), *Situated literacies: Reading and writing in context* (pp. 180–196). London and New York: Routledge.

Giddens, A. (1984). *The Constitution of Society: Outline of the Theory of Structuration.* Berkeley: University of California Press.

Giroux, H. A. (1987). Introduction. In P. Freire & D. Macedo, *Literacy: Reading the word and the world* (pp. 1–27). New York: Bergin & Garvey.

Giroux, H. A. (1988). Literacy and the pedagogy of voice and political empowerment. *Educational Theory, 38,* 61–75.

Giroux, H. A. (1989). Schooling as a form of cultural politics: Toward a pedagogy of and for difference. In H. A. Giroux & P. L. McLaren (Eds.), *Critical pedagogy, the state, and cultural struggle* (pp. 125–151). Albany: State University of New York Press.

Giroux, H. A. (1993). Literacy and the politics of difference. In C. Lankshear & P. L. McLaren (Eds.), *Critical literacy: Politics, praxis, and the postmodern* (pp. 367–377). Albany: State University of New York Press.

Goffman, E. (1961). *Asylums: Essays on the Social Situation of Mental Patients and Other Inmates.* Garden City: Anchor Books.

Goody, J., & Watt, I. (1968). The consequences of literacy. In J. Goody (Ed.), *Literacy in traditional societies* (pp. 27–68). Cambridge: Cambridge University Press.

Goody, J. (1986). *The logic of writing and the organization of society.* Cambridge: Cambridge University Press.

Gowen, S. G. (1992). *The politics of workplace literacy: A case study.* New York: Teacher's College Press.

Grabill, J. T. (2000). Shaping local HIV/AIDS services policy through activist research: The problem of client involvement. *Technical Communication Quarterly, 9,* 29–50.

Graff, H. J. (1988). The legacies of literacy. In E. R. Kintgen, B. M. Kroll, & M. Rose (Eds.), *Perspectives on literacy* (pp. 82–91). Carbondale: Southern Illinois University Press.

Graff, H. J. (1979). *The literacy myth: Literacy and social structure in the 19th century city.* London: Academic Press.

Greenwood, D.J., & Levin, M. (1998). *Introduction to action research: Social research for social change.* Thousand Oaks, CA: Sage.

Gutiérrez, G. (1988). *A theology of liberation: History, politics, and salvation.* (rev. ed.). (C. Inda & J. Eagelson, Trans.). Maryknoll, New York: Orbis.

Haas, C. (1996). *Writing technology: Studies on the materiality of literacy.* Mahwah, NJ: Lawrence Erlbaum.

Habermas, J. (1990). *Moral consciousness and communicative action* (C. Lenhardt & S.W. Nicholsen, Trans.). Cambridge, MA: The Massachusetts Institute of Technology Press.

Harris, J. (1989). The idea of community in the study of writing. *College Composition and Communication, 40,* 11–22.

Harvey, D. (1996). *Justice, nature, & the geography of difference.* Cambridge, MA: Blackwell.

Havelock, E. A. (1982). *The literate revolution in Greece and its cultural consequences.* Princeton, NJ: Princeton University Press.

Havelock, E. A. (1986). Orality, literacy, and star wars. *PRE/TEXT, 7,* 123–132.

Hawisher, G. E., LeBlanc, P., Moran, C., & Selfe, C. L. (1996). *Computers and the teaching of writing in American higher education, 1979-1994:*

A history. Norwood, NJ: Ablex and Computers and Composition.

Hawisher, G. E., & Sullivan, P. (1998). Women on the networks: Searching for e-spaces of their own. In S. C. Jarratt & L. Worsham, (Eds.) *Feminism and composition studies: In other words* (pp. 172–197). New York: Modern Language Association.

Heath, S. B. (1983). *Ways with words: Language, life, and world in communities and classrooms.* Cambridge: Cambridge University Press.

Heath, S. B. (1986). Critical factors in literacy development. In S. DeCastell, A. Luke, & K. Egan (Eds.), *Literacy, society, and schooling: A reader* (pp. 209–229). Cambridge: Cambridge University Press.

Heath, S. B. (1990). The fourth vision: Literate language at work. In A. A. Lunsford, H. Moglen, and J. Slevin (Eds.), *The right to literacy* (pp. 289–306). New York: Modern Language Association.

Hennelly, R. (1996). Forget computers: Kids without phones. *The Education Digest, 61*(5), 40–43.

Hirsch, E. D. (1987). *Cultural literacy: What every American needs to know.* Boston: Houghton Mifflin Company.

HotWired. (1996). Flux. *HotWired* [online publication]. Available <http://www.hotwired.com/wired/4.08/flux.html>.

Ivanič, R., & Moss, W. (1991). Bringing community writing practices into education. In D. Barton and R. Ivanic (Eds.), *Writing in the community* (pp. 193–223). Newbury Park, CA: Sage.

Johnson, R.R. (1998). *Usercentered technology: A rhetorical theory for computers and other mundane artifacts.* Albany: State University of New York Press.

Johnston, W. B., and Packer, A. E. (1987). *Workforce 2000: Work and workers for the 21ˢᵗ century.* Indianapolis: Hudson Institute.

Jolliffe, D. (1997). Finding yourself in the text: Identity formation in the discourse of workplace documents. In G. Hull (Ed.), *Changing work, changing workers: Critical perspectives on language, literacy, and skills* (pp. 335–349). Albany: State University of New York Press.

Jones, S. B. (1996). Specialized language as a barrier to automated information technologies. In P. Sullivan & J. Dautermann (Eds.), *Electronic literacies in the workplace: Technologies of writing* (pp. 23–40). Urbana, IL: National Council of Teachers of English.

Jonsen, A. R., & Toulmin, S. (1988). *The abuse of casuistry: A history of moral reasoning.* Berkeley: University of California Press.

Kaestle, C. F., Damon-Moore, H., Stedman, L. C., Tinsley, K., & Trollinger, W. V., Jr. (1991). *Literacy in the United States: Readers and reading since 1880.* New Haven, CT: Yale University Press.

Kintgen, E. R., Kroll, B. M., & Rose, M. (Eds.). (1988). *Perspectives on literacy.* Carbondale: Southern Illinois University Press.

Kline, D. (1996, January). Market forces: Who will give us push-button net access? *HotWired* [online publication]. Available <http://www.hotwired.com/market/96/03/index1a.html>.

Knoblauch, C. H. (1990). Literacy and the politics of education. In A. A. Lunsford, H. Moglen, & J. Slevin (Eds.), *The right to literacy* (pp. 74–80). New York: MLA.

Kozol, J. (1985). *Illiterate America.* New York: Doubleday.

Kozol, J. (1991). *Savage inequalities: Children in America's schools.* New York: Doubleday.

Kretzmann, J.P., & McKnight, J.L. (1993). *Building communities from the inside out: A path toward finding and mobilizing a community's assets.* Evanston, IL : ACTA Publications.

Kuhn, T. (1980). *The structure of scientific revolutions.* 2nd ed. Chicago: University of Chicago Press.

Laird, F.N. (1993). Participatory analysis, democracy, and technological decision making. *Science, Technology, & Human Values, 18,* 341–361.

Lankshear, C., & McLaren, P. L. (1993). Preface. In C. Lankshear & P. L. McLaren (Eds.), *Critical literacy: Politics, praxis, and the postmodern* (pp. xii–xx). Albany: State University of New York Press.

Lather, P. (1991). *Getting smart: Feminist research and pedagogy with/in the postmodern.* New York: Routledge.

Leitch, V. B. (1992). *Cultural criticism, literary theory, poststructuralism.* New York: Columbia University Press.

Lindsay, V. (1968). *Earth man & star thrower: Adventures, rhymes and designs.* New York: The Eakins Press.

Lopez, E. S. (1995). *The geography of computer writing spaces: A critical postmodern analysis.* Unpublished doctoral dissertation, Purdue University.

Luke, A. (1993). Introduction. In A. R. Welch & P. Freebody (Eds.), *Knowledge, culture and power: International perspectives on literacy as policy and practice* (pp. 1–5). Pittsburgh: University of Pittsburgh Press.

Lunsford, A. A., Moglen, H., & Slevin, J. (Eds.). (1990). *The right to literacy.* New York: MLA.

Lyotard, J-F. (1984). *The postmodern condition: A report on knowledge.* (G. Bennington and B. Massumi, Trans.). Minneapolis: University of Minnesota Press.

Lyotard, J-F., & Thébaud, J-L. (1985). *Just gaming.* (W. Godzich, Trans.). Minneapolis: University of Minnesota Press.

Massey, D. B. (1994). *Space, place, and gender.* Minneapolis: University of Minnesota Press.

McKee, S. (1994). Simulated histories. *Visible Language, 28,* 328–343.

McKnight, J. (1995). *The careless society: Community and its counterfeits.* New York: Basic Books.

McLaren, P. L. (1993). Introduction. In C. Lankshear & P. L. McLaren (Eds.), *Critical literacy: Politics, praxis, and the postmodern* (pp. 1–56). Albany: State University of New York Press.

McLaren, P. L. (1994). Postmodernism and the death of politics. In P. L. McLaren & C. Lankshear (Eds.), *Politics of liberation: Paths from Freire* (pp. 193–215). New York: Routledge.

Mikulecky, L., Henard, D., & Lloyd, P. (1992). *A guidebook for developing workplace literacy programs.* Indianapolis: Indiana's model workplace literacy training program.

Minter, D. W., Gere, A. R., & Keller-Cohen, D. (1995). Learning literacies. *College English, 57,* 669–687.

Mitchell, T. (1988). The product as illusion. In J. Thackara (Ed.), *Design after modernism: Beyond the object* (208–215). New York: Thames & Hudson.

Myers, L. (Ed.). (1993). *Approaches to computer writing classrooms: Learning from practical experience.* Albany: State University of New York Press.

National Literacy Act, Pub. L. No. 102-73 (1991).

National Telecommunications and Information Administration, Office of Telecommunications and Information Applications. (1995, June). Connecting the nation: Classrooms, libraries, and health care organizations in the information age. [Online]. Available: <http://www.ntia.doc.gov/ntiahome/newitems/connect.txt> [June 10, 1997].

National Telecommunications and Information Administration, Office of Telecommunications and Information Applications. (1997). Falling through the net II: New data on the digital divide. [Online]. Available: <http:// www.ntia.doc.gov/ntiahome/net2/falling.html> [July 30, 1998].

Negroponte, N. (1995, July). Affordable computing. *Wired* [online publication]. Available <http://www.wired.com/wired/3.07/departments/negroponte.html>.

Nystrand, M. (1989). A social-interactive model of writing. *Written Communication, 6,* 66–85.

O'Donnell, T. G. (1996). Politics and ordinary language: A defense of expressivist rhetorics. *College English, 58,* 423–439.

Ohmann, R. M. (1987). *Politics of letters.* Middletown, CT: Wesleyan University Press.

Olson, D. R. (1977). From utterance to text: The bias of language in speech and writing. *Harvard Educational Review, 47,* 257–279.

Olson, D. R. (1985). Introduction. In D. R. Olson, N. Torrance, & A. Hildyard (Eds.), *Literacy, language, and learning: The nature and consequences of reading and writing* (pp. 1–15). New York: Cambridge University Press.

Olson, D. R. (1986). The cognitive consequences of literacy. *Canadian Psychology/Psychologie Canadienne, 27,* 109–121.

Olson, D. R. (1994). *The world on paper: The conceptual and cognitive implications of writing and reading.* New York: Cambridge University Press.

Ong. W. J., S.J. (1982). *Orality and literacy: The technologizing of the word.* London: Routledge.

Peck, W. C. (1996, March). *Community literacy: Widening intersections of interest between urban teenagers and their parents through writing, reflection, and action.* Paper presented at the Conference on College Composition and Communication, Milwaukee, Wisconsin.

Peck, W. C., Flower, L., & Higgins, L. (1995). Community literacy. *College Composition and Communication, 46,* 199–222.

Piller, C. (1992, September). Separate realities: The creation of the technological underclass in America's public schools. *MacWorld, 9,* 218–230.

Porter, J.E., Sullivan, P., Blythe, S., Grabill, J.T., & Miles, L. (2000). Institutional critique: A rhetorical methodology for change. *College Composition and Communication, 51,* 610–642.

Porter, J.E. (1986). Intertextuality and the discourse community. *Rhetoric Review, 5,* 34–47.

Porter, J.E. (1992). *Audience and rhetoric: An archaeological composition of the discourse community.* Englewood Cliffs, NJ: Prentice Hall.

Porter, J.E. (1998). *Rhetorical ethics and internetworked writing.* Greenwich, CT: Ablex and Computers and Composition.

Purcell-Gates, V. (1995). *Other people's words: The cycle of low literacy.* Cambridge, MA: Harvard University Press.

Regan, Alison. (1993). "Type normal like the rest of us": Writing, power, and homophobia in the networked composition classroom. *Computers and Composition, 10*(4), 11–23.

Reich, R. B. (1992). *The Work of Nations : Preparing Ourselves for 21st Century Capitalism.* New York: Vintage Books.

Richardson, M., & Liggett, S. (1993). Power relations, technical writing theory, and workplace writing. *Journal of Business and Technical Communication, 7,* 112–136.

Rifkin, J. (1995). *The end of work: The decline of the global labor force and the dawn of the post-market era.* New York: Tarcher Putnam.

Robinson, S.K. (1998). Beyond basics: Workplace skills in the new manufacturing environment. In M.S. Garay & S.A. Bernhardt (Eds.), *Expanding literacies: English teaching and the new workplace* (pp. 99–118). Albany: State University of New York Press.

Romano, Susan. (1993). The Egalitarianism narrative: Whose story? Which yardstick? *Computers and Composition, 10*(3), 5–28.

Rush, R. T., Moe, A. J., & Storlie, R. L. (1986). *Occupational literacy education.* Newark, DE: International Reading Association.

Salinas, C. (1997, March). *Unequal spaces: Computers and class in first-year composition.* Paper presented at the Conference on College Composition and Communication, Phoenix, AZ.

Sandfort, S., & Frissell, D. (1995). IF: Net access for next to nothing. *Wired* [online publication]. Available <http://www.wired.com/wired/3.05/departments/access.if.html>.

Sawicki, D. S., & Craig, W. J. (1996). The democratization of data: Bridging the gap for community groups. *APA Journal, 62,* 512–523.

Scribner, S., & Cole, M. (1981). *The psychology of literacy.* Cambridge, MA: Harvard University Press.

Scribner, S. (1988). Literacy in three metaphors. In E. R. Kintgen, B. M. Kroll, & M. Rose (Eds.), *Perspectives on literacy* (pp. 71–81). Carbondale: Southern Illinois University Press.

Selfe, C. L. (1989). *Creating a computer-supported writing facility: A blueprint for action.* Houghton, MI and West Lafayette, IN: Computers and Composition.

Selfe, C. L. (1990). Technology in the English classroom: Computers through the lens of feminist theory. In C. Handa (Ed.), *Computers and community: Teaching composition in the twenty-first century* (pp. 118–139). Portsmouth, NH: Boynton/Cook Heinemann.

Selfe, C. L. (1996). Theorizing e-mail for the practice, instruction, and study of literacy. In P. Sullivan & J. Dautermann (Eds.), *Electronic literacies in the workplace: Technologies of writing* (pp. 255–293). Urbana, IL: National Council of Teachers of English.

Selfe, C. L. (1999). Technology and literacy: A story about the perils of not paying attention. *College Composition and Communication, 50,* 411–436.

Selfe, C. L., & Selfe, R. J., Jr. (1994). The politics of the interface: Power and its exercise in electronic contact zones. *College Composition and Communication, 45*, 480–504.

Sibley, D. (1995). *Geographies of exclusion: Society and difference in the West*. London: Routledge.

Simmons, M. (2000). *Building public rhetorics: A rhetorical approach to citizen participation in environmental public policy*. Unpublished doctoral dissertation, Purdue University.

Sims, T. A. (1997, March). *Not just computing race: Politics and culture from the black of the class*. Paper presented at the Conference on College Composition and Communication, Phoenix, AZ.

Smith, D. (1987). *The everyday world as problematic: A feminist sociology*. Toronto: University of Toronto Press.

Smith, F. (1985). A metaphor for literacy: Creating worlds or shunting information. In D. R. Olson, N. Torrance, & A. Hildyard (Eds.), *Literacy, language, and learning: The nature and consequences of reading and writing* (pp. 194–213). Cambridge: Cambridge University Press.

Sohng, S.S.L. (1995, November). *Participatory research and community organizing*. Paper presented at The New Social Movement and Community Organizing Conference, Seattle, WA. [Online]. <http://weber.u.washington.edu/~jamesher/sue.htm> [January 5, 1999].

Soifer, R., Irwin, M.E., Crumrine, B.M., Honzaki, E., Simmons, B.K., & Young, D.L. (1990). *The complete theory-to-practice handbook of adult literacy: Curriculum design and teaching approaches*. New York: Teachers College Press.

Soja, E. W. (1989). *Postmodern geographies: The reassertion of space in critical social theory*. London: Verso.

Soja. E.W. (1996). *Thirdspace: Journeys to Los Angeles and other real-and-imagined places*. Cambridge, MA: Blackwell.

Stanley, L., & Wise, S. (1993). *Breaking out again: Feminist ontology and epistemology*. London: Routledge.

Street, B. V. (1984). *Literacy in theory and practice*. Cambridge: Cambridge University Press.

Street, B. V. (1993). *Cross-cultural approaches to literacy*. Cambridge: Cambridge University Press.

Street, B. V. (1995). *Social literacies: Critical approaches to literacy in development, ethnography and education*. London: Longman.

Stuckey, J. E., & Alston, K. (1990). Cross-age tutoring: The right to literacy. In A. A. Lunsford, H. Moglen, & J. Slevin (Eds.), *The right to literacy* (pp. 245–254). New York: Modern Language Association.

Stuckey, J. E. (1991). *The violence of literacy*. Portsmouth, NH: Boynton/Cook.

Sullivan, W. M. (1995). Institutions as the infrastructure of democracy. In *New communitarian thinking: Persons, virtues, institutions, and communities* (pp. 170–180). Charlottesville: The University Press of Virginia.

Sullivan, P., & Dautermann, J. (Eds.). (1996). *Electronic literacies in the workplace: Technologies of writing*. Urbana, IL: National Council of Teachers of English.

Sullivan, P., & Porter, J. E. (1997). *Opening spaces: Writing Technologies and Critical Research Practices*. Greenwich, CT: Ablex and Computers and Composition.

Takayoshi, P. (1994). Building new networks from the old: Women's experiences with electronic communications. *Computers and Composition, 11*, 21–35.

United States Department of Labor, Secretary's Commission on Achieving Necessary Skills. (1991). *What work requires of schools: A SCANS report for America 2000*. Washington: Author.

United Way of Metropolitan Atlanta. (1999). Request for proposals (RFP) guidelines, instructions, and application. Fiscal year 2000 (July 1, 1999-June 30, 2000). Atlanta: Author.

van Toorn, J. (1994). Design and reflexivity. *Visible Language, 28,* 317–325.

Wade, R.C., (Ed.). (1997). *Community service-learning: A guide to including service in the public school curriculum.* Albany: State University of New York Press.

Wadsworth, Y. (1998). What is participatory action research? *Action Research International.* [Online]. <http://www.scu.edu.au/schools/sawd/ari/ari-wadsworth.html> [February 3, 1999].

Walters, K. (1990). Language, logic, and literacy. In A. A. Lunsford, H. Moglen, & J. Slevin (Eds.), *The right to literacy* (pp. 173–188). New York: Modern Language Association.

Welch, A. R., & Freebody, P. (1993). Introduction: Explanations of the current international "Literacy crises". In A. R. Welch & P. Freebody (Eds.), *Knowledge, culture and power: International perspectives on literacy as policy and practice* (pp. 6–22). Pittsburgh: University of Pittsburgh Press.

West, C. (1991). *The ethical dimensions of marxist thought.* New York: Monthly Review Press.

Western District Adult Basic Education. (1994). *Grant application for federal adult education funds.* Indianapolis: Author.

Western District Adult Basic Education. (no date). *Workplace literacy grant proposal.* Indianapolis: Author.

Western District Adult Basic Education. (1996). *Adult basic education center: An opportunity.* Indianapolis: Author.

Writers of the Greater Indianapolis Literacy League. (1994). *Writing our lives.* Indianapolis: The Greater Indianapolis Literacy League.

Yin, R. (1984, rev. ed.). *Case study research: Design and methods.* (rev. ed.). Beverly Hills, CA: Sage.

Young, I. M. (1990). *Justice and the politics of difference.* Princeton, NJ: Princeton University Press.

Index